Rhodius Apollonius, Francis Fawkes, Henry Meen

The Argonautics of Apollonius Rhodius

Rhodius Apollonius, Francis Fawkes, Henry Meen

The Argonautics of Apollonius Rhodius

ISBN/EAN: 9783337395933

Printed in Europe, USA, Canada, Australia, Japan

Cover: Foto ©ninafisch / pixelio.de

More available books at **www.hansebooks.com**

THE
ARGONAUTICS
OF
APOLLONIUS RHODIUS,

IN FOUR BOOKS,

By FRANCIS FAWKES:

THE WHOLE
REVISED, CORRECTED, AND COMPLETED,
By HIS COADJUTOR AND EDITOR;
WHO HAS ANNEXED A TRANSLATION OF
COLUTHUS'S GREEK POEM
ON THE
RAPE OF HELEN,
OR
THE ORIGIN OF THE TROJAN WAR;

WITH NOTES.

LONDON:
PRINTED FOR J. DODSLEY, IN PALL-MALL.

M,DCC,LXXX.

TO THE

MOST REVEREND FATHER IN GOD,

FREDERIC,

LORD ARCHBISHOP OF CANTERBURY,

PRIMATE OF ALL ENGLAND

AND METROPOLITAN,

THE FOLLOWING TRANSLATION OF

APOLLONIUS RHODIUS

IS, BY PERMISSION,

AND WITH ALL HUMILITY,

INSCRIBED,

BY HIS GRACE'S MOST DUTIFUL,

AND MOST OBLIGED SERVANT,

THE EDITOR.

the following lines, to that invidious spirit which prevailed in his scholar.

>'Ο φθόνος 'Απόλλωνος ἐπ' ὕατα λάθριος εἶπεν,
>'Ουκ ἄγαμαι τὸν ἀοιδὸν, ὃς ὑδ', ὅσα Πόντος, ἀείδει.
>
>Call. Hymn. ad Ap. v. 105.

For Apollonius, anxious to establish his own reputation, and jealous of his master's, had depreciated those more numerous, but lighter productions, in which the Muse of Callimachus excelled; epigrams, hymns, and elegies.

It will be no improper introduction to the following poem to trace the subject of it to its source: nor can we expect to be guided through its intricacies by a safer clue, than that which the ancients have afforded us.

Ino was the wife of Athamas, king of Orchomenos; from whom he was soon after divorced, and married Nephele. But she incurring his displeasure, he restored the repudiated Ino to his bed. By her he had two children, Learchus and Melicerta; by Nephele he had Phrixus and Helle. Ino beheld the children of her rival with a jealous eye. For they, being the eldest, had a prior claim to their father's inheritance. Resolved on their destruction, she concerted the following plan, as most likely to effect it. A grievous famine laying waste the country, it was judged expedient to consult the oracle about the means of suppressing it. Ino having gained

over

over the priests to her interest, prevailed on them to return this answer; that the ravages of famine could no otherwise be suppressed, than by the sacrifice of Nephele's children. Phrixus, who was made acquainted with the cruel purpose of Ino, freighted his vessel with his father's treasures, and embarked with his sister Helle for Colchis. The voyage proved fatal to her; and the sea, into which she fell, was named from her the Hellespont. But Phrixus arrived safe at Colchis; and was protected from the cruelties of his step-mother Ino, at the court of Æetes his kinsman, who bestowed on him his daughter Chalciope in marriage. Upon his arrival he consecrated his ship to Mars; on whose prow was represented the figure of a ram. This embellishment, it is supposed by some of the historians, gave rise to the fiction, of his having swam to Colchis on the back of that animal, of his having sacrificed it to Mars, and hung up its fleece in the temple of that God. It is this imaginary fleece which is celebrated by the poets for having given birth to the expedition of the Argonauts. A variety of whimsical conjectures have been formed concerning it. Some are of opinion, that it was a book of sheep-skins, containing the mysteries of the chymic art. Others have assured us, that it signified the riches of the country; with which their rivers, that abounded in gold, supplied its inhabitants: and that, from the sheep-skins made use of in collecting

collecting the golden duſt, it was called the Golden Fleece.

For a further illuſtration of the ſubject of this poem, it will be neceſſary to inſert the following hiſtory.

Tyro, the daughter of Salmoneus, had two ſons by Neptune, Neleus and Pelias: by Cretheus ſhe had Æſon, Pheres and Amithaon. The city of Iolcos in Theſſaly, which Cretheus built, was the capital of his dominions. He left his kingdom at his death to Æſon his eldeſt ſon; but made no proviſion for Pelias. Pelias, however, growing every day more powerful, at length dethroned Æſon. And hearing that his wife Alcimeda was delivered of a ſon, he was reſolutely bent on his deſtruction. For he had been forewarned by the oracle, that he muſt be dethroned by a prince, deſcended from Æolus, and who ſhould appear before him with one foot bare. Æſon and Alcimeda being informed of the tyrant's intention, conveyed their ſon to mount Pelion, where he was educated by Chiron. Having attained to maturity, he conſulted the oracle; who encouraged him to repair to the court of Iolcos. Pelias, hearing of the arrival of this ſtranger, and of the circumſtance of his appearance with only one ſandal, concluded that this muſt be the perſon, whom the oracle had foretold. Having made himſelf and his ſituation known to his uncle, Jaſon demanded of him the crown, which he had ſo

unjuſtly

unjuftly ufurped. Pelias was greatly alarmed at this requifition. But knowing that a thirft for glory is the darling paffion of youth, he contrived to appeafe his nephew's refentment by difclofing to him the means of gratifying his ambition. He affured him, that Phrixus, when he failed from Orchomenos, had carried with him a Fleece of Gold, the poffeffion of which would at the fame time enrich and immortalize him. The propofal had its defired effect. Jafon fignified his acceptance of it, and collected fpeedily the moft illuftrious princes of Greece, who were eager to embark in a caufe, that was at once advantageous and honourable. Who thefe heroes were, the route they took, the dangers with which they encountered, and the fuccefs they met with, are particulars recorded by Apollonius, and on which he has lavifhed all the graces of poetry.

Such is the hiftory of the Golden Fleece, as delivered down to us by the ancient poets and hiftorians. This celebrated expedition is generally fuppofed to be the firft æra of true hiftory. Sir Ifaac Newton places it about forty-three years after the death of Solomon, and nine hundred and thirty-feven years before the birth of Chrift. He apprehends, that the Greeks, hearing of the diftractions of Egypt, fent the moft renowned heroes of their country in the fhip Argo, to perfuade the nations on the coaft of the Euxine fea to throw off the Egyptian yoke, as the Lybians, Ethiopians, and Jews had before done. But Mr. Bryant has given us a far different account of this matter in his very learned fyftem of mythology: whofe fentiments on this head I have endeavoured to collect, and have ventured to give them a place in this preface. For the novelty of his hypothefis, and the learning and ingenuity with which it is fupported, cannot fail to entertain and inftruct us.

The main plot, fays the learned and ingenious mythologift, as it is tranfmitted to us, is certainly a fable, and replete with inconfiftencies and contradictions. Yet many writers, ancient and modern, have taken the account in grofs; and without hefitation, or exception to any particular part, have prefumed to fix the time of this tranfaction. And having fatisfied themfelves in this point, they have prefumed to make ufe of it for a ftated æra. Mr. Bryant is of opinion, that this hiftory, upon which Sir Ifaac Newton built fo much, did certainly not relate to Greece; though adopted by the people of that country. He contends, that Sir Ifaac's calculation refted upon a weak foundation. That it is doubtful, whether fuch perfons as Chiron or Mufæus ever exifted; and ftill more doubtful, whether they formed a fphere for the Argonauts. He produces many arguments to convince us, that the expedition itfelf was not a Grecian operation; and that this fphere at any rate was not a Grecian work: and if not from Greece, it muft certainly be the produce of Egypt. For the aftronomy of Greece confeffedly came from that country: con-

fequently

sequently the history to which it alludes, must have been from the same quarter. Many of the constellations, says our author, are of Egyptian original. The zodiac, which Sir Isaac Newton supposed to relate to the Argonautic expedition, was, he asserts, an assemblage of Egyptian hieroglyphics.

After having enumerated all the particulars of their voyage, the different routes they are supposed to have taken, and the many inconsistencies with which the whole story abounds, Mr. Bryant proceeds to observe, that the mythology, as well as the rites of Greece, was borrowed from Egypt and that it was founded upon ancient histories, which had been transmitted in hieroglyphical representations. These, by length of time, became obscure; and the sign was taken for the reality, and accordingly explained. Hence arose the fable about the bull of Europa, and the like. In all these is the same history under a different allegory and emblem. In the wanderings of Rhea, Isis, Astarte, Iona and Damater, is figured out the separation of mankind by their families, and their journeying to their places of allotment. At the same time, the dispersion of one particular race of men, and their flight over the face of the earth, is principally described. Of this family were the persons, who preserved the chief memorials of the ark in the Gentile world. They represented it under different emblems, and called it Demater, Pyrrha, Selene, Meen, Argo, Argus, Archas, and Archaius, or Archite. The Grecians, proceeds the learned writer, by taking this story of the Argo to themselves, have plunged into numberless difficulties. In the account of the Argo, we have undeniably the history of a sacred ship, the first that was ever constructed. This truth the best writers among the Grecians confess, though the merit of the performance they would fain take to themselves. Yet after all their prejudices they continually betray the truth, and shew that the history was derived to them from Egypt. The cause of all the mistakes in this curious piece of mythology arose from hence. The Arkites, who came into Greece, settled in many parts, but especially in Argolis and Thessalia; where they introduced their rites and worship. In the former of these regions, they were commemorated under a notion of the arrival of Da-naus, or Danaus. It is supposed to have been a person, who fled from his brother Ægyptus, and came over in a sacred ship given him by Minerva. This ship, like the Argo, is said to have been the first ship constructed; and he was assisted in the building of it by the same Deity, Divine Wisdom. Both histories relate to the same event. Danaus, upon his arrival, built a temple, called Argus, to Iona, or Juno; of which he made his daughters priestesses. The people of the place had an obscure tradition of a deluge, in which most perished, some few only escaping. The principal of these was Deucalion,

PREFACE. ix

who took refuge in the acropolis, or temple. Those who settled in Thessaly, carried with them the same memorials concerning Deucalion, and his deliverance; which they appropriated to their own country. They must have had traditions of this great event strongly impressed upon their minds; as every place, to which they gave name, had some reference to that history. In process of time, these impressions grew more and more faint, and their emblematical worship became very obscure and unintelligible. Hence they at last confined the history of this event to their own country; and the Argo was supposed to have been built, where it was originally enshrined. As it was reverenced under the symbol of the Moon, called Man or Mon, the people from this circumstance name their country Ai-mona, in after times rendered Aimonia.

This extract from the ingenious and learned mythologist will enable the reader to form some idea of his sentiments on this subject.

But whatever disgust the grave historian may have conceived at this unsightly mixture of the marvellous and the probable, the poet needs not be offended at it. Fiction is his province. He may be allowed to expatiate in the regions of fancy without controul, and to introduce his fiery bulls and sleepless dragons without the dread of censure.

The Argonautic expedition has been the admired subject of the Greek and Roman poets from Orpheus,

or

or rather from Onomacritus, who lived in the times of Pififtratus, to thofe of our author's imitators, who lived in the decline of the Roman empire. To weigh the merits of thefe ancient poets in the juft fcale of criticifm, and to appropriate to each his due fhare of praife, is a tafk too arduous and affuming for an humble editor to engage in. Yet fuch is the partiality of tranflators and editors to their favourite poets, that they wifh, either to find them feated above their rivals and contemporaries on the fummits of Parnaffus, or, if poffible, to fix them there. But vain are thefe wifhes, unlefs the teftimonies of the firft writers of antiquity concur to gratify them. The reputation of Apollonius can neither be impaired nor enhanced by the ftrictures of Scaliger and Rapin: the judgment of Quintilian and Longinus may, indeed, more materially affect it. They have delivered their opinions on our author in the following words:

Ἔπειτοι γε καὶ ἄπλωτος ὁ Ἀπολλώνιος, ὁ τῶν Ἀργοναυτικῶν ποιητής, ἀρ' ὃν Ὅμηρος ἂν μᾶλλον, ἢ Ἀπολλώνιος ἐθέλοις γενέσθαι; Sect. xxxiii. *Longin.* de Sublim.

Non contemnendum edidit opus æquali quadam mediocritate. *Quinctil.* Inft. Orat. L. x. c. 1.

Unfortunately, as it fhould feem, for the Rhodian, thefe celebrated ftrictures wear the double face of approbation and cenfure. The praife that is conveyed under the term ἄπτωτος, that he no where finks,

PREFACE. xi

finks, is loft in the implication, that he is no where elevated. The expreffion, *non contemnendum opus*, apparently a flattering meiofis, is limited to its loweft fenfe by the fubfequent obfervation, *æquali quadam mediocritate*. But we muft not defert our poet even in this extremity; for if imitation implies efteem and admiration, Apollonius's nobleft eulogy will be found in the writings of Virgil. Thofe applauded paffages in this poet, which are confeffedly imitated from our author, may ferve as a counterpoife to the fentence of the critics. Apollonius was Virgil's favourite author. He has incorporated into his Æneid his fimilies and his epifodes; and has fhewn the fuperiority of his judgment by his juft application and arrangement of them.

But it is not the Mantuan poet only, who has fetched from this ftorehoufe the moft precious materials. Valerius Flaccus, who has made choice of the fame fubject with the Rhodian, has difcovered through every part of his work a fingular predilection for him. He is allowed to have imitated the ftyle of Virgil with tolerable fuccefs; but he is indebted for the conduct of his poem chiefly to Apollonius. It is remarkable, that Quintilian, who has objected mediocrity to our author, has mentioned this his clofeft imitator in terms of the higheft refpect. Yet muft it be confeffed, that the genius of Flaccus feldom foars fo high, as when it is invigorated and enlightened by the Mufe of Apollonius.

But

But the admiration, in which this writer has been held by the Roman poets, did not expire with them. The rage of imitation, far from ceasing, has caught congenial spirits in every succeeding period; and the most approved passages in this elegant poem have been diffused through the works of the most admired moderns. It were needless to mention any others than Milton and Camoens. Milton's imitations of Apollonius are, many of them, specified in the notes inserted in Bishop Newton's valuable edition of all that writer's poetical works. Camoens, who has hitherto been known to the English reader only through the obscure and crude version of Fanshaw, has appeared of late greatly to advantage, in the very animated translation of Mr. Mickle. That the refined taste of Camoens was formed on the model of the Greek and Roman poets, is evident throughout the Lusiad; which abounds in allusions to the pagan mythology, and is enriched with a profusion of graces derived from the ancient classics. In the number of these it can be no disparagement to his poem to reckon Apollonius Rhodius; to the merit of whose work Camoens, if I misjudge not, was no stranger. The subject of the Portuguese poem bears a striking resemblance to that which our author has chosen. For the heroes both of Portugal and Greece traversed unknown seas, in pursuit of the wealth with which an unknown country was expected to supply them. Camoens not only alludes to Argo and

PREFACE. xiii

and her demigods, but feems particularly fond of drawing a comparifon betwixt the heroes of his country and thofe of Theffaly.

> Here view thine Argonauts, in feas unknown, &c.
> B. i. p. 9.

> With fuch bold rage the youth of Mynia glow'd,
> When the firſt keel the Euxine furges plow'd;
> When bravely venturous for the Golden Fleece,
> Orac'lous Argo fail'd from wondering Greece.
> B. iv. p. 172.

And foon after;

> While each prefaged that great as Argo's fame,
> Our fleet ſhould give fome ſtarry band a name.

" The folemnity of the night fpent in devotion, the affecting grief of their friends and fellow-citizens, whom they were never more to behold; and the angry exclamations of the venerable old man, give a dignity and interefting pathos to the departure of the fleet of Gama, *unborrowed from any of the claſſics.*" See *the concluding note* to B. iv.

Apollonius has admitted into his firſt book, on a fimilar occafion, moſt of the above-mentioned particulars, and many others equally interefting. The prayer of Jafon, and the facrifices previous to their embarkation, are circumſtantially related. The lamentations of Alcimeda at the lofs of her fon, the filent grief of Æfon his father, and the tears of his friends,

friends, contribute to make this parting scene the most pathetic imaginable. Through the whole of this affecting interview Camoens seems not to have lost sight of Apollonius. But, lest it should be said, that a similarity of situations naturally produces a similarity of sentiments; and that we ought not to interpret a resemblance like this, which might be casual only, to be the effect of studied imitation; another passage may be selected from the Lusiad, which is universally admired for its genuine sublimity, and is affirmed to be the happiest effort of unassisted genius. " The apparition, which in the night hovers athwart the Cape of Good Hope, is the grandest fiction in human composition; *the invention his own!*" See *the dissertation* prefixed to Mr. Mickle's translation of the Lusiad.

There is a passage in the third book of Apollonius, to which the description of the apparition at the Cape bears a striking resemblance; I mean, the appearance of the ghost of Sthenelus, standing on his tomb, and surveying the Argonauts as they sail beside him. The description of Camoens is indeed heightened by many additional circumstances, and enriched with a profusion of the boldest images. The colouring is his own; but the first design and outlines of the piece appear to be taken from our poet.

But it is time to quit the imitators of Apollonius, and to give some account of his translators.

Dr.

PREFACE.

Dr. Broome, well known in the literary world for the part he took in the tranflation of the Odyſſey, and for his notes annexed to it, has given an elegant verſion of the loves of Jaſon and Medea, and of the ſtory of Talus; which are publiſhed with his original poems. Mr. Weſt, who has transfuſed into his verſion of the odes of Pindar much of the ſpirit of his ſublime original, has preſented us in an Engliſh dreſs with one or two detached pieces from our author. Mr. Ekins has tranſlated the third book, and about two hundred lines of the fourth. Had this gentleman undertaken a verſion of the whole poem, Mr. Fawkes, I am confident, would have defiſted from the attempt. The public has long been in poſſeſſion of ſeveral tranſlations by this latter writer. Thoſe of Anacreon and Theocritus are acknowledged to have confiderable merit. The work before us was undertaken at the requeſt of Mr. Fawkes's particular friends: and the encreaſing number of his ſubſcribers encouraged him to perſevere in his deſign; but the completion of it was prevented by the premature ſtroke of fate. What part the editor has taken in this work, is a matter of too ſmall importance to need an explanation. But leſt his motive ſhould be miſtaken, and vanity ſhould be ſuppoſed to have inſtigated what friendſhip only ſuggeſted, he begs leave to add, as the beſt apology he can offer for engaging in this work; that with no other ambition than to aſſiſt his

friend,

friend, did he comply with his folicitations to become his coadjutor; and with no other motive does he now appear as his editor, than to enable the widow to avail herfelf of thofe generous fubfcriptions, for which fhe takes occafion here to make her thankful acknowledgments.

March 27,
1780.

THE
FIRST BOOK.

THE ARGUMENT.

This Book commences with the list and character of the Argonauts. Before they embark, two of the chiefs quarrel; but are pacified by the harmony of Orpheus. They set sail, and land at Lemnos, an island inhabited by female warriors; who, though they had slain their husbands and turned Amazons, are so charmed with these heroes, that they admit them to their beds. Thence they sail to the country of the Dolions, and are kindly received by their king Cyzicus. Loosing from thence in the night, and being driven back by contrary winds, they are mistaken for Pelasgians, with whom the Dolions were then at war. A battle ensues, in which Cyzicus and many of his men are slain. The morning discovers the unhappy mistake. Thence they sail to Mysia. Hercules breaks his oar; and while he is gone into a wood to make a new one, Hylas is stolen by a nymph, as he is stooping for water at a fountain. Hercules and Polyphemus go in search of him. Meanwhile the Argonauts leave them behind, and sail to Bithynia.

THE
ARGONAUTICS
OF
APOLLONIUS RHODIUS.

BOOK I.

INSPIR'D by thee, O Phœbus, I refound
The glorious deeds of heroes long renown'd,
Whom Pelias urg'd the Golden Fleece to gain,
And well-built Argo wafted o'er the main,
Through the Cyanean rocks. The voice divine   5
Pronounc'd this fentence from the facred fhrine;
' Erelong, and dreadful woes, foredoom'd by fate,
' Thro' that man's counfels fhall on Pelias wait,
' Whom he, before the altar of his God,
' Shall view in public with one fandal fhod.'   10
And, lo! as by this oracle foretold,
What time adventurous Jafon, brave and bold,
Anaurus paft, high fwoln with winter's flood,
He left one fandal rooted in the mud.

To Pelias, thus, the hasty prince repair'd, 15
And the rich banquet at his altar shar'd.
The stately altar, with oblations stor'd,
Was to his sire erected, ocean's lord,
And every Power that in Olympus reigns,
Save Juno, regent of Thessalia's plains. 20
Pelias, whose looks his latent fears express'd,
Fir'd with a bold adventure Jason's breast;
That, sunk in ocean, or on some rude shore
Prostrate, he ne'er might view his country more.
Old bards affirm this warlike ship was made 25
By skilful Argus, with Minerva's aid.
'Tis mine to sing the chiefs, their names and race,
Their tedious wanderings on the main to trace,
And all their great achievements to rehearse:
Deign, ye propitious Nine, to aid my verse. 30

   First in the list, to join the princely bands,
The tuneful bard, enchanting Orpheus, stands;
Whom fair Calliope, on Thracia's shore,
Near Pimpla's mount, to bold Œagrus bore.
Hard rocks he soften'd with persuasive song, 35
And sooth'd the rivers as they roll'd along.
Yon beeches tall, that bloom near Zona, still
Remain memorials of his vocal skill:

                                          His

His lays Pieria's liftening trees admire,
And move in meafures to his melting lyre.   40
Thus Orpheus charm'd, who o'er the Biftons reign'd,
By Chiron's art to Jafon's intereft gain'd.
Afterion next; whofe fire rejoic'd to till
Pirefian valleys by Phylleion's hill,
Born near Apidanus, who fportive leads   45
His winding waters thro' the fertile meads;
There where, from far, Enipeus, ftream divine,
And wide Apidanus their currents join.
The fon of Elatus, of deathlefs fame,
From fair Lariffa, Polyphemus came.   50
Long fince, when in the vigour of his might,
He join'd the hardy Lapithæ in fight
Againft the Centaurs; now his ftrength declin'd
Thro' age, yet young and martial was his mind.
Not long at Phylace Iphiclus ftaid,   55
Great Jafon's uncle; pleas'd he join'd his aid,
And march'd to meet th' adventurous band from far,
Urg'd by affinity and love of war.
Nor long Admetus, who at Pheræ reign'd,
Near high Chalcodon's bleating fields remain'd.   60
Echion, Erytus, for wiles renown'd,
Left Alope, with golden harvefts crown'd;

The gainful sons of Mercury: with these
Their brother came, the bold Æthalides;
Whom fair Eupolema, the Phthian, bore   65
Where smooth Amphrysos rolls his watery store:
Those, Menetus, from thy fair daughter sprung,
Antianira, beautiful and young.
Coronus came, from Gyrton's wealthy town,
Great as his sire in valour and renown,   70
Cæneus his sire; who, as old bards relate,
Receiv'd from Centaurs his untimely fate.
Alone, unaided, with transcendent might,
Boldly he fac'd, and put his foes to flight.
But they, reviving soon, regain'd their ground;   75
Yet fail'd to vanquish, and they could not wound.
Unbroke, unmov'd, the chief his breath resigns,
O'erwhelm'd beneath a monument of pines.
From Titaresus Mopsus bent his way,
Inspir'd an augur by the God of day.   80
Eurydamas, to share fair honour's crown,
Forsook near Xynias' lake his native town,
Nam'd Ctimena: Menœtius join'd the band,
Dismiss'd from Opuns by his sire's command.
Next came Eurytion, Irus' valiant son,   85
And Eribotes, seed of Teleon.

Oïleus

Oïleus join'd thefe heroes, fam'd afar
For ftratagems and fortitude in war;
Well fkill'd the hoftile fquadrons to fubdue,
Bold in attack, and ardent to purfue. 90
Next, by Canethus, fon of Abans, fent,
Ambitious Canthus from Eubœa went;
Doom'd ne'er again to reach his native fhore,
Nor view the towers of proud Cerinthus more.
For thus decreed the deftinies fevere, 95
That he and Mopfus, venerable feer,
After long toils and various wanderings paft,
On Afric's dreary coaft fhould breathe their laft.
How fhort the term affign'd to human woe,
Clos'd, as it is, by death's decifive blow! 100
On Afric's dreary coaft their graves were made,
From Phafis diftant far their bones were laid;
Far as the eaft and weftern limits run,
Far as the rifing from the fetting fun.
Clytius and Iphitus unite their aid, 105
Who all the country round Œchalia fway'd;
Thefe were the fons of Eurytus the proud,
On whom his bow the God of day beftow'd;
But he, devoid of gratitude, defy'd,
And challeng'd Phœbus with a rival's pride. 110

The sons of Æacus, intrepid race!
Separate advanc'd, and from a different place.
For when their brother unawares they flew,
From fair Ægina diverse they withdrew.
Fair Salamis king Telamon obey'd,   115
And valiant Peleus Phthia's sceptre sway'd.
Next Butes came from fam'd Cecropia far,
Brave Teleon's son, a chief renown'd in war.
To wield the deadly lance Phalerus boasts,
Who, by his sire commission'd, joins the hosts: 120
No son, save this, e'er bless'd the hoary sage,
And this heaven gave him in declining age:
Yet him he sent, disdaining abject fears,
To shine conspicuous 'midst his gallant peers.
Theseus, far more than all his race renown'd,   125
Fast in the cave of Tænarus was bound
With adamantine fetters, (dire abode!)
E'er since he trod th' irremeable road
With his belov'd Pirithoüs: had they sail'd,
Much had their might, their courage much avail'd. 130
Bœotian Tiphys came, experienc'd well
Old ocean's foaming surges to foretell,
Experienc'd well the stormy winds to shun,
And steer his vessel by the stars, or sun.

            Minerva

Minerva urg'd him by her high command, 135
A welcome mate to join the princely band.
For she the ship had form'd with heavenly skill,
Tho' Argus wrought the dictates of her will.
Thus plann'd, thus fashion'd, this fam'd ship excell'd
The noblest ships by oar or sail impell'd. 140
From Aræthyrea, that near Corinth lay,
Phlias, the son of Bacchus, bent his way:
Bless'd by his sire, his splendid mansion stood
Fast by the fountains of Asopus' flood.
From Argos next the sons of Bias came, 145
Areius, Talaus, candidates for fame,
With bold Leodocus, whom Pero bore,
Neleus' fair daughter, on the Argive shore;
For whom Melampus various woes sustain'd,
In a deep dungeon by Iphiclus chain'd. 150
Next Hercules, endued with dauntless mind,
At Jason's summons, stay'd not long behind.
For warn'd of this adventurous band, when last
The chief to Argos from Arcadia past,
(What time in chains he brought the living boar, 155
The dread, the bane of Erymanthia's moor,
And at the gate of proud Mycenæ's town,
From his broad shoulders hurl'd the monster down:)

Unask'd

Unafk'd the ftern Mycenian king's confent,
Inftant to join the warlike hoft he went. 160
Young Hylas waited with obfequious care,
The hero's quiver and his bow to bear.
Next came, the lift of demigods to grace,
He who from Danaüs deriv'd his race,
Nauplius; of whom fam'd Prætus was the fon, 165
Of Prætus Lernus; thus the lineage run:
From Lernus Naubolus his being claim'd,
Whofe valiant fon was Clytoneüs nam'd.
In navigation's various arts confefs'd
Shone Nauplius' fkill, fuperior to the reft: 170
Him to the fea's dread lord, in days of yore,
Danaüs' fair daughter, Amymone bore.
Laft of thofe chiefs who left the Grecian coaft,
Prophetic Idmon join'd the gallant hoft;
(Full well he knew what cruel fate ordain'd; 175
But dreaded more than death his honour ftain'd)
The fon of Phœbus by fome ftolen embrace,
And number'd too with Æolus's race,
He learn'd his art prophetic from his fire,
Omens from birds and prodigies from fire. 180
Illuftrious Pollux, fam'd for martial force,
And Caftor, fkill'd to guide the rapid horfe,

Ætolian

Ætolian Leda sent from Sparta's shore:
Both at one birth in Tyndarus' house she bore.
No boding fears her generous mind deprefs'd; 185
She thought like them whom Jove's embrace had blefs'd.
Lynceus and Idas, from Arene's wall,
Heard fame's loud summons, and obey'd her call:
The sons of Aphareus, of matchlefs might,
But Lynceus stands renown'd for piercing sight: 190
So keen his beam, that ancient fables tell,
He saw, thro' earth, the wondrous depths of hell.
With these bold Periclymenus appears,
The son of Neleus, most advanc'd in years
Of all his race; his sire's unconquer'd pride: 195
Him with vast strength old ocean's lord supply'd,
And gave the power, when hard in battle prefs'd,
To take whatever form might suit him best.
From Tegea's towers, where bore Aphidas sway,
Amphidamas and Cepheus took their way, 200
The sons of Aleus both; and with them went
Ancæus, by his sire Lycurgus sent.
Of those the brother, and by birth the first,
Was good Lycurgus; tenderly he nurs'd
His sire at home; but bade his gallant son 205
With the bold chiefs the race of glory run.

On

On his broad back a bear's rough spoils he wore,
And in his hand a two-edg'd pole-axe bore,
Which, that the youth might in no danger share,
Were safe secreted by his grandsire's care.   210
Augeas too, lord of the Elean coast,
Sail'd, brave associate, with the warlike host.
Rich in possessions, of his riches proud,
Fame says his being to the Sun he ow'd.
Ardent he wish'd to see the Colchian shore,   215
And old Æeta who the sceptre bore.
Asterius and Amphion, urg'd by fame,
The valiant sons of Hyperasius, came
From fair Pellene, built in days of yore
By Pelle's grandsire on the lofty shore.   220
From Tænarus, that yawns with gulf profound,
Euphemus came, for rapid race renown'd.
By Neptune forc'd, Europa gave him birth,
Daughter to Tityus, hugest son of Earth.
Whene'er he skimm'd along the watery plain,   225
With feet unbath'd he swept the surging main,
Scarce brush'd the surface of the briny dew,
And light along the liquid level flew.
Two other sons of Neptune join'd the host,
This from Miletus on th' Ionian coast,   230

Erginus

Erginus nam'd, but that from Samos came,
Juno's lov'd isle, Ancæus was his name;
Illustrious chiefs, and both renown'd afar
For the joint arts of sailing and of war.
Young Meleager, Œneus' warlike son, 235
And sage Laocoon march'd from Calydon.
From the same father he and Œneus sprung;
But on the breasts of different mothers hung.
Him Œneus purpos'd with his son to send,
A wise companion, and a faithful friend. 240
Thus to the royal chiefs his name he gave,
And green in years was number'd with the brave.
Had he continu'd but one summer more
A martial pupil on th' Ætolian shore,
First on the lists of fame the youth had shone, 245
Or own'd superior Hercules alone.
His uncle too, well-skill'd the dart to throw,
And in th' embattled plain resist the foe,
Iphiclus, venerable Thestius' son,
Join'd the young chief, and boldly led him on. 250
The son of Lernus, Palæmonius, came,
Olenian Lernus; but the voice of fame
Whispers, that Vulcan was the hero's sire,
And therefore limps he like the God of fire.

Of nobler port or valour none could boaſt; 255
He added grace to Jaſon's godlike hoſt.
From Phocis Iphitus with ardour preſs'd
To join the chiefs; great Jaſon was his gueſt,
When to the Delphic Oracle he went,
Conſulting fate, and anxious for th' event. 260
Zetes and Calaïs of royal race,
Whom Orithyïa bore in wintry Thrace
To bluſtering Boreas in his airy hall,
Heard fame's loud ſummons, and obey'd the call.
Erectheus, who th' Athenian ſceptre ſway'd, 265
Was parent of the violated maid,
Whom dancing with her mates rude Boreas ſtole,
Where the fam'd waters of Iliſſus roll;
And to his rock-fenc'd Sarpedonian cave
Convey'd her, where Erginus pours his wave: 270
There, circumfus'd in gloom and grateful ſhade,
The god of tempeſts woo'd the gentle maid.
They, when on tip-toe rais'd, in act to fly,
Like the light-pinion'd vagrants of the ſky,
Wav'd their dark wings, and, wondrous to behold! 275
Diſplay'd each plume diſtinct with drops of gold;
While down their backs, of bright cerulean hue,
Looſe in the winds their wanton treſſes flew.

Not

Not long with Pelias young Acastus stay'd;
He left his sire to lend the Grecians aid.   280
Argus, whom Pallas with her gifts inspir'd,
Follow'd his friend, with equal glory fir'd.
  Such the compeers of Jason highly fam'd;
And all these demigods were Minyans nam'd.
The most illustrious heroes of the host   285
Their lineage from the seed of Minyas boast;
For Minyas' daughter, Clymena the fair,
Alcimeda, great Jason's mother, bare.
  When all was furnish'd by the busy band
Which vessels destin'd for the main demand;   290
The heroes from Iolcos bent their way
To the fam'd port, the Pagasæan bay;
And deep-environ'd with thick-gathering crowds,
They shone like stars resplendent thro' the clouds.
Then thus among the rout, with wondering look,   295
Some swain survey'd the bright-arm'd chiefs and spoke:
' Say, what can Pelias, mighty Jove, intend,
' Far, far from Greece so great a force to send?
' Sure, should Æeta spurn the sons of Greece,
' And to their claims refuse the golden Fleece,   300
' That self-same day shall see his palace crown'd
' With glittering turrets, levell'd to the ground.

                                                 ' But

' But endlefs toils purfue them as they go,
' And Fate hath mark'd their defperate fteps with woe.'
Thus, when he faw the delegated bands, 305
Spoke the rude fwain with heaven-uplifted hands:
The gentler females thus the Gods implore;
" Safe may they reach again their native fhore:"
And thus fome matron mild her mind exprefs'd;
(Tears in her eye, and terrors at her breaft) 310
' Unfortunate Alcimeda, thy fate
' Now frowns malignant, tho' it frowns fo late;
' Nor wills the tenor of thy life to run
' Serene and peaceful, as it firft begun.
' On Æfon too attend unnumber'd woes; 315
' Far, better far, a lingering life to clofe,
' And bury all his forrows in the tomb,
' Unconfcious of calamities to come.
' Oh! had both Phrixus and the ram been drown'd,
' When Helle perifh'd in the gulf profound: 320
' But the dire monfter was with voice endu'd,
' And human accents from his mouth enfu'd,
' To fad Alcimeda denouncing ftrife,
' And woes to cloud the evening of her life.'
Thus fpoke fome matron as the heroes went; 325
Around their lords the menial train lament:

Alcimeda

Alcimeda embrac'd her son with tears,
Each breast was chill'd with sad presaging fears.
Age-drooping Æson heard the general moan,   329
Wrapp'd in soft robes, and answer'd groan for groan.
But Jason sooths their fears, their bosom warms,
And bids his servants bring the burnish'd arms.
They, with a downcast look and lowly bow,
Obey their chief with silent steps and slow.
The pensive Queen, while tears bedew her face,   335
Her son still circles with a fond embrace.
Thus to her nurse an infant orphan springs,
And weeps unceasing as she closely clings;
Experienc'd insults make her loath to stay
Beneath a step-dame's proud, oppressive sway.   340
Thus in her royal breast the sorrows pent
Forc'd sighs and tears, and struggled for a vent.
Still in her arms she held her favourite son,
And comfortless with faltering speech begun:
' Oh had I died on that detested day,   345
' And with my sorrows sigh'd my soul away,
' When Pelias publish'd his severe decree,
' Severe and fatal to my son and me!
' Thyself had then my aged eyelids clos'd,
' And those dear hands my decent limbs compos'd;   350

C   ' This

18   *The* ARGONAUTICS *of*   Book I.

' This boon alone I wiſh'd thee to impart,
  This wiſh alone lay dormant at my heart.
' But now, alas! tho' firſt of Grecian names,
' Admir'd and envy'd by Theſſalian dames,
' I, like an hand-maid, now am left behind,   355
' Bereav'd of all tranquillity of mind.
' By thee rever'd, in dignity I ſhone,
' And firſt and laſt for thee unloos'd my zone.
' For unrelenting hate Lucina bore,
' Thee, one lov'd ſon, ſhe gave, but gave no more. 360
' Alas! not ev'n the viſions of the night
' Foretold ſuch fatal woes from Phrixus' flight.'
  Thus mourn'd Alcimeda; her handmaids hear,
Sigh back her ſighs, and anſwer tear with tear.
Then Jaſon theſe conſoling words addreſs'd,   365
To ſooth the riſing anguiſh of her breaſt:
" Ceaſe, mother, ceaſe exceſs of grief to ſhow,
" Oh! ceaſe this wild extravagance of woe.
" Tears cannot make one dire diſaſter leſs;
" They cheriſh grief, and aggravate diſtreſs,   370
" Wiſely and juſtly have the Gods aſſign'd
" Unthought-of miſeries to all mankind.
" The lot they give you, tho' perchance ſevere,
" Confiding in Minerva, bravely bear.

" Minerva

" Minerva firſt this bold adventure mov'd, 375
" Apollo, and the Oracles approv'd.
" Theſe calls of heaven our confidence command,
" Join'd with the valour of this princely band.
" Haſte, royal mother, to your native tow'rs,
" Paſs with your handmaids there the peaceful hours.
" Forebode not here calamities to come: 381
" Your female train will re-conduct you home."
He ſpoke; and from the palace bent his way,
Graceful of port; ſo moves the god of day
At Delos, from his odour-breathing fanes, 385
Or Claros ſituate on Ionian plains,
Or Lycia's ample ſhores, where Xanthus leads
His winding waters thro' irriguous meads.
Thus Jaſon march'd majeſtic thro' the crowd,
And Fame auſpicious rais'd her voice aloud: 390
When lo! the prieſteſs of Diana came,
Their guardian Goddeſs, Iphias was her name,
Bending with age, and kiſs'd the chief's right hand;
In vain ſhe wiſh'd to ſpeak; the haſty band
With ſpeedy footſteps from the dame withdrew, 395
And Jaſon mingled with his valiant crew.
Then from the tower-fenc'd town he bent his way,
And reach'd ere long the Pagaſæan bay;

There

There join'd his comrades waiting on the coaft,
And there faluted his confederate hoft.   400
When from Iölcos, lo, the wondering train
Obferve Acaftus haftening o'er the plain,
And with him Argus, his compeer and friend;
Unknown to Pelias, to the ſhip they tend.
Argus around his brawny ſhoulders flung   405
A bull's black ſpoils that to his ancles hung.
Acaftus wore a mantle rich and gay,
Wrought by his fifter, lovely Pelopa.
Thus rob'd, the chiefs approach'd the crowded ſhore;
Illuftrious Jafon ftay'd not to explore   410
What caufe fo long detain'd them, but commands
To council all the delegated bands.
On ſhrouds and fails that cover'd half the beach,
And the tall, tapering maft, in order each,
The heroes fat; then rifing o'er the reft,   415
His bold aſſociates Jafon thus addrefs'd:

' Since now the ftores lie ready on the ftrand,
' And fince our chiefs and arms are all at hand,
' No longer let us wafte the golden day,
' But the firft fummons of the breeze obey.   420
' And, fince we all with equal ardour burn
' For Colchian ſpoils, and hope a fafe return,

' Impartial

' Impartial choose some hero fam'd afar
' To guide the vessel, and conduct the war,
' Let him, your sovereign chief, with foreign foes   425
' The terms of treaty, and of fight propose.'
  He spoke; with earnest eyes the youthful band
Mark bold Alcides for supreme command;
On him with voice unanimous they call,
Own him their leader, and the lord of all.   430
In the mid circle sat the godlike man,
His broad right hand he wav'd, and thus began:
  " Let none to me this arduous task assign,
  " For I the glory with the charge decline.
  " Jason alone shall lead this valiant band,   435
  " The chief who rais'd it, let that chief command."
  Thus briefly spoke th' unconquerable man;
Loud approbation thro' the circle ran:
Then Jason rose, (complacence fill'd his breast)
And thus the pleas'd, attentive throng addres'd: 440
  ' Friends and associates, since your wills decree
' This great, this honourable trust to me,
' No longer be our enterprize delay'd:
' To Phœbus first be due oblations paid;
' Let then a short repast our strength renew: 445
' And, till my herdsmen to our gallant crew

C 3   ' With

'With beeves return, the beft my ftalls contain,'
'Strive we to launch our veffel in the main.
'And when clofe ftow'd our military ftores,
'Each take his poft, and ply the nimble oars.   450
'To Phœbus firft, Embafian Phœbus, raife
'The fmoaking altar; let the victims blaze.
'He promis'd, if due rites to him I pay,
'To point thro' ocean's paths our dubious way.'
  He faid, and inftant to the tafk he flew;   455
Example fir'd his emulative crew.
They heap'd their veftments on a rock, that ftood
Far from the infults of the roaring flood,
But, in times paft, when wintry ftorms prevail'd,
Th' encroaching waves its towering top affail'd. 460
As Argus counfel'd, with ftrong ropes they bound,
Compacting clofe, the veffel round and round;
Then with ftout nails the fturdy planks they join'd,
To brave the fury of the waves or wind:
Next delv'd with fpades a channel deep and wide, 465
Thro' which the fhip might launch into the tide.
Near to the water deeper was the way,
Where wooden cylinders tranfverfely lay;
On thefe they heav'd the veffel from the plain,
To roll her, fmoothly-gliding, to the main.   470

Then

Then to the benches, tapering oars they fix'd;
A cubit's meafure was the fpace betwixt:
This was the ftation for the labouring bands,
To tug with bending breafts, and out-ftretch'd hands.
Firft Tiphys mounted on th' aerial prow   475
To iffue orders to the train below,
That at his word, their ftrength uniting, all
Might join together, and together haul.
With eager look th' attentive heroes ftand,
And wait impatient till he gave command;   480
Then all at once, with full exerted fway,
They move her from the ftation where fhe lay,
And pufhing inftant, as the pilot guides,
On fmooth round rollers Pelian Argo glides;
Glibly fhe glides; loud fhouts the jovial band; 485.
They haul, they pull, they pufh her from the ftrand.
Beneath the huge hulk groan the rollers ftrong;
Black fmoke arifes as fhe moves along;
With fwift defcent fhe rufhes to the main:
Coercive ropes her rapid race reftrain.   490
Then, next, their fails they hoifted, fix'd their oars,
The maft erected, and embark'd the ftores.
By lots on benches were the heroes plac'd,
And with two heroes every bench was grac'd.

On great Alcides, formidable name, 495
And on Ancæus, who from Tegea came,
With voice unanimous, the martial hoft
Beftow'd the centre's honourable poft.
To watchful Tiphys was the helm affign'd,
To ftem the waves, and catch the favouring wind. 500
This done, with ftones befide the fhore which lay,
They rear'd an altar to the God of day,
Embafian Phœbus, and the furface round
With the dry branches of an olive crown'd.
Meanwhile the herdfmen drove two beeves well fed
From Jafon's ftalls; youths to the altar led 506
The victims; fome brought water from the lake;
Some the due offering of the falted cake.
Jafon, while thefe the facrifice prepare,
Thus to his parent God prefers his pray'r: 510
' Patron of Pagafæ, thine ear we claim,
' Guard of the city grac'd with Æfon's name:
' When to confult thine oracle I went,
' It promis'd to reveal this great event,
' The final iffue of our bold emprife: 515
' On thee, chief author, all our hope relies.
' Conduct my comrades to the far-fam'd Fleece,
' Then fafe reftore them to the realms of Greece.

' And

'And here I vow, whatever chiefs return,
'So many bulls shall on thine altar burn;   520
'A sacrifice at Delphos is decreed,
'And in Ortygia shall the victims bleed.
'But now thefe humble offerings which we pay,
'Gracious accept, far-darting God of day.
'Be thou, O father, our aufpicious guide,   525
'When hence we fail acrofs the founding tide.
'Smooth the rough billows, and let breezes bland
'Propitious waft us to the Colchian land.'
Thus pray'd he fuppliant, and prepar'd to make
The facred offering of the falted cake.   530
Alcides, fam'd for manly ftrength and fway,
And bold Ancæus rofe the beeves to flay.
Alcides' club imprefs'd a deadly wound
On the fteer's front, and fell'd him to the ground.
Thy axe, Ancæus, at one fturdy ftroke,   535
The fteer's fkull fractur'd, and the neck-bone broke,
Down fell the victim, floundering with the blow,
Prone on his horns, and plough'd the fand below.
The ready train, that round in order ftood,
Stab the fallen beeves, and fhed the life-warm blood;
Then from the body ftrip the fmoaking hide,   541
The beafts they quarter, and the joints divide;

The

The thighs devoted to the Gods they part,
On thefe the fat, involv'd in cawls, with art
They fpread, and as the lambent flame devours,   545
The Grecian chief the pure libation pours.
Joy fill'd the breaft of Idmon to behold,
How from the thighs the flame relucent roll'd
In purple volumes, and propitious fmoke;
And thus the feer, infpir'd by Phœbus, fpoke: 550
' Tho' various perils your attempt oppofe,
' And toils unnumber'd bring unnumber'd woes;
' Yet fhall ye fafe return, ye fons of Greece,
' Adorn'd with conqueft, and the golden Fleece.
' Me cruel Fate ordains on Afia's fhore   555.
' To die, nor e'er behold my country more.
' And tho' my deftiny long fix'd I knew,
' Yet, ftill refolv'd, I join'd the martial crew;
' Inflam'd with glory to the hoft I came,
' Of life regardlefs, emulous of fame.'   560
Thus he; the hoft the fate of Idmon mourn,
But joy tranfports them for their wifh'd return.
The fun, remitting now his fiercer ray,
Pours from the weft the faint remains of day:
Low as he finks, the lofty rocks expand   565
Their lengthen'd fhadows o'er the diftant land,

On

On leafy couches now the warlike train
Repose along the beach that skirts the main.
Before the chiefs are savoury viands plac'd,
And generous wines, delicious to the taste. 570
The hours in mutual converse they employ,
In festive songs and undissembled joy.
Thus at the banquet sport the young and gay,
When Mirth breaks in, and Envy skulks away.
But not unmark'd was Jason's pensive look; 575
Idas beheld him, and licentious spoke:

' What doubts, what fears do Æson's son perplex?
' What dangers fright him, and what sorrows vex?
' Proclaim thy thoughts: or is thy dubious mind
' Dismay'd with terrours of the dastard kind? 580
' Now by this stout, unconquer'd lance, I swear,
' On which in war victorious wreaths I bear,
' (Scorning from Jove's assistance to receive
' Those palms, which this resistless lance can give)
' No foes shall brave, no wiles of war withstand, 585
' Tho' Jove frown adverse, this impetuous hand.
' Such Idas is, for prowess fam'd afar,
' Arene's boast, the thunder-bolt of war.'

This said, the boaster seiz'd a goblet, fill'd
With racy wine, and to the bottom swill'd. 590

O'er

O'er his black beard and cheeks the liquor flow'd:
Th' affembled hoft with indignation glow'd.
Then Idmon rofe and boldly thus reply'd:
" Vain wretch! to brand our leader and our guide;
" And more irreverent ftill, thus flufh'd with wine, 595
" To dare reproach fuperior powers divine.
" Far different fpeech muft cheer the focial train;
" Thy words are brutifh, and thy boafts are vain.
" Thus, fame reports, the Aloïdæ ftrove
" Long fince to irritate the powers above   600
" By vile afperfions, infamoufly free;
" Yet they in valour far exceeded thee.
" Slain by the fhafts of Phœbus, down they fell,
" Tho' high afpiring, to the depths of Hell."
  He faid; but Idas, with farcaftic fneer,   605
Laughing, provok'd the venerable feer:
' Declare, wife augur, if the Gods decree,
' The fame perdition fhall be hurl'd on me,
' Which fam'd Aloëus' impious fons befell
' When flain by Phœbus, and condemn'd to hell.   610
' Meantime efcape, or manfully withftand,
' Vain feer, the fury of this vengeful hand.'
  Thus Idas fpoke, impatient of controul,
And rifing rage inflam'd his fiery foul;

Nor

Nor had they here ceas'd fiercely to conteſt, 615
But Jaſon and his friends their wrath repreſs'd.
'Twas then, the jarring heroes to compoſe,
Th' enchanting bard, Oeagrian Orpheus roſe,
And thus, attuning to the trembling ſtrings
His ſoothing voice, of harmony he ſings: 620
" How at the firſt, beneath chaotic ſway,
" Heaven, earth and ſea in wild diſorder lay;
" Till nature parted the conflicting foes,
" And beauteous order from confuſion roſe.
" How in yon bright etherial fields above 625
" The lucid ſtars in conſtant orbits move;
" How the pale queen of night and golden ſun,
" Thro' months, and years their radiant journeys run:
" Whence roſe the mountains, clad with waving woods,
" The cryſtal founts, and hoarſe-refounding floods, 630
" With all their nymphs; from what celeſtial ſeed
" Springs the vaſt ſpecies of the ſerpent breed:
" How o'er the new-created world below,
" On high Olympus' ſummits crown'd with ſnow,
" Ophion, and, from ocean ſprung of old, 635
" The fair Eurynome reign'd uncontroll'd:
" How haughty Saturn, with ſuperior ſway
" Exil'd Ophion from the realms of day;

" Eurynome

" Eurynome before proud Rhea fled,
" And how both funk in ocean's billowy bed.   640
" Long time they rul'd the bleft Titanian Gods,
" While infant Jove poffefs'd the dark abodes
" Of Dicte's cave; yet uninform'd his mind
" With heavenly wifdom, and his hand confin'd.
" Forg'd by earth's giant fons, with livid rays   645
" Flam'd not as yet the lightning's piercing blaze;
" Nor roar'd the thunder thro' the realms above,
" The ftrength and glory of almighty Jove."
Here the fweet bard his tuneful lyre unftrung,
And ceas'd the heavenly mufic of his tongue;   650
But, with the found entranc'd, the liftening ear
Still thought him finging, and ftill feem'd to hear:
In filent rapture every chief remains,
And feels within his heart the thrilling ftrains.
Forthwith the bowl they crown with rofy wine,   655
And pay due honours to the powers divine;
Then on the flaming tongues libations pour,
And wait falubrious fleep's compofing hour.
Soon as the bright-ey'd morning's fplendid ray
On Pelion's fummit pour'd the welcome day,   660
Light fkimm'd the breezes o'er the liquid plain,
And gently fwell'd the fluctuating main;

          Then

Then Tiphys rose, and, summon'd by his care,
Embark the heroes, and their oars prepare.
Portentous now along the winding shores 665
Hoarse sounding Pagasæan Neptune roars:
From Pelian Argo's keel loud murmurs broke,
Urgent to sail; the keel of sacred oak,
Endu'd with voice, and marvellously wrought,
Itonian Pallas from Dodona brought. 670
Now on their destin'd posts, arrang'd along,
In seemly order sat the princely throng;
Fast by each chief his glittering armour flames:
The midmost station bold Ancæus claims,
With great Alcides, (whose enormous might 675
Arm'd with a massy club provokes the fight,)
Close plac'd beside him: in the yielding flood
The keel deep-sinking owns the demigod.

Their hausers now they loose, and on the brine
To Neptune pour the consecrated wine: 680
Then from his native shore sad Jason turns
His oft-reverted eye, and silent mourns.
As in Ortygia, or the Delphic fane,
Or where Ismenus laves Bœotia's plain,
Apollo's altar round, the youthful quire, 685
The dance according with the sounding lyre,

The

The hallow'd ground with equal cadence beat,
And move in meafure their alternate feet;
Together fo Theffalia's princes fweep
With well-tim'd oars the filver-curling deep: 690
While, raifing high the Thracian harp, prefides
Melodious Orpheus, and the movement guides.
Dafh'd by their oars the foaming billows broke,
And loud remurmur'd to each mighty ftroke.
Swift fail'd the fhip, the fun refulgent beam'd, 695
And bright as flame their glittering armour gleam'd.
While to their outftretch'd oars the heroes bow,
The parted ocean whitening foams below.
So fhines the path, along fome graffy plain,
Worn by the footfteps of the village-fwain. 700

    Th' immortal powers that Jove's proud palace crown,
All on that memorable day look'd down,
The godlike chiefs and Argo to furvey,
As thro' the deep they urg'd their daring way.
Then too on Pelion's cloud-capt fummit ftood 705
The Nymphs that wander in that facred wood;
Wondering they view'd below the failing pine,
(Itonian Pallas fram'd the work divine)
And bold Theffalia's labouring heroes fweep
With ftretching oars the navigable deep. 710

Lo!

Lo! from the mountain's topmost cliff descends
The Centaur Chiron; to the shore he bends
His hasty footsteps: on the beach he stood,
And dipp'd his fetlocks in the hoary flood.
He hail'd the heroes with his big, broad hand, 715
And wish'd them safe to gain their native land.
With Chiron came Chariclo to the shore;
The young Achilles in her arms she bore.
Peleus, his sire, with secret pleasure smil'd,
As high in air she rais'd the royal child. 720
And now the winding bay's safe precincts past,
Thessalian Argo plough'd the watery waste;
On Tiphys' care the valiant chiefs rely'd,
To steer the vessel o'er the foaming tide,
The smooth well-modell'd rudder to command, 725
Obsequious to the movement of his hand.
And next inserting in the keel below
The mast tall-tapering, to the stern and prow,
With ropes that thro' the rolling pulleys glide,
They rear upright, and firm on every side. 730
Then high in air the swelling sails they raise,
While on their bosoms buxom Zephyr plays.
With favouring gales their steady course they keep
To where Tisæum frowns upon the deep.

D Meanwhile

Meanwhile sweet Orpheus, as they sail'd along, 735
Rais'd to Diana the melodious song,
Who sav'd them, where her guardian power presides,
From treacherous rocks that lurk beneath the tides.
The fish in shoals, attentive to his lay,
Pursu'd the poet o'er the watery way; 740
And oft emerging from their liquid sphere,
Strove more distinct his heavenly notes to hear.
As sheep in flocks thick-pasturing on the plain
Attend the footsteps of the shepherd-swain,
His well-known call they hear, and fully fed, 745
Pace slowly on, their leader at their head;
Who pipes melodious, as he moves along,
On sprightly reeds his modulated song:
Thus charm'd with tuneful sounds, the scaly train
Pursu'd the flying vessel o'er the main. 750
And now the winds with favouring breezes blew,
Corn-crown'd Thessalia lessen'd to the view,
The Grecian heroes pass by Pelion's steep,
Whose rocky summit nodded o'er the deep.
Now Sepias' cliffs beneath the waves subside, 755
And sea-girt Sciathos surmounts the tide.
Next, but far distant, was Piresiæ seen,
(Built on Magnesia's continent serene)

And

And Dolops' tomb, for this pacific shore,
Blest with mild evening's soften'd gales, they bore.
To him with victims was an altar crown'd, 761
While night prevail'd, and ocean roar'd around.
Two days they tarried, till propitious gales
Rose with the third, and bellied all their sails.
Assiduous then, the well-known shore they fill, 765
The shore call'd Aphetæ of Argo still.
Next Melibœa, on Thessalia's shore,
They pass, where winds and thundering tempests roar.
At early dawn, incumbent o'er the deep,
They view high Omole's aspiring steep. 770
Next by the streams of Amyrus they steer,
And where thy vales, Eurymena, appear,
And Ossa and Olympus' shady brow;
Loud from deep caverns gush the waves below.
By night beside Pallene's heights they sail, 775
And rough Canastra frowning o'er the vale.
But when the morn display'd her orient light,
Tall Athos rose conspicuous to the sight;
Which tho' from Lemnos far remov'd it lay,
As far as ships can sail till noon of day, 780
Yet the proud mountain's high-exalted head,
A gloom umbrageous o'er Myrina spread.

All day till eve the soft, indulgent gales
Their succour lent, and fill'd the swelling sails.
But when with eve the breezes ceas'd to blow, 785
The mariners to Sintian Lemnos row,
Ill-fated island! where the female train
Had all the males, the year preceding, slain.
For, deep-enamour'd with the nymphs of Thrace,
The men declin'd the conjugal embrace; 790
Their wives they slighted, and unwary led
War's pleasing spoils, fair captives, to their bed.
For angry Venus robb'd of love's delights
The Lemnian females, for neglected rites.
Ah miserable train! with envy curs'd 795
And jealousy, of passions far the worst!
One fatal night this unrelenting crew
Their mates, and all the lovely captives, slew,
And every male; left in the course of time
Should rise some hero to revenge the crime. 800
Hypsipyla alone, illustrious maid,
Spar'd her sire Thoas, who the sceptre sway'd.
With pious care, in reverence to his age,
In a capacious ark she plac'd the sage,
Confiding in the mercy of the wave 805
The monarch from the massacre to save.

         Some

Some faithful fifhers, to their mandate juft,
Convey'd with care the delegated truft
Safe to a neighbouring, fea-furrounded fhore,
Œnœa nam'd, fo nam'd in days of yore,   810
Now Sicinum; from Sicinus it takes
Its title, whom a naiad of the lakes,
The nymph Œnœa, beautiful and fair,
Comprefs'd by Thoas, to the monarch bare.
The widow'd Lemnians, tho' by waves fecur'd,   815
Oft fhone in arms, to martial toils inur'd.
To feed their cattle was their daily care,
Or cleave the furrow with the crooked fhare:
Expert at thefe, Minerva's arts they fcorn'd,
Which once employ'd them, and which once adorn'd.
Oft to the main, opprefs'd with dire alarms,   821
They look'd; for much they fear'd the Thracian arms.
And when Theffalian Argo caught their view,
Quick from Myrina to the fhore they flew.
All clad in glittering arms they prefs'd the ftrand,
Impetuous; (like the Bacchanalian band,   826
When with raw flefh their horrid feafts they clofe;)
They deem'd the veffel ftor'd with Thracian foes,
Hypfipyla advanc'd among the reft,
In the bright armour of her father drefs'd;   830

Anxious,

Anxious, aftonifh'd all the dames appear,
And by their filence teftified their fear.
Meanwhile Æthalides the heroes fend;
To him their peaceful mandates they commend.
Invefted with the office of the God,   835
They grace their herald too with Hermes' rod,
Hermes his fire; who blefs'd his favourite heir
With memory nor time, nor place impair.
In vain around him Acheron's waters roll;
They pour no dull oblivion o'er his foul.   840
To him the fates this privilege beftow,
By turns to wander with the fhades below;
By turns with men to view the golden day,
And feel the fun's invigorating ray.
But why expatiate on fuch themes as thefe?   845
Why tell the fame of great Æthalides?
The herald to Hypfipyla addrefs'd,
With mild benevolence, this joint requeft;
That now, at evening-clofe, the friendly land
Might hofpitably treat this gallant band,   850
Who fear'd at morn to hoift their fwelling fails,
For Boreas blew with unpropitious gales.

    The queen had fummon'd to the council-hall
The Lemnian dames, the dames obey'd her call:

Who

Who mildly, with perfuafion in her look, 855
In order rang'd, the heroines befpoke :
' Let us, my mates, and ye my words attend,
' Commodious prefents to thefe ftrangers fend;
' Such as their friends to mariners confign,
' Salubrious viands, and delicious wine; 860
' So will they peaceful on our borders ftay,
' Nor need compel them to the town to ftray.
' Here will they learn the ftory of our guilt,
' The vows we broke, the kindred blood we fpilt;
' And fure a tale, thus horrid, muft appear 865
' Cruel and impious to a foreign ear.
' Thefe are the counfels of your faithful friend,
' Prompt to advife, and fteady to defend.
' She who can furnifh counfel more difcreet,
' Now let her offer—for this caufe we meet.' 870
Thus fpoke the queen, and prefs'd her father's throne,
A royal feat, compos'd of folid ftone.
Then rofe Polyxo, venerable dame,
Once the queen's nurfe, opprefs'd with age, and lame;
A ftaff fuftain'd her (for her limbs were weak) 875
Tottering with age, yet vehement to fpeak.
Near her four damfels, blooming, frefh and fair,
Sat crown'd with ringlets of the whiteft hair.

D 4 Full

Full in the midſt ſhe ſtood, then rais'd her head,
Her back was bent with years, and thus ſhe ſaid: 880
' The queen's advice I greatly muſt commend,
' Commodious preſents to our gueſts to ſend.
' And what more ſaving counſel ſhall I give
' To thoſe my friends who ſhall hereafter live;
' Whene'er the ſons of Thrace, or hoſtile hoſts 885
' From other kingdoms ſhall infeſt our coaſts;
' Which well may happen, we muſt all allow,
' As this invaſion that alarms us now?
' But ſhould ſome God avert th' impending ill,
' Yet greater evils may befall, and will. 890
' For when the oldeſt die, as die they muſt,
' And our wiſe matrons be transform'd to duſt,
' And you, now young, oppreſs'd at laſt with age,
' Shall unprolific tread life's irkſome ſtage:
' What wretched mortals ye, who then ſurvive! 895
' Who to their labour, then, the ſteers ſhall drive?
' Will oxen then their necks ſpontaneous bow
' Beneath the yoke, and drag the ponderous plough?
' Or will they reap the harveſt on the plain,
' And every autumn houſe the golden grain? 900
' I, tho' preſerv'd to this important day,
' (For death from me abhorrent turns away,)

' Yet,

' Yet, ere the fun compleats his annual round,
' If right I judge, shall mingle with the ground,
' Lodg'd in the lap of Earth, at Nature's call,   905
' And 'scape the ruin that involves you all.
' Hear then, young damsels, what my years advise;
' Before you now the fair occasion lies:
' Commit your city to these strangers' care,
' Let them your mansions and possessions share.'   910
She spoke, pleas'd murmurs fill'd the spacious hall;
Polyxo's counsel was approv'd by all.
From her sire's throne Hypsipyla arose,
Thus in few words the conference to close:
" My mates, since all this sage advice commend,   915
" An instant message to the ship I send."
She said, and to Iphinoa gave command;
" Haste, find the leader of yon martial band,
" Invite him (of our amity a proof)
" To lodge beneath my hospitable roof;   920
" There time will furnish leisure to relate
" The genius and the manners of our state.
" But let his comrades rove, as pleasure leads,
" And pitch their tents along the fertile meads;
" Or to the tower-defended town repair,   925
" Assur'd of safety, and our royal care."

Th'

Th' assembly rose, as thus the princess spoke,
Then to the regal dome her way she took.
Iphinoa, mindful of the queen's command,
Approach'd the Minyans scatter'd o'er the strand, 930
Who throng'd around her, eager to explore
Wherefore she came, and what commands she bore.
Then thus she said; 'Strangers, to you as friends
' Hypsipyla, the seed of Thoas, sends
' Her faithful herald, with this strict command 935
' To find the leader of your martial band;
' Him she invites (of amity a proof)
' To lodge beneath her hospitable roof:
' There time will furnish leisure to relate
' The genius, and the manners of our state. 940
' But let his comrades rove, as pleasure leads,
' And pitch their tents along the fertile meads;
' Or to the tower-defended town repair,
' Assur'd of safety, and the royal care.'
These words were grateful to the warlike band; 945
From her they learn'd whose sceptre rul'd the land;
Instant they urg'd their chief's assent, and all
Prepar'd obsequious to accept the call.
A mantle doubly lin'd, of purple hue,
The son of Æson o'er his shoulders threw. 950

This

This Pallas gave him, when, with wondrous art,
She plann'd his ship, and meafur'd every part.
'Twere fafer to furvey the radiant globe
Of rifing Phœbus, than this fplendid robe.
Full in the middle beam'd a crimfon blaze,   955
The verge furrounding darted purple rays.
In every part hiftoric fcenes were wrought;
The moving figures feem'd inform'd with thought.
Here, on their work intent, the Cyclops ftrove
Eager to forge a thunder-bolt for Jove;   960
Half-rough, half-form'd the glowing engine lay,
And only wanted the fire-darting ray;
And this they hammer'd out on anvils dire;
At each collifion flafh'd the fatal fire.
Not diftant far, in lively colours plann'd,   965
Two brothers, Zethus and Amphion ftand,
Sons of Antiopa: no turrets crown'd
Thy city, Thebes, but walls were rifing round.
A mountain's rocky fummit Zethus bore
On his broad back, but feem'd to labour fore.   970
Behind, Amphion tun'd his golden fhell,
Amphion, deem'd in mufic to excel:
Rocks ftill purfu'd him as he mov'd along,
Charm'd by the mufic of his magic fong.

       Crown'd

Crown'd with soft tresses, in a fairer field, 975
Gay Venus toy'd with Mars's splendid shield.
Down from her shoulder her expanded vest
Display'd the swelling beauties of her breast.
She in the brazen buckler, glittering bright,
Beheld her lovely image with delight. 980
On a rich plain appear, not distant far,
The Taphians, and Electryon's sons at war;
Fat steers the prize for which the swains contend,
Those strive to plunder, these their herds defend;
The meads were moist with blood and rosy dew: 985
The powerful many triumph'd o'er the few.
Two chariots next roll'd lightly o'er the plains,
This Pelops drove, and shook the founding reins;
Hippodamia at his side he view'd:
In the next chariot, Myrtilus pursu'd, 990
And with him Oenomas; approaching near,
At Pelops' back he aim'd the vengeful spear;
The faithless axle, as the wheels whirl'd round,
Snapp'd short, and left him stretch'd along the ground.
Here young Apollo stood, in act to throw 995
The whirring arrow from the twanging bow,
At mighty Tityus aim'd, who basely strove
To force his mother, erst belov'd by Jove:

He

He from fair Elara deriv'd his birth,
Tho' fed and nourish'd by prolific Earth. 1000
There Phryxus stoop'd to listen to the ram,
On whose broad back the Hellespont he swam.
The beast look'd speaking; earnest could you gaze,
The lively piece would charmingly amaze.
Long might you feast your eye, and lend an ear,
With pleasing hope the conference to hear. 1006
   Such was the present of the blue-ey'd maid—
In his right hand a missile lance he sway'd,
Which Atalanta, to reward the brave,
Sure pledge of friendship, to the hero gave, 1010
When on the breezy Mænalus she rov'd,
And wish'd the company of him she lov'd;
But he, of suitors' amorous strife afraid,
Repress'd the fond intention of the maid.
Thus rob'd, thus arm'd, he to the city went, 1015
Bright as a star that gilds the firmament,
Which maids assembled view with eager eyes
High o'er their roof in orient beauty rise.
On the bright signal, as it darts its rays,
Attentive they with silent transport gaze. 1020
Each, with this omen charm'd, expects, tho' late,
Return'd from distant climes her destin'd mate.

Thus

Thus shone the chief, for high achievements known,
Majestic as he mov'd to Lemnos' town.
The noble heroines his footsteps meet, 1025
With courteous joy the Grecian guest to greet,
Whose downcast eye ne'er wander'd, till he came
To the proud palace of the royal dame;
Obsequious damsels at the portal wait,
And quick unbar the double-folding gate: 1030
Then thro' the various courts extending wide,
And stately rooms, Iphinoa was his guide;
On a bright throne, with rich embroidery grac'd,
Fronting her sovereign she the hero plac'd.
Th' embarrass'd queen, her face with blushes spread,
In courteous terms addrefs'd the prince, and said:
‘ Why, gentle stranger, should your warlike train
‘ At distance far, without the walls remain?
‘ The men who till'd these ample fields before,
‘ Now turn rich furrows on the Thracian shore. 1040
‘ But hear, while I our matchless woes relate;
‘ So shall you know the story of our fate.
‘ When o'er this realm my father Thoas reign'd,
‘ The Lemnian youth, to fraud and rapine train'd,
‘ On Thracian borders seiz'd the trembling prey,
‘ And brought whole flocks, and lovely maids away.
                                    ‘ This

' This Venus plann'd, with mifchievous intent,
' And fierce among them fatal difcord fent.
' Their wives they loath'd, and vainly impious led
' War's fpoils, fair captives, to the lawlefs bed. 1050
' Long we endur'd, forgiving infults paft,
' And hop'd the faithlefs would reform at laft.
' In vain; each day but doubled our difgrace,
' Our children yielded to a fpurious race.
' The widow'd mother, the difcarded maid, 1055
' Forlorn, neglected thro' the city ftray'd.
' No tender pity touch'd the parent's breaft,
' To fee his darling child abus'd, opprefs'd
' Beneath a ftep-dame's proud, imperious fway:
' No fons would then maternal duty pay, 1060
' Nor, as before, their mother's caufe defend;
' No fifter then to fifter prov'd a friend:
' But the gay troops of Thracian captives fair
' Inthrall'd the men, and challeng'd all their care;
' At home, abroad, the firft, at pleafure's call, 1065
' To fhare the banquet, and conduct the ball.
' At length, but ftrange! fome favouring power divine
' In female minds infpir'd this bold defign,
' That, when return'd from Thracia's hateful fhore,
' Our roofs thefe traitors might protect no more;

' That,

' That, thus conſtrain'd, they might forego their
  crimes, 1071
' Or with their captives flee to diſtant climes.
' They fail, return, the few remaining males
' Demand, then quit us with auſpicious gales;
' And now the frigid fields of Thrace they plough,
' And countries whiten'd with Sithonian ſnow. 1076
' Haſte then, conduct your comrades to the town:
' Here fix your feat, and Lemnos is your own.
' And if to high dominion you aſpire,
' Reign here, and wield the ſceptre of my ſire. 1080
' You muſt approve; for not ſo fair a coaſt,
' Or iſle ſo fertile can the Ægean boaſt.
' Haſte to your friends, and make my pleaſure known,
' Nor let them longer lodge without the town.'
    Artful ſhe ſpoke, forbearing to relate   1085
How in one night each woman ſlew her mate.
    Then Jaſon thus: " Whate'er your bounty grants,
" Stores for our voyage, or our preſent wants,
" Pleas'd we accept: I to my valiant bands
" Will ſpeed to ſignify your kind commands, 1090
" Then ſoon conduct my comrades to the town:
" But ſtill, O Queen, ſtill wear your father's crown.
" Not from diſdain I ſhun imperial ſway,
" But great achievements call me hence away."

He

He spoke, and gently press'd her fair right hand,
Then sought his comrades scatter'd o'er the strand.
Unnumber'd damsels round the hero wait,
Gazing with joy, and follow to the gate;
Then grateful presents in swift cars convey
To the land's margin, where the warriours lay. 1100
When Jason now to his adventurous bands
Had signified Hypsipyla's commands,
With eager joy the Minyans haste to share
Her friendly roofs, and hospitable fare.
The Queen of Love Thessalia's chiefs inspires, 1105
For Vulcan's sake, with amorous desires;
That Lemnos, Vulcan's sacred isle, agen
May flourish, peopled with a race of men.
Great Jason hastens to the regal walls;
The rest proceed where chance or pleasure calls, 1110
Save great Alcides; with a chosen train,
Ambitious he in Argo to remain.
Eager with joy the jolly crowds advance
To share the genial feast, or lead the dance;
To Venus' and to Vulcan's fane they throng, 1115
And crown the day with victims and with song.
Sunk in soft ease th' enamour'd heroes lay,
(Their voyage still deferr'd from day to day)

E. And

And longer ftill, and longer had declin'd,
Full loath to leave the lovely place behind, 1120
Had not Alcides, the fair dames apart,
Thus fpoke incens'd the language of his heart:
' Miftaken comrades, does our kindred, fay,
' From our own country drive us far away?
' Or are we fondly thus enamour'd grown 1125
' Of foreign damfels, and defpife our own?
' Here fhall we ftay to till the Lemnian fields?
' Small fame to heroes this bafe commerce yields;
' No God, propitious to the fons of Greece,
' Without our toil, will grant the golden Fleece.
' Our courfe purfue we; for the breeze invites; 1131
' And let him revel in Love's foft delights,
' Who here but ftays to propagate his kind,
' And leave a memorable name behind.'
 Alcides thus: none dar'd to lift his eye, 1135
To breathe a murmur, or to make reply;
But keenly ftung with this farcaftic ftile,
They hafte to leave the lov'd Vulcanian ifle.
Soon as the damfels their fix'd purpofe knew,
Around the chiefs in bufy crowds they flew. 1140
As bees from fome deep-cavern'd rock proceed,
Buzz o'er the lilies of the laughing mead,

2   The

Book I. APOLLONIUS RHODIUS. 51

The sweets of all ambrosial herbs devour,
And suck the soul of every fragrant flow'r;
Thus they in swarms the parting Greeks address, 1145
With hands salute, with soothing words caress;
Then to the Powers above with fervour pray,
Safe to their arms the heroes to convey.
Hypsipyla the hand of Jason press'd,
And thus with tears the parting chief address'd: 1150
" Adieu!—and may you with the sons of Greece
" Return triumphant with the golden Fleece.
" Here shall you then my father's sceptre sway,
" And his domains your sovereign will obey.
" The neighbouring states will furnish large supplies,
" And a vast empire by your wisdom rise. 1156
" But if on nobler plans your thoughts are bent,
" And vainly I presage the wish'd event;
" Absent or present, to my memory kind,
" Still let Hypsipyla possess your mind. 1160
" And if with offspring heaven should bless me, say,
" How shall I then my Jason's will obey?"
The prince beheld the queen with rapturous look,
And thus with mild benevolence bespoke:
' May these events, foredoom'd by heaven's decree,
' Successful prove, Hypsipyla, to thee. 1166

E 2 ' But

'But still of Jason nobler thoughts retain:
'Enough for me o'er my own realms to reign;
'May but the powers of heaven (I ask no more)
'Safe reconvey me to my native shore. 1170
'If that's denied, and you, my source of joy,
'Bear, the soft token of our loves, a boy;
'Him, when mature, in kindness to your friend,
'My parents' solace, to Iölcos send;
'If then perchance the venerable pair 1175
'Survive their woes, and breathe this vital air.
'There may he live, from Pelias far remov'd,
'By Grecians honour'd, who his father lov'd.
He spoke his last farewell: then first ascends
The ship, and with him his illustrious friends. 1180
In their due stations plac'd, each seiz'd an oar,
While Argus loos'd the cable from the shore.
With active strokes the vigorous heroes sweep
The founding bosom of the billowy deep.
As Orpheus counsel'd, and mild evening near, 1185
To Samothrace, Electra's isle, they steer;
That there initiated in rites divine,
Safe might they sail the navigable brine.
But, Muse, presume not of these rites to tell:
Farewell, dread isle! dire deities, farewell! 1190

Let

Let not my verse these mysteries explain;
To name is impious, to reveal profane.
Thence the black main they lash'd with all their might,
Thrace on their left, and Imbros on the right;
And safely, with the now-declining sun, 1195
To far-projecting Chersonesus run.
Then stemm'd they, aided by the southern gales,
The stormy Hellespont with swelling sails,
Left the high-surging sea with morning light,
And reach'd Sigæum with approaching night. 1200
Dardania past, and high exalted Ide,
They saw Abydos on the stormy tide.
Thence sail'd they by Percote's pasture lands,
Pityëa's meadows, and Abarnis' sands:
And nightly, favour'd by the friendly blast, 1205
The purple-foaming Hellespont they past.
An ancient island in Propontis lies,
That towering lifts its summit to the skies;
Near Phrygia's corn-abounding coast it stands,
And far-projecting all the main commands; 1210
An island this, save where the isthmus' chain
Connects both lands, and curbs the boisterous main.
Round its rough sides the thundering tempests roar,
And a safe bay is form'd on either shore.

Æsepus' waters near this isthmus fall: 1215
And bordering tribes the mountain Arcton call.
On this rough mountain, barbarous, fierce and bold,
Dwell mighty giants, hideous to behold;
And, wonderful to tell! each monster stands
With six huge arms, and six rapacious hands; 1220
Two pendent on their shaggy shoulders grow,
And four deform their horrid sides below.
The lowland isthmus, verging to the main,
The Dolions till'd, and all the fertile plain.
O'er these reign'd Cyzicus the brave, the young, 1225
Who from the gallant warriour, Æneus, sprung.
The daughter of Euforus, first in fame,
Bore Cyzicus, Æneta was her name.
Secure they liv'd, and free from war's alarms,
Tho' Earth's huge sons were terrible in arms. 1230
Sprung from the monarch of the hoary tide,
On Neptune's aid the Dolian race rely'd.
To this fair port, with gentle-breathing gales,
This friendly shore, Thessalian Argo sails.
Here the rope-fasten'd stone they heave on shore, 1235
Which serv'd as anchor to the ship before,
But now too light, so Typhis bids, they bring,
And leave it at the pure Artacian spring;

Then

Then choose another on the rocky bay,
More ponderous far, the rolling ship to stay.   1240
There the first stone unnumber'd years remain'd,
Till, as Apollo's oracle ordain'd,
Th' Ionians found, with rites mysterious grac'd,
And sacred to Jasonian Pallas plac'd.
Soon as the Dolians, near approaching, knew   1245
Thessalian Argo, and the godlike crew,
Led on by Cyzicus they haste to meet
The princely band, and amicably greet;
Invite them down the winding bay to fall,
And fix their cable near the city-wall.   1250
Thus friendly treated, the Pelasgic train
Strive with their oars th' interiour port to gain.
Then first Ecbasian Phœbus they adore,
And rear an altar on the founding shore.
To them the king dispatch'd, with heart benign,   1255
Fat sheep, and strong, exhilarating wine.
For thus the sacred oracle foretold,
' When here arrives a band of heroes bold,
' With kind complacence treat the godlike crew,
' Meet not in arms, but pay them honours due!'   1260
Scarce had the down the monarch's cheeks o'erspread;
No children yet had bless'd the nuptial bed.

Clita,

Clita, his lovely queen, the young, the fair,
Renown'd for beauty, and her golden hair,
Sprung from Percofian Merops, ftill remains   1265
A ftranger to Lucina's cruel pains.
Late from her father's court the king convey'd,
With ample dower enrich'd, the blamelefs maid;
Yet he neglects the genial bed, and feafts,
All fears far banifhing, with foreign guefts.   1270
Oft he enquires of Pelias' ftern command,
And why the heroes left their native land.
As oft they afk'd what cities neighbouring lay,
And in Propontis which the fafeft bay.
But fcanty knowledge could the king beftow,   1275
Tho' it behov'd them much thefe truths to know.
When morning rofe, the Dindymean fteep
Some mount, to view the navigable deep,
And all its winding bays; the road they came
They honour'd with illuftrious Jafon's name.   1280
The chiefs, who chofe aboard the fhip to ftay,
Remov'd her from the moorings where fhe lay.
Mean while the fons of Earth, a numerous train,
From their bleak mountains rufh into the plain,
Befiege the pervious bay, and ftrive to block   1285
Its mouth with maffy fragments from the rock;

                                 Intending

Intending there Theffalia's pine to keep
Hemm'd up, like fome huge monfter of the deep.
But Hercules remain'd; his bow he drew,
And heaps of giants with his arrows flew. 1290
The reft enrag'd, rough, rocky fragments tore,
Hurl'd high in air, and thunder'd from the fhore.
(This labour ftill for Hercules remain'd,
By Juno, Jove's imperial queen, ordain'd)
And fiercely now the glowing battle burn'd, 1295
When lo! the chiefs from Dindymus return'd,
Attack'd the defperate giants in the rear,
And dealt deftruction with the dart and fpear;
Till Earth's fierce fons, defil'd with wounds and gore,
Dropp'd dead; their bodies cover'd half the fhore. 1300
As near the fea's broad brink, with fturdy ftrokes,
Affiduous woodmen fell afpiring oaks;
Then draw them in due order from the flood,
And thus well drench'd they cleave with eafe the wood:
Thus at the entrance of the hoary bay, 1305
The frequent corfe of many a giant lay;
Some, tumbled headlong, made the fea their grave,
While their legs rofe above the briny wave;
Some o'er the fands their horrid vifage fhow,
Their feet deep-rooted in the mud below, 1310

Thus

Thus their huge trunks afford abundant fare
To Neptune's fishes, and the birds of air.
Soon as concluded was the bloody fray,
And favouring breezes call'd the chiefs away,
They loos'd; o'er swelling ocean southern gales 1315
Breath'd all day long, and fill'd their bellying sails.
Night rose, the favouring gales no longer laſt,
The ship drives backward with the stormy blaſt.
Again they harbour on the friendly coaſt,
Where late the Dolians entertain'd the hoſt; 1320
And round the rock the steady cable bind,
The rock ev'n now to sacred fame consign'd.
Here thro' the gloom of night again they came,
And knew not that the country was the same.
Nor knew the Dolians, so dark night prevail'd, 1325
That back to Cyzicum the Greeks had sail'd;
But deem'd the chiefs a band of Macrian foes:
To arms they call, and force to force oppose.
A gleamy luſtre glanc'd along the field,
While spear met spear, and shield encounter'd shield.
In sun-scorch'd bushes thus the bickering blaze 1331
Flames forth, and crackling on the branches preys.
Dire was the conflict; on the fatal plain
Their prince, alas! was number'd with the slain,
His queen and bridal bed beheld he ne'er again.

For

For Jason spy'd the prince advancing near, 1336
And thro' his bosom plung'd the furious spear;
The ribs it broke, and circumscrib'd his date,
Wing'd with th' inevitable will of Fate.
Fate, like a wall, devoted man surrounds, 1340
And fast confines him in its circling bounds.
Himself he deem'd, in that disorder'd fight,
Vainly he deem'd! protected by the night:
The favouring night, alas! produc'd his bane,
And chiefs unnumber'd with their prince were slain.
For Hercules, with his all-conquering bow, 1346
Dispatch'd Telecles to the shades below,
And Megabrontes: by Acastus' hand
Pale Sphodris lay extended on the strand.
Peleus to Pluto's dark dominions gave 1350
Zelys the hardy, and Gephyrus brave.
Bold Telamon, well-skill'd the lance to wield,
Left Basileus expiring on the field.
Next Idas vanquish'd Promeus by his side;
By warlike Clytius Hyacinthus died. 1355
Fair Leda's sons, in bloody combat skill'd,
Fierce Megalossacus and Phlogius kill'd,
And Meleager added two to these,
Itymoneus and valiant Artaces.

These

Thefe all were chiefs in fighting fields approv'd, 1360
Deplor'd as heroes, and as brothers lov'd.
The reft for fafety on their flight rely;
(As trembling doves before the falcon fly)
Then to the city-gates tumultuous prefs,
And raife the piercing cry of deep diftrefs; 1365
The city mourn'd: they deem'd, return'd from far,
That hoftile Macrians had renew'd the war.

But when the rofy morn began to wake,
All found their irretrievable miftake.
Heart-rending grief opprefs'd the Grecian train, 1370
To fee the hofpitable monarch flain,
A clay-cold corfe, extended on the fhore,
Deform'd with duft, and all befmear'd with gore.
The Greeks and Dolians, funk in deep defpair,
Mourn three long days, and rend their graceful hair.
A tomb they rear upon the rifing ground, 1376
And clad in brazen arms thrice march around;
Then for the monarch, on Limonia's plain,
Of rites obfervant, funeral-games ordain.
There ftands the tomb, adorn'd with honours due,
Which diftant ages will with forrow view. 1381
When the fad news at Clita's ear arriv'd,
Not long the queen her monarch's fate furviv'd;

But

But woe augmenting, round her neck she tied
The noose dishoneft, and unseemly died. 1385
Her mournful dirge the weeping Dryads sung,
While Dindymus with lamentations rung;
And all the tears that from their eye-lids fell,
The Gods transform'd, in pity, to a well;
In cryftal ftreams it murmurs ftill, and weeps, 1390
And ftill the name of wretched Clita keeps.
A day so difmal, so replete with woes,
Till this sad day, to Dolians never rose.
Deep, deep immers'd in sorrow they remain'd,
And all from life-supporting food abftain'd; 1395
Save such poor pittance as man's needs require,
Of corn unground, or unprepar'd by fire.
And annual, on this day, the Dolians ftill
Sift coarfeft meal, and at the public mill.

 Thenceforth twelve days and nights dire ftorms
  prevail, 1400
Nor could the chiefs unfurl the swelling sail.
The following night, by sleep's soft power opprefs'd,
Once more in Cyzicum the heroes reft;
Mopsus alone and brave Acaftus keep
The watch nocturnal, while their comrades sleep;
When, lo! a Halcyon, of cerulean hue, 1406
O'er the fair head of slumbering Jason flew,

          In

In airy circles, wondrous to behold,
And, screaming loud, the ceasing storm foretold.
The grateful sound attentive Mopsus heard, 1410
And mark'd the meaning of the sea-bred bird;
(Which gently rising from the deck below,
Perch'd on the summit of th' aerial prow)
Then rous'd he Jason from his fleecy bed,
Of sheeps' soft skins compos'd, and thus he said; 1415
' O son of Æson, hear! be this thy care,
' Haste, to the fane of Dindymus repair;
' There Cybele with sacrifice implore,
' So will the winds tempestuous cease to roar.
' For this proclaim'd the boding Halcyon true, 1420
' As round thee, sunk in deep repose, she flew.
' By Cybele's dread power the vast profound,
' And all the winds in harmony are bound.
' By her subsists prolific earth below,
' And high Olympus, ever crown'd with snow. 1425
' Jove yields, when she ascends the courts of day,
' And all the powers immortal own her sway.'
To Jason thus the venerable seer;
And welcome came the tidings to his ear.
Instant the chief, exulting with a bound, 1430
Sprung from the bed, and wak'd his comrades round.

Elate

Elate with joy his looks, his words unfold
The glad presage which Mopsus had foretold.
Then from the stalls the youths appointed drove
Selected oxen to the heights above.   1435
Some from the rock unloos'd the corded stay,
And with fleet oars approach'd the Thracian bay.
From thence the top of Dindymus they gain'd;
Few were the heroes that aboard remain'd:
By those the Macrian rocks, and Thracian land   1440
Directly opposite, appear'd at hand;
The Thracian Bosphorus here, involv'd in shade,
And Mysia's rising mountains were survey'd;
There, where his waters black Æsepus pours,
Nepea's plain, and Adrasteia's tow'rs.   1445
A vine's vast trunk adorn'd with branches stood,
Though old, yet sound, and long had grac'd the wood:
This trunk they hew'd, and made, by Argus' skill,
An image of the Goddess of the hill;
Which on the rocky eminence they plac'd,   1450
With the thick boughs of circling beeches grac'd.
They rear an altar, then, on rising ground,
Of stones that readiest lay, and wide around
Dispose the branches of the sacred oak,
And Dindymus's deity invoke,   1455

The

The guardian power of Phrygia's hills and woods,
The venerable mother of the Gods.
On Tityas and Cyllenus too they call,
Of all her priests most lov'd, and honour'd most of all:
For skill prophetic they alone are fam'd; 1460
Ideän Dactyli these priests are nam'd;
Both whom Anchiala in Dicte's cave
Brought forth, where chill Oaxis rolls his wave.
While on the burning victims Jason pours
Libations due, the Goddess he implores 1465
To smile propitious on the Grecian train,
And still the tempests of the roaring main.
Then Orpheus call'd, and youthful chiefs advance,
All clad in arms, to lead the martial dance;
With clashing swords they clatter'd on their shields,
And fill'd with festive sounds th' aerial fields. 1471
Lost in these sounds was every doleful strain,
And their loud wailings for their monarch slain.
The Phrygians still their Goddess' favour win
By the revolving wheel and timbrel's din. 1475
Of these pure rites the mighty mother show'd
Her mind approving, by these signs bestow'd;
Boughs bend with fruit, Earth from her bosom pours
Herbs ever green, and voluntary flow'rs.

Fierce

Fierce foreſt-beaſts forſake the lonely den, 1480
Approach with gentleneſs, and fawn on men.
A pleaſing omen, and more wondrous ſtill
The Goddeſs gave: the Dindymean hill,
That ne'er knew water on its airy brow,
Burſts into ſtreams, and founts perennial flow. 1485
This wonder ſtill the Phrygian ſhepherds ſing,
And give the name of Jaſon to the ſpring.
Then on the mount the chiefs the feaſt prolong,
And praiſe the venerable queen in ſong.
But when the morning roſe, they plied their oars, 1490
And, the wind ceaſing, left the Phrygian ſhores.
Then fair contention fir'd the princely train,
Who beſt the toil of rowing could ſuſtain.
For now the howling ſtorm was lull'd to ſleep;
Etherial mildneſs had compos'd the deep. 1495
On the calm ſea the labouring chiefs rely'd;
Fleet flew the ſhip along the yielding tide;
Not Neptune's ſteeds ſo ſwift, with looſen'd reins,
Skim the light level of the liquid plains.
But when with even-tide the bluſtering breeze 1500
Bruſh'd the broad boſom of the ſwelling ſeas,
The wearied chiefs their toilſome courſe repreſs'd,
And all, ſave great Alcides, ſunk to reſt.

Swift thro' the waves his arm unaided drew
The ship, deep-laden with the drowsy crew.   1505
Thro' all her planks the well-compacted pine
Shook, as his oar dispers'd the foamy brine.
But soon the heroes view'd the Mysian shore,
As by the mouth of Rhyndacus they bore.
On Phrygia's fields a wishful look they cast,   1510
And huge Ægæon's promontory pass'd,
When great Alcides, at one luckless stroke,
His oar, hard straining, near the middle broke.
One part was swallow'd in the whelming main,
One, though he fell, his grasping hands retain; 1515
Backward he fell, but soon his seat regain'd,
And, loathing rest, in mute amaze remain'd.
What time the weary labourer, wanting rest,
Hies to his cot with pining fast oppress'd;
Ev'n in the entrance of his rural door   1520
His tottering knees he bends, and moves no more;
His dusty limbs he views, and callous hands,
And curses hunger's insolent demands:
Then, nor till then, the chiefs to Chius row,
Chius, whose streams around Arganthon flow.   1525
The friendly Mysians on their peaceful coast
Receive with hospitality the host;

Abundant

Abundant ſtores they ſend, with hearts benign,
Fat ſheep, and ſtrong exhilarating wine.
Some bring dry wood, and ſome in order ſpread   1530
Soft leaves and herbage for a ſpacious bed;
Some from the flint elicit living fire;
Some mix the wines that generous deeds inſpire:
The feaſt they crown, and rites to Phœbus pay,
Ecbaſian Phœbus, at the cloſe of day.   1535
But Hercules the genial feaſt declin'd,
And ſought the wood, a fitting oar to find.
Nor long he ſought before a fir he found;
Few leaves adorn'd it, and few branches crown'd;
Yet as the poplar's ſtem aſpires on high,   1540
This fir, ſo ſtout and tall, attracts his eye.
On the green graſs his bow he laid aſide,
His arrowy quiver, and the lion's hide.
Firſt with his club the ſolid ſoil he ſhook,
Then in both arms, aſſur'd, the fir-tree took;   1545
Firm on his feet he ſtood, with bended knee;
His big broad ſhoulder lean'd againſt the tree;
Then heav'd it up, deep-rooted in the ground,
Clogg'd with the ſoil's impediments around.
As when, beneath Orion's wintry reign,   1550
The ſudden tempeſt ruſhes from the main,

Some tall ship's mast it tears, and every stay,
And all the cordage, all the sails away:
Thus he the trunk; then took, in haste to go,
The hide, the club, his arrows and his bow. 1555
  Meanwhile, preparing for his friend's return
A ready supper, with his brazen urn
Alone rov'd Hylas o'er the fields, to bring
The purest water from the sacred spring.
For to such tasks Alcides train'd his squire, 1560
Whom first he took an infant from his sire
Theodamas; but him with sword severe
He slew, who churlish had refus'd a steer.
For when Theodamas, opprefs'd with care,
Turn'd the fresh furrow with his shining share, 1565
He disobey'd, ah wretch! the chief's command,
Who claim'd the labouring ox that till'd the land.
But know, Alcides sought for cause to bring
War on Dryopia's kingdom and the king,
For barbarous acts, and rights neglected long. 1570
  But rove not, Muse, digressive from the song.
Soon faithful Hylas to the fountain came,
Which Mysian shepherds crystal Pegæ name;
It chanc'd the nymphs, in neighbouring streams that
    dwell,
Then kept a concert at the sacred well. 1575

In Dian's praife they rais'd the nightly fong,
All who to high, aerial hills belong;
All who in caverns hide, or devious rove
The mountain-foreft, or the fhady grove.
When from her fpring, unfullied with a ftain, 1580
Rofe Ephydatia, to attend the train,
The form of Hylas rufh'd upon her fight,
In every grace of blufhing beauty bright:
For the full moon a beamy luftre fhed,
And heighten'd all the honours of his head. 1585
Fir'd with love's fudden flame, by Venus rais'd,
The frantic naiad languifh'd as fhe gaz'd:
And foon as, ftooping to receive the tide,
He to the ftream his brazen urn apply'd,
In gufh'd the foaming waves; the nymph with joy
Sprung from the deep to kifs the charming boy. 1591
Her left arm round his lovely neck fhe threw,
And with her right hand to the bottom drew.
Firft Polyphemus heard, as wandering nigh
This fatal fount, the youth's diftrefsful cry, 1595
(In fearch of Hercules he rov'd the wood)
And hied with hafty footfteps to the flood.
As when a lion from his cavern'd rock,
At diftance hears the bleatings of the flock,

To seize his prey he springs, with hunger bold, 1600
But faithful shepherds had secur'd the fold;
Defeated of his prize, he roars amain,
Rends his hoarse throat, and terrifies the swain:
Thus Polyphemus call'd with voice profound,
And vainly anxious rov'd the forest round. 1605
At length retreating, he the path explor'd
Thro' which he came, and drew his trusty sword,
Lest savage beasts should seize him for their prey,
Or nightly robbers intercept his way.
And as he brandish'd the bright burnish'd blade, 1610
He met Alcides in the gloomy shade,
Unknown at first, but as he nearer drew,
His friend returning to the ship he knew.
Though his breath falters, and his spirits fail,
He thus reveals the melancholy tale: 1615
‘ Hard is my lot, and much averse my will,
‘ To be the first sad messenger of ill;
‘ Young Hylas went to fetch fresh water late,
‘ Not yet return'd; I tremble for his fate:
‘ By robbers seiz'd or beasts, 'tis hard to guess; 1620
‘ I heard his cry, the signal of distress:’
Thus he: the sweat from great Alcides flow'd,
And the black blood thro' all his body glow'd:

Enrag'd,

Enrag'd, the fir-tree on the ground he threw,
And, where his feet or frenzy hurried, flew. 1625
As when a bull, whom galling gadflies wound,
Forsakes the meadows, and the marshy ground,
The flowery food, the herd and herdsmen shuns,
Now stands stock-still, and restless now he runs;
Stung by the breese, he maddens with the pain, 1630
Tosses aloft his head, and roars amain:
Thus ran the raging chief with matchless force,
Then sudden stopp'd he, wearied with the course.
Anxious in vain, he rov'd the forest round,
The distant hills and vales his voice rebound. 1635
Now o'er the lofty mountains rose in view
The morning-star, and mildest breezes blew:
That instant Tiphys bade the heroes sail,
Ascend the vessel, and enjoy the gale.
The ready crew obey the pilot's word, 1640
Their anchor weigh, and haul the cords aboard;
Then give the stretching canvass to the wind,
And leave the Posidean rocks behind.
When from the rosy orient, beaming bright,
Aurora tipp'd the foot-worn paths with light; 1645
And o'er moist meads the glittering dew-drops shin'd,
They mifs'd those friends their folly left behind.

Then rose contention keen, and pungent grief,
For thus abandoning their braveſt chief.
In ſilence Jaſon ſat, and long ſupprefs'd, 1650
Though griev'd, the labouring anguiſh of his breaſt.
Brave Telamon, with anger kindling, ſpoke:

'Mute is thy tongue, and unconcern'd thy look:
' To leave unconquer'd Hercules behind
' Was a baſe project, and by thee deſign'd; 1655
' Left, when to Greece we ſteer the ſailing pine,
' His brighter glories ſhould out-dazzle thine,
' But words avail not——I renounce the band,
' Whoſe ſelfiſh wiles this ſtratagem have plann'd:'

Thus ſpoke Æacides, inflam'd with ire, 1660
His eye-balls ſparkling like the burning fire;
On Tiphys then, by rage impell'd, he flew:
And once more Myſia had receiv'd the crew;
Again the heroes the ſame courſe had ſail'd,
Though roaring winds and raging waves prevail'd,
Had not bold Boreas' ſons the chief addrefs'd, 1666
And, nobly daring, his rough rage reprefs'd.
(Ill fated youths! for that heroic deed
Doom'd by the hands of Hercules to bleed.
For, when returning home their courſe they ſped, 1670
From funeral games perform'd for Pelias dead,

In

In sea-girt Tenos he the brothers slew,
And o'er their graves in heapy hillocks threw
The crumbling mould; then with two columns crown'd,
Erected high the death-devoted ground; 1675
And one still moves, how marvellous the tale!
With every motion of the Northern gale—
But these are facts reserv'd for future years)
Lo! sudden, Glaucus to their sight appears,
Prophet of Nereus, rising from the main, 1680
Most skill'd of all his fate-foretelling train.
High o'er the waves he rear'd his shaggy head,
With his strong hand the rudder seiz'd; and said:
' Why strive ye thus, tho' Jove's high will with-
stands,
' To bear Alcides to the Colchian lands? 1685
' He must at Argos, so the fates ordain,
' And so Eurystheus has decreed, sustain
' Twelve mighty labours, thence be rais'd above,
'· To high Olympus, and the court of Jove.
' Cease for Amphytrion's son, your murmurs cease,
' And lull the sorrows of your souls to peace. 1691
' In Mysia, where meandering Chius strays,
' Must Polyphemus a proud city raise:
' Then, mid' the Calybes, a desperate clan,
' Expires on Scythian plains the gallant man. 1695

' But

' But ſtrange is Hylas' fate: his youthful charms
' Entic'd a nymph, who claſp'd him in her arms.
' Now the bleſt pair the bands of Hymen bind;
' In ſearch of him the chiefs are left behind.'

This ſaid, he plung'd into the gulf profound, 1700
The purple ocean foam'd in eddies round.
The God deſcending with reſiſtleſs ſway,
Impell'd the hollow veſſel on her way.
The chiefs rejoic'd this prodigy to view,
And inſtant Telamon to Jaſon flew 1705
In friendly ſort, and in his right he took
The prince's hand, and thus embracing ſpoke:
' Illuſtrious chief, let not thine anger riſe.
' At aught I ſaid impetuous and unwiſe.
' Grief for my friend has made me indiſcreet, 1710
' And utter words for Jaſon's ear unmeet;
' Thoſe to the winds wide-ſcattering let us give,
' And, as before, in friendly concord live.'

Then Jaſon thus; " Thy cenſures wound my mind,
" Which ſay, I left the braveſt Greek behind. 1715
" Yet though thy words reproachful guilt ſuggeſt,
" Rage dwells not long in Jaſon's generous breaſt;
" Since not for flocks or riches we contend,
" But a bold hero, and a faithful friend.

" And

" And thou, I truſt, if reaſon calls, wilt be   1720
" As firm and warm an advocate for me."
  He ſpoke; and now, the hateful conteſt o'er,
The chiefs reſum'd the feats they held before.
But for thoſe heroes, whom they left behind,
By Jove's decree are various cares deſign'd.   1725
Nam'd from its ſtream, the boaſt of future days,
Muſt one on Myſian plains a city raiſe:
One (great Alcides) other toils muſt ſhare,
And learn Euriſtheus' ſtern commands to bear.
Long time he threaten'd, for his Hylas loſt,   1730
Inſtant deſtruction to the Myſian coaſt,
Unleſs the Myſians to his arms reſtor'd,
Alive or dead, the partner of his board.
Of all their bands the choiceſt youths they choſe,
And them as pledges of their faith propoſe;   1735
Then ſwore they all, their ſearch ſhould never end,
Till haply they had found the hero's friend.
Still to this day the fond Cianians ſeek
(All who at Trachin dwell) the lovely Greek.
For beauteous youths, to Trachin's walls convey'd,
Were there as pledges to Alcides paid.   1741
  Meanwhile all day and night briſk breezes blew,
Fleet o'er the foaming flood the veſſel flew;

But

But when the dawn gave promise of the day,
The winds expiring gently died away. 1745
A land projecting o'er the bay below
The chiefs discover'd, and to this they row;
This peaceful port awhile the Minyans chose,
And, as they reach'd it, grateful morning rose.

END OF THE FIRST BOOK.

THE
SECOND BOOK.

THE ARGUMENT.

This Book contains the combat between Amycus and Pollux; the former of whom is slain. A battle ensues between the Argonauts and Bebrycians, in which the Argonauts come off conquerors. They sail to Salmydessus, a city of Thrace, where they consult Phineus, a soothsayer, on the success of their expedition. He promises, if they would deliver him from the Harpies, to direct them safely to Colchos. His request is granted, and he gives them instructions. The story of Paræbius, Cyrene and Aristæus. They sail through the Symplegades, and thence to the island Thynia, where they land. Apollo, who here appears to them, is rendered propitious by sacrifice. The course of the river Acheron is described. They land on the coast of the Mariandyni, and are hospitably entertained by Lycus, the king of that country. Here Idmon is killed by a wild boar, and here Tiphys dies. Ancæus is appointed pilot in his stead. They sail by the monument of Sthenelus, whose ghost is released by Proserpine, and gratified with the sight of the Argonauts. At the island of Mars they meet the sons of Phrixus, who had just before been shipwrecked. They are kindly received by the Argonauts, who take them on board. Sailing by Mount Caucasus they come in sight of the eagle that preys on the entrails of Prometheus. The end of their voyage.

THE

THE
ARGONAUTICS
OF
APOLLONIUS RHODIUS.

BOOK II.

TENTS o'er the beach Bebrycia's king had fpread,
And ftalls erected where fat oxen fed.
To genial Neptune a Bithynian dame
Bore the fierce tyrant, Amycus his name,
Proudeft of men; who this hard law decreed,   5
That from his realm no ftranger fhould recede,
Till firft with him compell'd in fight to wield
The dreadful gauntlet in the lifted field.
Unnumber'd guefts his matchlefs prowefs flew:
Stern he accofts fwift Argo's valiant crew,   10
Curious the reafon of their courfe to fcan,
Who, whence they were; and fcornful thus began:
' Learn what 'tis meet ye knew, ye vagrant hoft;
' None that e'er touches on Bebrycia's coaft,

' Is

'Is thence by law permitted to depart, 15
' Till match'd with me he prove the boxer's art.
' Choose then a chief who can the gauntlet wield,
' And let him try the fortune of the field:
' Should ye contemptuous scorn my fix'd decree,
' Know, your proud hearts shall yield to fate and me.'
Thus spoke the chief with insolent disdain, 21
And rous'd resentment in the martial train;
But Pollux most his vaunting words provoke,
Who thus, a champion for his fellows, spoke:
" Threat not, whoe'er thou art, the bloody fray; 25
" Lo, we obsequious thy decrees obey!
" Unforc'd, this instant, to the lists I go,
" Thy rival I, thy voluntary foe."
Stung to the heart with this severe reply,
On him he turn'd his fury-flaming eye: 30
As the grim lion, pierc'd by some keen wound,
Whom hunters on the mountain-top surround;
Though close hemm'd in, his glaring eye-balls glance
On him alone who threw the pointed lance.
The Greek stript off his mantle richly wrought, 35
Late from the Lemnian territory brought,
Which some fair nymph, who had her flame avow'd,
The pledge of hospitable love bestow'd;

His

His double cloak, with clasps of sable hue,
Bebrycia's ruler on the greensword threw,   40
And his rough sheep-hook of wild olive made,
Which lately flourish'd in the woodland shade.
Then sought the heroes for a place at hand
Commodious for the fight, and on the strand
They plac'd their friends, who saw, with wondering eyes;   45
The chiefs how different, both in make and size;
For like Typhœus' race the tyrant stood
Enormous, or that miscreated brood
Of mighty monsters, which parturient Earth,
Incens'd at Jove, brought forth, a hideous birth.   50
But Pollux shone like that mild star on high,
Whose rising ray illumes fair Evening's sky.
Down spread his cheek, ripe manhood's early sign,
And in his eye-balls beam'd the glance divine.
But like a lion, glorying in his might,   55
Stood Jove's puissant son, prepar'd for fight.
His arms he poiz'd, advancing in the ring,
To try if still they kept their pristine spring;
If pliant still, and vigorous as before,
Nor rigid grown with labouring at the oar.   60
Trial like this the haughty king disdain'd:
Aloof and silent Amycus remain'd.

                G   Full

Full on his foe his vengeful eyes he turn'd,
For blood he thirsted, and for conquest burn'd.
With that his squire Lycoreus, full in view, 65
Two pair of gauntlets in the circle threw,
Of barbarous fashion, harden'd, rough and dry'd.
Then thus the king, with insolence and pride:
' Lo, two stout pair; the choice I leave to thee;
' (No lot appoints them) choose, and blame not me.
' Bind them secure, and after trial tell, 71
' How greatly I in either art excel,
' Whether to form the cestus firm and good,
' Or stain the cheeks of mighty men with blood.'
He spoke: brave Pollux nothing deign'd to say, 75
But smiling chose the pair which nearest lay.
To cheer their champion, Castor, honour'd name!
And Talaüs, the son of Bias, came;
Firm round his arms the gloves of death they bind,
And animate the vigour of his mind. 80
Aratus, and bold Ornytus his friend,
To Amycus their kind assistance lend:
Fools! for they knew not, this one conflict o'er,
Those gauntlets never should be buckled more.
Accoutred thus each ardent hero stands, 85
And raises high in air his iron hands;

With clashing gauntlets fiercely now they close,
And mutual meditate death-dealing blows.
First Amycus a furious onset gave,
Like the rude insult of the battering wave,   90
That, heap'd on high by driving wind and tide,
Bursts thundering on some gallant veffel's side;
The wary pilot, by superior skill,
Forefees the storm, and shuns the menac'd ill.
Thus threatening Amycus on Pollux press'd,   95
Nor suffer'd his antagonist to rest:
But Jove's brave son observes each coming blow,
Quick leaps aside, and difappoints the foe;
And where a weak unguarded part he fpies,
There all the thunder of his arms he plies.   100
As busy shipwrights stoutly labouring strive
Through sturdy planks the piercing spikes to drive,
From head to stern repeated blows go round,
And ceaseless hammers send a various sound;
Thus from their batter'd cheeks loud echoes sprung,
Their dash'd teeth crackled, and their jaw-bones rung:
Nor ceas'd they from the strokes that threaten'd death,
Till tir'd with toil they faintly gasp'd for breath:
Awhile they then remit the bloody fray,
And panting wipe the copious sweat away.   110

But adverse soon they meet, with rage they glow,
Like bulls fierce fighting for some favourite cow.
Then Amycus, collecting all his might,
Rose to the stroke, resolv'd his foe to smite,
And by one blow the dubious war conclude: 115
The wary prince, his ruin to elude,
Bent back his head; defeated of its aim,
The blow impetuous on his shoulder came.
Then Pollux with firm steps approaching near,
Vindictive struck his adversary's ear; 120
Th' interior bones his ponderous gauntlet broke;
Flat fell the chief beneath his dreadful stroke:
The Grecians shouted, with wild rapture fir'd,
And, deeply groaning, Amycus expir'd.

The griev'd Bebrycians saw their monarch slain, 125
And big with vengeance rush'd into the plain;
With season'd clubs and javelins arm'd they ran,
And aim'd their fury at the conquering man.
Their keen-edg'd swords the friends of Pollux drew,
And to the succour of their comrade flew. 130
First Castor slaughter'd, with victorious hand,
A hero of the bold Bebrycian band,
The griding sword at once his head divides,
And on his shoulders hang the parted sides.

Mimans,

Mimans, Itymoneus of giant-size, 135
Each by the arm of conquering Pollux dies.
On this his foot impress'd a deadly wound
Full on his side, and stretch'd him on the ground:
His right hand dash'd, with unresisted sway,
Mimans' left eye, and tore the ball away. 140
Orcides, Amycus's proud compeer,
Then launch'd at Talaüs his brazen spear;
Just near his flank the point he lightly felt,
That ras'd the skin beneath his broider'd belt.
Aratus, with his club of harden'd oak, 145
Aim'd at brave Iphitus a deadly stroke:
Vain thought! too soon, alas! it is decreed,
The hero by his brother's sword must bleed.
Then rush'd, to succour the Thessalian band,
Ancæus, with his pole-axe in his hand; 150
O'er his broad back a bear's dark spoils he threw,
And boldly mingled with the hostile crew.
The sons of Æacus, renown'd for might,
And Jason join'd them in the fields of fight.
As when, what time both dogs and shepherds keep 155
Close in warm cots, neglectful of their sheep,
Wolves, pinch'd with hunger and bleak winter's cold,
Leap o'er the fence, and terrify the fold,

With ravening eyes the crowded sheep survey,
And doubt where first to rend the trembling prey; 160
Thus the bold Greeks, as near their foes they drew,
Intimidate the congregated crew.

As swains with smoke, of honey studious, strive
From some rock's cleft the swarming bees to drive;
Alarm'd and trembling, with a murmuring sound, 165
They crowd to all their waxen rooms around;
But if the fumes prevail, their wings they ply,
And rove uncertain thro' the various sky:
Dispersing thus, the wild Bebrycians fled,
And loud proclaim'd that Amycus was dead. 170
Ah, hapless race of men! they little knew,
That, soon, far greater evils must ensue:
Soon must they see, their monarch now no more,
Their lands a drear, depopulated shore;
Their vineyards spoil'd, and wasted all their coast 175
By Lycus, and the Mariandine host:
For 'twas their fate, with spear and steely brand,
Hard lot! to battle for an iron land.
The Greeks then seiz'd their herds, an easy prey,
And from the sheep-folds drove the flocks away; 180
The live provision to their ship they sent:
Then thus some sailor gave his boasting vent;

‘ What

' What had thefe mifcreants done, with fears dif-
   may'd,
' Had heaven indulg'd us with Alcides' aid?
' No fierce contention then, I judge, had been,   185
' No bloody boxing on the lifted green:
' The chief's ftout club had tam'd the tyrant's pride,
' And fet his execrable laws afide.
' But now, impell'd by fwelling waves and wind,
' We leave at land the matchlefs chief behind;   190
' Whofe lofs diftrefs to every Greek will prove.'
   He faid;------but all things own the will of Jove.
All night the heroes on the coaft remain,
To heal the bruifes of the wounded train.
Firft to the gods they give the honours due,   195
And next, a banquet for the princely crew.
Nor can night's fhades the chiefs to fleep incline,
Or o'er the facrifice, or o'er the wine;
Mirthful they fit, their brows with laurel crown'd:
To a green laurel was the cable bound.   200
While Orpheus ftrikes the lyre, the hymn they raife,
And Jove's fam'd offspring, mighty Pollux, praife:
Soft breathes the breeze, the billows ceafe to roar,
And feftive joy exhilarates the fhore.
But when the fun illum'd the hills and plains,   205
Dank with the dew, and rous'd the fhepherd-fwains,

They fent abundant flocks and herds aboard,
And from the laurel-ftem unloos'd the cord;
And while the favourable winds prevail'd,
Thro' the rough-rolling Bofphorus they fail'd. 210
When, lo! a wave by gathering furges driv'n,
Swoln big for burfting, is up-heav'd to heav'n,
Still rifes higher, and ftill wider fpreads,
And hangs a watery mountain o'er their heads;
Like a black cloud it frowns, prepar'd to fall, 215
And threatens quick deftruction to them all.
Yet the train'd pilot, by fuperior fkill,
Well knows to 'fcape this laft impending ill :
Safe through the ftorm the veffel Tiphys fteer'd,
And fav'd the heroes from the fate they fear'd. 220

Fronting Bithynia's coaft, next morn, they reach
New land, and fix their halfers on the beach.
There on the margin of the beating flood
The mournful manfions of fad Phineus ftood,
Agenor's fon ; whom heaven ordain'd to bear 225
The grievous burden of unequall'd care.
For, taught by wife Apollo to defcry
Unborn events of dark futurity,
Vain of his fcience, the prefumptuous feer
Deign'd not Jove's awful fecrets to revere; 230

But

But wantonly divulg'd to frail mankind
The sacred purpose of th' omniscient mind:
Hence Jove indignant gave him length of days,
But dimm'd in endless night his visual rays.
Nor would the vengeful God indulge his taste 235
With the sweet blessings of a pure repast,
Tho' (for they learn'd his fate) the country round
Their prophet's board with every dainty crown'd.
For, lo! descending sudden from the sky,
Round the pil'd banquet shrieking Harpies fly, 240
Whose beaks rapacious, and whose talons tear
Quick from his famish'd lips th' untasted fare.
Yet would some slender pittance oft remain,
Life to support, and to perpetuate pain.
Such odours still the nauseous scraps exhal'd, 245
That with the stench the loathing stomach fail'd.
Aloof the guests amaz'd and hungry stood,
While their sick hearts abhorr'd the putrid food.

 But now the princely crew approaching near,
The welcome sound invades the prophet's ear; 250
Taught by almighty Jove, that now was come
The long-wish'd period of heaven's vengeful doom;
When, by these heroes' destin'd aid restor'd,
Peace should hereafter bless his feastful board.

           Then

Then heaves he from the couch his haggard head, 255
(Like some pale, lifeless, visionary shade)
Propp'd on his staff his way explores, and crawls
With lingering step along the lonely walls:
Diseas'd, enfeebled, and by age unbrac'd,
Thro' every limb he trembled as he pass'd; 260
Shrunk was his form, with want aduft and thin,
The pointed bones seem'd bursting thro' his skin:
But faint and breathless as he reach'd the gate,
Down on the threshold, tir'd with toil, he sat.
In dizzy fumes involv'd, his brain runs round, 265
And swims beneath his feet the solid ground;
No more their functions the frail senses keep,
But speechless sinks he in a death-like sleep.

 This saw the chiefs amaz'd, and gather'd round;
When from his labouring lungs a hollow sound 270
(His breath and utterance scarce recover'd) broke,
And thus th' enlighten'd seer prophetic spoke:

 ' Princes of Greece, attend; if ye be they
' Whom o'er the main Thessalia's pines convey,
' And Jason leads to Colchos' magic land; 275
' Such is your cruel tyrant's stern command,
' Yes, ye are they; for yet my mental eye
' Undimm'd, past, present, future can descry:

' Thanks

' Thanks to thy fon, Latona, who beftows
' This grace, this only folace of my woes, 280
' By Jove, to whom the fuppliant's caufe belongs,
' Who hates the cruel, and avenges wrongs;
' By Phœbus, and by Juno, from on high
' Who marks your progrefs with compaffion's eye,
' Aid me, and, oh! a fufferer's pangs affuage, 285
' And bid corrofive famine ceafe to rage:
' Leave me not thus, unpitied and unblefs'd;
' But ere you fail, ah! pity the diftrefs'd.
' For not thefe orbs alone, depriv'd of fight,
' Vindictive Heaven hath veil'd in doleful night; 290
' But to extreme old age his cruel law
' Dooms me th' unwafting thread of life to draw.
' Still weightier woes from forrow's lengthen'd chain
' Depend, and pain is ever link'd to pain.
' From fecret haunts, aërial, unexplor'd, 295
' Flights of devouring Harpies vex my board;
' Swift, inftantaneous, fudden they defcend,
' And from my mouth the tafteful morfel rend.
' Meanwhile my troubled foul, with woe opprefs'd,
' No means of aid, no comfort can fuggeft. 300
' For when the feaft I purpofe to prepare,
' They fee that purpofe, and prevent my care:

' But

' But cloy'd, and glutted with the luscious spoil,
' With noisome ordure parting they defile
' Whate'er remains, if aught perchance remain, 305
' That none approaching may the stench sustain,
' Tho' his strong heart were wrapp'd in plated mail,
' The filthy fragments such dire steams exhale.
' Yet me fell hunger's all-subduing pain
' Compels reluctant, loathing to remain; 310
' Compels the deadly odours to endure,
' And gorge my craving maw with food impure.
' From these invaders (so hath Fate decreed)
' By Boreas' offspring shall my board be freed.
' Nor on a stranger to your house and blood, 315
' O sons of Boreas, is your aid bestow'd.
' Phineus behold, Agenor's hapless son,
' Once for prophetic skill and riches known;
' Who, while I sway'd the Thracian sceptre, led
' Your portion'd sister to my spousal bed.' 320

Here Phineus ceas'd, and touch'd each pitying
chief:

But Boreas' sons were pierc'd with double grief;
Compassion kind was kindled in their breast:
Their tears abating, friendly Zetes press'd
His trembling hand, and thus the seer address'd:

'' O most

" O moft difaftrous of all human kind, 326
" Whence fpring thefe evils that o'erwhelm thy mind?
" Haft thou, intrufted with the book of Fate,
" By folly merited celeftial hate?
" Hence falls this indignation on thy head? 330
" Fain would the fons of Boreas grant thee aid;
" Fain would they execute what heaven ordains,
" But awful dread their willing hands reftrains.
" To frighted mortals well thy fufferings prove
" How fierce the vengeance of the Gods above. 335
" Swear, or we dare not, as we wifh, effay
" To drive thefe hateful Harpies far away:
" Swear that the fuccours, which our arms intend,
" Shall no fuperior deity offend."

 He fpoke; and ftraight to heaven difclofing wide
His fightlefs eye-balls, thus the feer reply'd: 341
' My fon, th' injuftice of thy tongue reftrain,
' Nor let fuch thoughts thy pious foul profane.
' By Phœbus, heavenly augur, who infpires
' My confcious bofom with prophetic fires; 345
' By every woe fate deftines me to bear,
' And by thefe eyes, involv'd in night, I fwear;
' By the fell demons of the realms below,
' (Whom ever unpropitious may I know,

       ' From

' From their refentment not in death fecure, 350
' If falfly their dread godheads I adjure;)
' That, fhould a captive by your arms be freed,
' No God vindictive will avenge the deed.'
Then acquiefcing in the folemn pray'r,
To aid the prophet Boreas' fons prepare. 355
The youthful train a banquet fpread; the laft
Which thofe fell Harpies were decreed to tafte.
Nigh ftand the brothers, ardent to oppofe
With glittering falchions their invading foes.
But fcarce the firft fweet morfel Phineus took, 360
When from the clouds with fwift prevention broke,
(Swift as the lightning's glance, or ftormy blaft,
Whofe rapid fury lays the foreft wafte)
Shrill-clamouring for their prey, the birds obfcene;
The watchful heroes fhouting rufh'd between; 365
But they with fpeedieft rage the cates devour'd,
And round intolerable odours pour'd;
Then o'er th' Ægean far away they flew;
The fons of Boreas arm'd with fwords purfue;
Clofe they purfue; for Jove, that fignal day, 370
Their ftrength proportion'd to the defperate fray;
The ftrength he gave had Jove, that day, deny'd,
In vain their pinions had the brothers plied.

For

For when to Phineus furious they repair,
Or quitting Phineus feek the fields of air, 375
The light-wing'd monfters, fleeter than the wind,
Leave the careering Zephyrs far behind.
As when fwift hounds, experienc'd in the chace,
Through fome wide foreft, o'er the fcented grafs
The bounding hind, or horned goat purfue, 380
Near, and more near their panting prey they view;
And eager ftretching, the fhort fpace to gain,
They fnap, and grind their gnafhing fangs in vain:
 Thus ever near, the rapid chiefs purfu'd,
The Harpies thus their grafping hands elude. 385
But now far off in the Sicilian main,
By the wing'd brothers, fons of Boreas, flain,
The Harpy-race, tho' every God withftood,
Had ftain'd the Plotian ifles with facred blood;
Their fore diftrefs had Iris not furvey'd, 390
And darting from the fkies the heroes ftaid:
' O fons of Boreas, the dread laws above
' Permit you not to wound the *dogs of Jove*:
' And, lo! my oath I pledge, that never more
' Shall thefe fell *dogs* approach the Thracian fhore.'
 This faid, adjuring the tremendous floods, 396
Moft fear'd, moft honour'd by immortal Gods;

By

By the flow-dripping urn of Styx she swore;
The prophet's peaceful manfions on the shore
For ever from those spoilers should be free;   400
Such was the fatal sisters' fix'd decree.
The Goddess swore, the brothers straight obey,
And back to Argo wing their airy way:
The Strophades from thence derive their name,
The Plotian islands styl'd by ancient fame.   405
Disparting then, to different regions flew
The maid celestial and the monster-crew.
Those to the grots retir'd, the dark retreat
Of Dicte's caverns in Minoian Crete;
While the gay Goddess of the watery bow   410
Soar'd on fleet pinions to Olympus' brow.

Mean-while the princes, with unwearied pains,
Wash from their feet the Harpies' filthy stains:
Next from the spoils, which on Bebrycia's shore
From vanquish'd Amycus brave Pollux bore,   415
The fleecy victims they select with care;
And sooth the Gods with sacrifice and pray'r.
Then in the palace each heroic guest
Partakes the pleasures of the sumptuous feast:
With them sat Phineus, and refresh'd his soul   420
With favoury viands, and the cheering bowl:

While

Book II. APOLLONIUS RHODIUS. 97

While yet he feasts, infatiate still he seems,
And shares a bliss beyond the bliss of dreams.
Tho' now the rage of hunger was repress'd,
And generous wine had open'd every breast; 425
Yet still the chiefs prolong the banquet late,
And for the feather'd sons of Boreas wait.
Plac'd in the midst, before the cheerful fire,
Thus of their voyage spoke the sacred sire:

' Hear what the Gods permit me to relate; 430
' For 'tis profane to publish all your fate.
' Unnumber'd woes I felt, and feel them still,
' For erst divulging Jove's almighty will:
' To man he gives Fate's dark events to scan
' In part, but always leaves dependent man. 435
' When hence your destin'd voyage ye pursue,
' Two rocks will rise, tremendous to the view,
' Just in the entrance of the watery waste,
' Which never mortal yet in safety past:
' Not firmly fix'd; for oft with hideous shock 440
' Adverse they meet, and rock encounters rock:
' The boiling billows dash their airy brow,
' Loud thundering round the ragged shore below.
' Safe if ye hope to pass, my counsel hear,
' Be rul'd by prudence, and the Gods revere; 445

H ' Nor

' Nor on your unexperienc'd youth depend,
' The want of caution brings you to your end.
' First from your ship a nimble dove let fly,
' And on the sure prognostic bird rely ;
' Safe thro' the rocks if she pursue her way,   450
' No longer ye the destin'd course delay ;
' Steer for the strait, and let the rowers sweep
' With stretching oars the close-contracted deep :
' For not in prayers alone your safety stands ;
' But nervous vigour, and the strength of hands.   455
' Ply then your oars, and strain at every stroke ;
' But first with prayer the Deities invoke.
' The dove's sad fate should you desponding view,
' Crush'd by the closing fragments as she flew,
' Steer back, lest you against those rocks be driv'n,
' Steer back ; 'tis safest to submit to Heav'n.   461
' 'Twere death thro' them to force the foaming keel,
' Tho' heaven-built Argo were compos'd of steel.
' O friends, be warn'd by me, nor rashly dare
' To venture farther than my words declare ;   465
' Me though ye deem the righteous Gods pursue
' With direful vengeance, threefold more than due ;
' Tempt not without the dove this dangerous strait,
' For man must suffer what's ordain'd by Fate.

' But

' But if with active oars ye safely gain, 470
' Through these tremendous rocks, the distant main;
' Close to Bithynia let your vessel run,
' And on the left the dangerous shallows shun;
' Till Rhebas, rapid-rolling stream, ye reach,
' The gloomy shore, and Thynia's sheltering beach.
' Thence o'er the billows fronting Thynia's strand,
' Soon will ye gain the Mariandine land.
' Here lies the path to Pluto's dreary caves,
' Here Acherusia frowns above the waves,
' Whose skirts the gulfy Acheron divides, 480
' And from deep whirlpools disembogues his tides.
' Thence, not far distant, with the western gale,
' Near Paphlagonia's towering heights ye sail,
' The hardy sons of which inclement coast
' Enetean Pelops for their founder boast. 485
 ' Full to the north a promontory fam'd
' Lifts the high head in air, Carambis nam'd;
' The northern winds below its summit sweep,
' So loftily it rises o'er the deep.
' This point once doubled, a new coast expands 490
' Its ample plains, and on the limit stands
' A cape far-jutting, from whose rocky shores
' The rapid Halys in old ocean roars.

H 2   ' Near

' Near him clear Iris draws his humbler train,
' In silver torrents foaming to the main.   495
' Beyond projects an headland tall and steep,
' And forms a peaceful harbour in the deep.
' Here o'er extensive fields Thermodon pours,
' Near Themiscyria's heights, his watery stores.
' Next lie the spacious Dœan plains, and near   500
' Three cities of the Amazons appear:
' And next the Chalybes, inur'd to toil,
' Work at the forge, and turn the stubborn soil.
' Near these the wealthy Tiberenians till,
' Sacred to Jove, the Genetæan hill.   505
' The Moffynœcians, next, the country round
' Possess, with mountains and with forests crown'd.
' In towers they live of solid timber fram'd,
' Moffynes call'd, and thence the nation nam'd.
' When these are past, an island bleak and bare   510
' Lies full in view, there guide your ship with care,
' And thence with care those noxious birds expel,
' Which on the desert shore unnumber'd dwell.
' Here form'd of solid stone, and seen from far,
' Stands the rough temple of the God of war.   515
' Two Amazonian queens, renown'd for arms,
' Had rais'd the fane, when stunn'd with war's alarms.

' Steer

' Steer to this ifland through the ftormy main,
' And, all that mariners can wifh, ye gain.
' But why fhould I each circumftance difclofe, 520
' And make again the powers of heaven my foes?
' Beyond that ifle, but on the fronting fhores,
' The Philyreans feed their fleecy ftores:
' The brave Macronians till the neighbouring coaft;
' Next thefe the numerous Bechirian hoft: 525
' Near them Sapirians and Byzerians dwell,
' And next the Colchians, who in arms excel.
' But ye, your fteady courfe in Argo keep,
' Shun the falfe fhores, and plough fecure the deep,
' Till that rich coaft ye reach, where Phafis leads 530
' From Amarantine hills o'er Colchian meads
' His liquid ftores, and through fam'd Circe's plain ;
' Then rolls his widening current to the main.
' To this fam'd ftream purfue your watery way,
' Soon will your eyes Æeta's towers furvey, 535
' And Mars's grove, where, wondrous to behold!
' Hangs on a fpreading oak the fleecy gold.
' A hideous dragon of enormous fize
' Turns all around his circumfpective eyes:
' O'er the bright fpoil the ftricteft watch he keeps; 540
' He never flumbers, and he never fleeps.'

He spoke, and terror curdled all their blood;
Deep fix'd in silence long the warriors stood.
At length thus Jason, though possess'd with fear:
" Tell us, O tell us, venerable seer,   545
" Th' event of all our toils; the sign explain
" How safely we may pass into the main
" Thro' those dire rocks: and, O! indulgent, say,
" Shall we once more our native land survey?
" Unskill'd am I, unskill'd our martial train; 550
" How shall I act, how measure back the main?
" For far as ever flying sails were furl'd
" Lies Colchos, on the limits of the world."
 Thus Jason spoke; and thus the prophet old:
' Those dangerous rocks once pass'd, my son, be
    bold.   555
' Some God from Æa shall thro' seas untry'd,
' Skirted by others coasts, your vessel guide,
' But you, to Æa sailing, on your crew confide.
' But, friends, to Venus be due honours paid;
' Still in remembrance keep her secret aid.   560
' On all your toils she kindly will bestow
' A glorious end------expect no more to know.'
 Scarce had he spoke, when speeding back repair
The sons of Boreas through the fields of air,

At

At the seer's door with nimble feet they light; 565.
Up rose the chiefs rejoicing at the sight.
When Zetes trembling, and with toils opprefs'd,
While thick short sobs inceffant heav'd his chest,
Tells how they drove the Harpies far away,
How Iris screen'd them, and forbad to slay, 570
And pledg'd her solemn oath: while they retreat
To the huge caves of mountain-cover'd Crete.
These joyful tidings cheer'd the hearts of all,
But most the prophet's, in the feastful hall;
Whom Jason thus: "Sure from his heavenly state 575
" Some God look'd down, and wail'd thy woeful fate,
" And fore-decreed from far our bands to send,
" That Boreas' sons might their affistance lend.
" Should the same God restore thy long-lost sight,
" My gladden'd soul would feel as great delight, 580
" As ev'n my native country could bestow."
    Then thus sage Phineus with dejected brow:
' My eyes, alas! shall ne'er behold the day;
' Shrunk are these balls, and quench'd the visual ray:
' Heaven round me soon death's gloomy shade shall
        spread, 585
' And every honour will await me dead.'
    With converse thus the fleeting hours they cheer'd,
When rosy morning beaming bright appear'd.

The neighbouring peasants round, with early day,
Flock to the seer, their due regards to pay;   590
This daily custom love and reverence taught,
And some provision for the sage they brought.
All came to learn by his prophetic lore;
He to the rich divin'd, and to the poor:
For numerous votaries he reliev'd from dread,   595
Who dearly lov'd him, and who daily fed.
With these his steady friend Paræbius came,
Who saw with joy these gallant sons of fame.
To him prophetic Phineus had foretold,
That a young band of Grecians, brave and bold, 600
Should, in their voyage to the Colchian shore,
In Thynia's bay their well-built vessel moor,
And from these coasts, those ravenous birds of prey,
The Harpies drive, though sent by Jove, away.
The seer well pleas'd dismiss'd his friendly train, 605
But bade Paræbius with the Greeks remain,
And fetch him instant from his numerous stock
A sheep, the best and fairest of the flock.
The willing swain obey'd the seer's request,
And Phineus thus the mariners addrefs'd: 610
' We are not all unciviliz'd and rude,
' My friends, nor guilty of ingratitude.

' That

' That shepherd to my mansion came of late,
' To learn from me the colour of his fate;
' For the more labours and fatigues he bore, 615
' Pale, pining want opprefs'd him still the more;
' New woes succeeded to the woes that past,
' And every day was darker than the last:
' And yet no crime had poor Paræbius wrought,
' Alas! he suffered for his father's fault: 620
' Who, when alone, and on the mountain's brow,
' With cruel axe he laid the forest low,
' Deaf to a doleful Hamadryad's pray'r,
' The nymph neglected, and refus'd to spare,
' Though oft she urg'd this lamentable plea; 625
" Pity, ah! pity my coeval tree,
" Where I so many blissful ages dwelt!"
' But his hard heart no soft compassion felt;
' The tree he fell'd; and for this foul disgrace
' The nymph ordain'd him woes, and all his race. 630
' To me Paræbius' came opprefs'd with fear,
' The cause I found, and counsell'd him to rear
' An altar to the goddess of the shore,
' And pardon for his father's crimes implore.
' Thus was the guilt aton'd; e'er since the man 635
' Pays all regards that grateful mortal can;

' For

'For ever at my side he loves to stay,
'And always goes unwillingly away.'
Thus Phineus spoke, when from his fleecy flock
His friend brought two, the fairest of the flock. 640
Then Jason rose, and, urg'd by Phineus blind,
Rose the bold offspring of the northern wind;
Their sacred offerings on the flames they lay,
Invoking Phœbus at the dawn of day.
The choicest viands with affiduous care 645
The younger heroes for their friends prepare.
Thus feasted, some their vessel's cordage press'd,
Some in the prophet's mansion sunk to rest.
Etesian breezes with the morning blow,
Which, sent by Jove, o'er every region flow. 650
 The nymph Cyrene, in old times, 'tis said,
Her flocks beside Thessalian Peneus fed,
Pleas'd with the honours of her virgin name,
Till day's bright God seduc'd the rural dame.
Far from Hæmonia he convey'd the fair, 655
Brought to the nymphs, and trusted to their care,
The mountain-nymphs that in parch'd Libya keep
Their airy mansions on Myrtosia's steep.
Cyrene there, along the winding shore,
Thee, Aristæus, to Apollo bore. 660

To

To whom rich swains, who in Theſſalia live,
The names of Agreus, and of Nomius give.
With length of days the God her love repaid,
And fix'd her huntreſs of the woodland ſhade;
But the young boy to Chiron's care he gave, 665
To reap inſtruction in his learned cave.
To him, when blooming in the prime of life,
The Muſes gave Autonoë to wife;
And taught their favourite pupil to excel
In arts of healing, and divining well. 670
To him they gave their numerous flocks to feed,
Which Phthia's Athamantine paſtures breed;
And thoſe that ſtray on Othrys' lofty brow,
Or where Apidanus' fam'd waters flow.
But when fierce Syrius ſcorch'd the Cyclades, 675
The realms of Minos, in th' Ægean ſeas,
Nought could the burning malady allay;
The iſlanders implor'd the God of day,
Who ſent young Ariſtæus to their aid,
By whom the fatal peſtilence was ſtaid. 680
At his ſire's call he left fair Phthia's land,
Attended by a bold Arcadian band,
Who from Lycaon their extraction boaſt,
And ſail'd to Ceos with his numerous hoſt.

He there an altar rais'd to fhowery Jove,   685
And made oblation on the heights above
To the red ftar that defolates the land,
And to heaven's king; at whofe fupreme command
Th' Etefian winds, while forty days they blow,
Refrefh with balmy gales the foil below.   690
Ev'n now the Cean priefts pay rites divine
Before the burning ftar begins to fhine.
Thus fame reports; and by thefe winds detain'd,
With Phineus ftill the Argonauts remain'd.
The grateful Thynians daily, while they ftaid,   695
To their lov'd feer abundant ftores convey'd.
Yet, ere they leave this hofpitable land,
To the twelve Gods erect they on the ftrand
An altar, and with facrifice and pray'r
Appeafe the powers of heaven, and to their fhip repair,
Eager their long-neglected oars to prove;   701
Yet not unmindful of the timorous dove:
Which fafely faften'd by a flender band
Euphemus carry'd trembling in his hand.
Quick from the ftay they lopp'd the doubled cord: 705
Minerva faw the heroes hafte aboard:
On a thin cloud fhe lighted from above,
(The cloud upheld the mighty feed of Jove)

And

And fped her voyage to the Euxine main,
For much fhe lov'd the delegated train. 710
So when fome fhepherd quits his native home,
(As men adventurous much delight to roam)
No roads too diftant, or too long appear,
In thought he fees, and thinks his manfion near;
O'er fea, o'er land with keen enquiring eyes 715
He views all ways, and in idea flies:
Thus to the Thynian fhore, from heaven above,
Swift flew the daughter of imperial Jove.

When now the heroes through the vaft profound
Reach the dire ftraits with rocks encompafs'd round,
Though boiling gulphs the failing pine detain'd, 721
Still on their way the labouring Grecians gain'd,
When the loud-juftling rocks increas'd their fears:
The fhores refounding thunder'd in their ears.
High on the prow Euphemus took his ftand, 725
And held the dove that trembled in his hand.
The reft with Tiphys on their ftrength rely'd,
To fhun the rocks, and ftem the roaring tide.
Soon, one fharp angle paft, the joyful train
Saw the cleft crags wide opening to the main. 730
Euphemus loos'd the dove, the heroes ftood
Erect to fee her fkim the foaming flood.

She

She through the rocks a ready paffage found;
The dire rocks met, and gave a dreadful found.
The falt-fea fpray in clouds began to rife;   735
Old ocean thunder'd; the cerulean fkies
Rebellow'd loudly with the fearful din;
The caves below remurmur'd from within.
O'er wave-worn cliffs, the coaft's high margin o'er
Boil'd the light foam, and whiten'd all the fhore. 740
Round whirl'd the fhip; the rocks with rapid fway
Lopp'd from the dove her fteering tail away;
Yet ftill fecurely through the ftraits fhe flew:
Loud joy infpir'd the circumfpective crew.
But Tiphys urg'd the chiefs their oars to ply,   745
For the rocks yawn'd, tremendous to the eye.
Then terror feiz'd them, when with fudden fhock
The refluent billows forc'd them on the rock;
With chilling fears was every nerve unftrung,
While o'er their heads impending ruin hung.   750
Before, behind they faw the fpacious deep,
When inftant, lo! a billow, vaft and fteep,
Still rifes higher, and ftill wider fpreads,
And hangs a watery mountain o'er their heads.
The heroes ftoop'd, expecting by its fall   755
That mighty billow would o'erwhelm them all;

But

But Tiphys' art reliev'd the labouring oars:
On Argo's keel the impetuous torrent pours,
Which rais'd the ship above the rocks so high,
She seem'd sublimely sailing in the sky.   760
Euphemus haftening urg'd the valiant crew
Their course with all their vigour to pursue.
Shouting they plied their oars, but plied in vain;
For the rough billows beat them back again.
And as the heroes unremitting row,   765
Their labouring oars were bent into a bow.
Swift down the mountainous billows Argo glides,
Like a huge cylinder along the tides,
Entangled with thick, craggy rocks around,
Her seams all bursting, and her planks unbound. 770
In that nice moment the Tritonian maid
To sacred Argo lent the timely aid.
Her left-hand heav'd her from the craggy steep,
Her right dismiss'd her gently to the deep:
Then like an arrow from th' elastic yew,   775
Swift o'er the foaming waves the vessel flew.
Yet had the clashing rocks with adverse sway
Torn the tall prow's embellishments away.
When thus the Greeks had safely reach'd the main,
To heaven Minerva wing'd her flight again.   780

The

The parted rocks at once concurrent stood,
Fix'd on one firm foundation in the flood:
This had been long determined by the fates,
If mortal ever paſt thoſe dangerous ſtraits.
Now freed from fears, the Greeks with eager eyes 785
View the broad ocean and ſerener ſkies:
Their anxious doubts for Argo they diſpel,
And deem her reſcued from the jaws of hell.
Then Tiphys thus: ' Sure to this ſhip we owe
' That fearleſs ſafety we experience now. 790
' For tho' wiſe Argus with ingenious art
' Form'd the fair ſhip compact in every part,
' Vigour divine propitious Pallas gave,
' And power aſſign'd her o'er the wind and wave.
' All now is ſafe: fear not thy haughty lord, 795
' But mark, illuſtrious chief, the prophet's word,
" The rocks eſcap'd, no future fears remain,
" Your toils are eaſy, and your voyage plain."

Thus he; and ſteering through the ſpacious ſea,
Near fair Bithynia plough'd the liquid way. 800
Then Jaſon mild the pilot thus addreſs'd:
" Why, Tiphys, this to me with grief oppreſs'd?
" Yes, I have err'd---my faults afflict my ſoul:
" When Pelias gave command without controul,

" 'Twas

" 'Twas mine to've shunn'd this wild-projected plot,
" Though inftant death had been my certain lot. 806
" Now fears and cares my tortur'd bofom rend;
" I dread thofe ills that from the deep impend,
" I dread the favage coaft, and every place
" Where dwells the bloody, or the barbarous race. 810
" No peace by day, no fleep at night I take,
" Since thefe brave chiefs affembled for my fake.
" With cold indifference may'ft thou look down,
" For no man's fafety anxious but thy own;
" But I, the leaft folicitous for mine, 815
" Feel for this friend's, that comrade's, and for thine.
" Much fhall I feel for all this martial band,
" Unlefs they fafe regain their native land."
Thus fpoke the prince, his gallant hoft to try;
With animating founds they rend the fky. 820
The loud acclaim was grateful to his ears,
And thus he boldly hails his brave compeers:
" Your valour, friends, encourages my foul:
" And fince no fears your gallant hearts controul,
" Boldly will I each coward-thought repel, 825
" Though doom'd to enter the abyfs of hell.
" For thefe rocks paft, no dangers can difmay,
" If we the counfel of the feer obey."

I   The

The Greeks applauding what their leader spoke,
Ply their stout oars and bend to every stroke; 830
And first by Rhebas, rapid stream, they fly,
And where Colona's rocks invade the sky,
And where the black-brow'd promontory low'rs,
'And where lov'd Phillis his broad current pours.
There Dipsacus receiv'd, in days of yore, 835
Young Phryxus landing on his friendly shore,
When, exil'd from Orchomenos, he swam
On the broad shoulders of the gold-fleec'd ram.
For to that stream a nymph of rural race
Bore Dipsacus, who, fearful of disgrace, 840
Dwelt with his mother, and along the mead
Chose, near his father's stream, his fleecy flocks to feed.
The chiefs soon pass'd his celebrated fane,
The river Calpis, and th' extended plain;
And all the night, along the tranquil tide, 845
And all the day their oars inceffant ply'd.
As when laborious steers, inur'd to toil,
With the bright plow-share turn the stubborn soil;
Sweat from their sides diftils in foamy smoke;
Their eyes obliquely roll beneath the yoke; 850
Their scorching breath heaves quick with panting
  found,
While all day long they tread the weary ground:

So

So toil'd the Greeks; nor yet the morning-light
Had pafs'd the doubtful confines of the night,
But, faintly glimmering on this earthly ball, 855
Produc'd what mortals morning-twilight call.
To Thynia's neighbouring ifle their courfe they bore,
And fafely landed on the defert fhore;
When bright Apollo fhew his radiant face,
From Lycia haftening to the Scythian race. 860
His golden locks, that flow'd with grace divine,
Hung cluftering like the branches of the vine:
In his left hand, his bow unbent he bore,
His quiver pendent at his back he wore:
The confcious ifland trembled as he trod, 865
And the big rolling waves confefs'd the God.
Nor dar'd the heroes, feiz'd with dire difmay,
The fplendors of his countenance furvey,
But on the ground their downward eyes they caft:
Meanwhile Apollo o'er the watery wafte, 870
And through thin ether on his journey flew.
Then thus fpoke Orpheus to the martial crew:
" Let us, my honour'd chiefs, with joint acclaim
" This ifland facred to bright Phœbus name,
" Who early here to all this hoft appear'd; 875
" Here let an altar on the fhore be rear'd,

I 2 " And

" And paid the rites divine: and if he deign
" That fafe we reach our native land again,
" Young horned goats fhall on his altars bleed,
" And the choice thighs to Phœbus be decreed. 880
" Now, comrades, due libations let us pay:
" Be gracious, O be gracious, God of day!"

 Thus he: and fome the ftony altar raife,
And fome explore the foreft's devious maze;
Haply within its lone retreats to find   885
A kid wild wandering, or a bounding hind:
Latona's fon foon led them to the prey;
Then on the altar, blazing bright, they lay
The choiceft parts involv'd in facred fmoke,
And fair Apollo, early God, invoke.   890
Around the flame in fprightly dance they fpring,
And Iö Pæan, Iö Pæan fing.
Then on the Thracian harp Oeager's fon
In foothing ftrains his tuneful tale begun:

 How once beneath Parnaffus' rocky brow   895
He lanch'd an arrow from his deadly bow,
And the fell ferpent flew; though young and fair
And beardlefs yet, but grac'd with golden hair:
(O prove propitious, thou whofe radiant head
Is deck'd with curls unclip'd, that never fhed, 900
            Worthy

Book II.   APOLLONIUS RHODIUS.   117

Worthy thyself! Latona only knows
With nicest art those ringlets to dispose)
Corycian nymphs their joys in rapture show'd,
And Iö, Iö Pæan call'd aloud:
Encomium grateful to the God of day.   905
Thus having prais'd him in the solemn lay,
They swear devoutly, due libations made,
To league for ever, and lend mutual aid;
Then touch the hallow'd altar with their hands
Concordant; and ev'n now a temple stands   910
Sacred to Concord, by the Grecians rais'd,
When here that mighty Deity they prais'd.

Now the third morn began on earth to smile,
When with fresh gales they left the lofty isle.
The foaming Sangar at a distance seen,   915
The Mariandine meads for ever green,
And Lycus' winding waters they forsake
All on the right, and Anthemoisia's lake.
So fast before the wind the vessel went,
Crack'd was the cordage, and the canvass rent: 920
But the gale ceasing with the dawning day,
Joyful they reach the Acherusian bay,
Begirt with rocks so towering tall and steep,
They frown tremendous on Bithynia's deep;

And yet so firmly founded in the main, 925
The raging billows round them roar in vain :
Above, upon the promontory's brow,
Umbrageous planes in beauteous order grow.
Thence, downward, thro' a deep and dreary dell,
Descends the path-way to the cave of hell, 930
With woods and shaggy rocks obscure; from whence
Exhaling vapours, chilly, damp and dense,
Scatter hoar frost along the whitening way,
Which melts before the sun's meridian ray.
On these rough cliffs, which many a storm molests, 935
The pleasing power of silence never rests.
From hollow caverns through the leafy boughs,
Above, the whistling wind for ever blows;
And while mad billows lash the founding shores,
Below, the raging main for ever roars. 940
There, bursting from the promontory's sides,
Sad Acheron along the valley glides ;
Deep-hollow'd beds his turbid streams convey,
As eastward to the main he winds his way.
This sable flood, in ancient story fam'd, 945
The Megarensians Soönautes nam'd
In after ages, when their course they bore
By ocean to the Mariandine shore :

For

For when the deep in deathful billows heav'd,
This peaceful port their shatter'd ships receiv'd. 950
To this the labouring Grecians bent their way,
Row'd round the cape, and anchor'd in the bay.
When Lycus and his Mariandine hoſt,
Lycus, the mighty monarch of the coaſt,
Knew theſe brave Greeks who Amycus had ſlain, 955
They welcom'd Jaſon and his conquering train:
But moſt on Pollux fix'd their wondering eyes,
And view'd him as a hero from the ſkies:
For long the fierce Bebrycians' rude alarms
Had rouz'd the Mariandyni to arms. 960
That day, the Grecian band with one conſent
To the king's hoſpitable palace went:
Cheerful they there on choiceſt dainties din'd,
And there with converſe ſweet regal'd the mind.
Then Jaſon to the king recounts the name, 965
And race of all theſe choſen ſons of fame,
Who lent their aid at Pelias' dire command;
Their ſtrange adventures on the Lemnian land;
What griefs, what woes at Cyzicus they bore;
And how they landed on the Myſian ſhore, 970
Where Hercules, diſtreſs'd his friend to find,
They left at land, unwillingly, behind.

I 4   What

What Glaucus fpoke prophetic from the main,
How with his fubjects Amycus was flain,
The prince relates: what Phineus poor and old, 975
Worn out with fufferings to the chiefs foretold;
How thro' Cyanean rocks they fafely fteer'd,
And in what ifle the God of day appear'd.
The king rejoic'd his guefts fo well had fped,
But griev'd that Hercules was left, and faid: 980
' Think how, my friends, this hero's aid deny'd,
' Rafhly ye tempt a length of feas untry'd.
' Full well I knew that valiant fon of fame,
' When here on foot thro' Lydia's coaft he came
' (For here my hofpitable father dwelt) 985
' To fetch Hippolita's embroider'd belt.
' The hero found me then a beardlefs fwain,
' Mourning my brother by the Myfians flain;
' (The nation dearly lov'd the blooming chief,
' And ftill lament in elegies of grief) 990
' Then at the funeral games he prov'd his might,
' And vanquifh'd Titias in the gauntlet-fight;
' Tho' young and ftout, and eager for the fray,
' From his bruis'd jaws he dafh'd the teeth away.
' The Myfian country, and the Phrygian plains 995
' The conqueror added to my fire's domains;

' And

Book II.   APOLLONIUS RHODIUS.   121

' And the rude nations that Bithynia till,
' To foaming Rhebas and Colona's hill;
' And Paphlagonia to its utmost bounds,
' Which fable Billis with his waves surrounds. 1000
' But now proud Amycus, and all his host,
' Since Hercules has left the neighbouring coast,
' Have spoil'd my realms, and spread their hostile
    bands
' Wide as where Hipias' streams enrich the lands.
' At length their lawless insolence they rue,   1005
' And by your hands have suffer'd vengeance due.
' And sure some God afforded his relief
' When Pollux slew that proud Bebrycian chief.
' I for this deed my due regard will show;
' 'Tis what the meanest to the mighty owe.   1010
' My son, your comrade, shall at my command
' Attend o'er distant seas your gallant band:
' O'er distant seas, with Dascylus your guide,   ⎫
' You still with faithful friends shall be supply'd, ⎬
' Far as Thermodon rolls his foaming tide.   1015 ⎭
' Meanwhile on yon bold cape that mates the skies
' To Leda's sons a sacred fane shall rise,
' Admir'd by all that cross the boundless main,
' For all shall venerate the sacred fane:

' To

'To them will I, as to the powers divine, 1020
'Some fruitful acres near the town affign.'
Converfing thus, the genial feaft they fhare,
And to the fhip at early day repair:—
With his brave fon the friendly Lycus went,
Who ftore of viands to the fhip had fent. 1025
'Twas here the cruel deftinies decreed
That Idmon, fam'd for augury, fhould bleed:
The fate of others he had oft forefhown,
But fail'd, unhappy! to prevent his own,
Here, in a covert near the reedy flood, 1030
A fell wild boar lay deep immers'd in mud.
With horrid tufks fo dreadful he appear'd,
The fountain-nymphs the favage monfter fear'd:
No living wight in miry marfh or moor
E'er faw fo fierce, fo horrible a boar. 1035
On the lake's verge as lucklefs Idmon ftood,
From his clofe covert, in the reedy mud,
Up fprung the furious beaft with might and main,
Tore the chief's thigh, and fnapp'd the bone in twain;
He groans, he falls, and on the bank he lies, 1040
His griev'd companions anfwer to his cries;
When Peleus inftantly approaching near,
Lanch'd at the boar his unavailing fpear:

But

But Idas aim'd his pointed dart so well,
Low in the marsh the dying monster fell. 1045
The chiefs with Idmon to the ship retir'd,
Who deeply groaning in their arms expir'd:
Immers'd in grief, they now neglect to sail;
For three whole days their comrade they bewail;
But on the fourth, with pensive sorrow, paid 1050
The last sad honours due to Idmon's shade.
The king, the people join'd the mournful crew,
And, loud-lamenting, numerous victims slew:
They dug the grave, and on the greensword raise
A tomb on which posterity will gaze: 1055
For near the tomb a tall wild olive grows,
Beneath the cape, and beautifully blows.
Me would the Nine commission to unfold
This truth, which Phœbus had long since foretold,
This, this is he, the tutelary lord, 1060
Henceforth to be by mighty states ador'd:
For here Bæotians and Megarians join'd,
Near the wild olive wavering in the wind,
To build a city; though due honours they
To Agamestor, not to Idmon, pay. 1065
 Who fell beside? for, lo! the chiefs intend
Another tomb for some lamented friend.

Ev'n

Ev'n now two mournful monuments appear:
Tiphys, Fame says, was stretch'd upon the bier.
Him cruel fate ordain'd no more to roam; 1070
He died far distant from his native home.
For while to Idmon funeral rites they pay,
Untimely sickness snatch'd the chief away.
Then heart-felt sadness seiz'd the pensive train,
Who, prostrate on the margin of the main, 1075
Forgetful of their necessary food,
Mourn'd in sad silence to the roaring flood.
For they, now skilful Tiphys is no more,
Despair'd returning to their native shore;
And here had staid, with bitter grief oppress'd, 1080
Had not Saturnia in Ancæus' breast
Breath'd courage: him Astypalæa bore,
Near winding Imbrasus on Samos' shore,
To ocean's God; a chief expert to guide
The flying vessel o'er the foaming tide. 1085
Then thus to Peleus, Neptune's valiant son,
By heaven inspir'd, in cheering terms begun:
' Ill suits the brave in foreign climes to stay,
' And waste, O Peleus, precious time away.
' I left not Samos less for sailing skill'd 1090
' Than fierce contention in the fighting field.

' For

'   For Argo cherish not one abject fear,
'   Since many skill'd, besides myself, are here,
'   And he, to whom the steerage we ordain,
'   Will safely guide the vessel o'er the main.   1095
'   'Tis thine to stimulate the fainting crew
'   With ready oars their voyage to pursue.'
He spoke, and transport touch'd the Phthian's breast,
Instant he rose, and thus the host addrefs'd:
   " Why are we here by fruitless grief detain'd? 1100
   " Two friends are dead, and this the fates ordain'd;
   " Yet many pilots in this host remain,
   " To steer firm Argo o'er the watery plain.
   " To sorrows unavailing bid adieu!
   " Let us, bold peers, our destin'd course pursue." 1105
He said, and Jason anxious thus reply'd;
'   Where are those pilots, say, our course to guide?
'   For those whom late we boasted as the best
'   And ablest chiefs, are most with grief opprefs'd.
'   I therefore deem a like sad fate attends   1110
'   On us, as on our late departed friends,
'   If neither in Æeta's ports we moor,
'   Nor thro' those rocks regain our native shore,
'   But here inactive and inglorious stay,
'   Years following years, and linger life away.' 1115.

He

He spoke; Ancæus seiz'd the steerage, driv'n
By power instinctive from the queen of heav'n:
Erginus next the glorious charge desir'd;
Euphemus, Nauplius to the helm aspir'd..
But these the congregated chiefs declin'd, 1120
And bold Ancæus to the post assign'd.

 With the twelfth rising morn the heroes sail;
Favonius breath'd a favourable gale;
And soon they leave sad Acheron behind,
Then give the swelling canvass to the wind: 1125
On the smooth sea the ship serenely rides,
And light along the liquid level glides.
Ere long with stretching sails the coast they gain,
Where broad Callichorus augments the main.
To Thebes returning from his Indian fights, 1130
Here Bacchus solemniz'd mysterious rites,
The dance before the sacred cave ordain'd,
And here full many a doleful night remain'd.
This name the country to the river gave,
Callichorus; and Aulion to the cave. 1135

 Still as their course the daring Greeks pursue,
The monument of Sthenelus they view.
With honours grac'd, obtain'd in realms afar,
Returning from the Amazonian war,

On

On the bleak shore (Alcides at his side) 1140
Pierc'd by a fatal dart the hero died.
Slow sail'd they on, for, eager to survey
His kindred warriours on the watery way,
At his request, from her infernal coast
Pluto's grim queen releas'd the pensive ghost. 1145
The pensive ghost beheld with eager ken
From the tall monument the ship and men.
As arm'd for war the martial phantom seem'd;
Four crests high-towering on his helmet beam'd,
With purple rays intolerably bright; 1150
Then soon it sunk beneath the shades of night.
In mute amazement stood the Grecian host;
But Mopsus counsel'd to appease the ghost
With offerings due; the chiefs approach the strand,
And round the tomb of Sthenelus they stand. 1155
They pour libations, and the victims slay,
And on the fire the destin'd offerings lay.
Apart, to guardian Phœbus next they raise
An altar meet, and bid the victims blaze.
Here Orpheus plac'd his lyre for music fam'd; 1160
Apollo's altar hence was Lyra nam'd.
And now, invited by the favouring gales,
They climb the ship and spread their swelling sails;
Swift

Swift o'er the deep the winged veffel flies,
Swift as the rapid hawk that cleaves the fkies, 1165
And lightly thro' the liquid ether fprings,
Nor moves, felf-poiz'd, his wide-expanded wings.
Thence by Parthenius fail'd the focial train,
The gentleft ftream that mingles with the main.
Fatigued with traverfing the mazy grove, 1170
Here, ere fhe re-afcends the courts of Jove,
The chafte Diana, huntrefs of the wood,
Bathes her fair limbs, and gambols in the flood.
Then during night by Sefamus they fail,
And Erythinus rifing o'er the vale; 1175
By Cromna and Crobrialus, and where
Thy groves, Cytorus, ever green appear.
Thence with the rifing fun they ftoutly row
Near where Carambis lifts his rocky brow.
All day, all night with unremitted oar 1180
They coaft along Ægialus's fhore.
Then to the Syrian clime the heroes fped,
Where Jove, by hafty promifes mifled,
Sinope plac'd, and, all fhe wifh'd to claim,
Gave her the honours of a virgin's name. 1185
For, know, the God, by Love's ftrong power oppref'd,
Promis'd to grant whate'er fhe might requeft;

           And

And this requeft th' infidious damfel made,
That her virginity might never fade.
Hence Phœbus foil'd could no one wifh obtain; 1190
Hence winding Alys wooed the maid in vain.
No mortal force fuch virtue could o'ercome,
Defeat Jove's promife, and impair her bloom.
Here dwelt Deïmachus's offspring fam'd,
Deileon, Autolycus and Phlogius nam'd, 1195
What time they ceas'd with Hercules to roam,
And at Sinòpe found a fettled home.
They, when they faw the bold Theffalian band,
Met them on fhore and welcom'd them to land;
And, loathing longer in thefe climes to ftay, 1200
Join'd the brave crew, and with them fail'd away.
Blefs'd with the zephyr's breeze that brifkly blew,
Near Halys' ftream and Ifis' fail'd the crew;
Near Syria's coaft, and, ere night's fhades abound,
Near th' Amazonian cape, for many a bay renown'd.
Where Hercules furpriz'd, in days of yore, 1206
Bold Menalippe wandering on the fhore:
A belt Hippolyta her fifter paid,
And for this ranfom he reftor'd the maid.
Here in Thermòdon's bay firm Argo moor'd; 1210
For lafh'd with tempefts the vex'd ocean roar'd.

K No

No river like the fam'd Thermodon leads
Such numerous currents o'er the fertile meads:
A hundred ſtreams to him their waters owe;
Yet from one ſource, one only ſource they flow. 1215
On Amazonian hills, that reach the ſkies,
The great Thermodon firſt begins to riſe;
Hence ſoon emerging many a courſe he takes,
Sinks but to mount, and various channels makes.
The different ſtreams from different founts diſtil, 1220
In ſoft meanders wandering down the hill;
Some public notice and fair titles claim,
Some flow obſcurely, and without a name;
But confluent ſoon, along the winding plain,
He rolls his waves, and foams o'er half the main. 1225

Had the Greeks landed on this hoſtile coaſt,
War would have ſoon purſu'd the gallant hoſt:
(For the fierce Amazons regard not right,
Strife is their ſport, and battles their delight:
From Mars and Harmony theſe warlike maids 1230
Sprung where Acmonius ſpreads its bowery ſhades)
But favour'd with the ſoft Favonian wind,
The heroes left the crooked ſhore behind,
Where the bold Amazons, perceiv'd from far,
Stood ſheath'd in arms, prepar'd for ſpeedy war. 1235

Not

Not in one city dwelt this martial band,
But in three parties scatter'd o'er the land:
The first tribe at Themiscyra remain'd,
O'er this Hippolyta, their empress, reign'd;
There dwelt the fair Lycastian dames apart, 1240
Here the Chadesians, skill'd to lance the dart.
Th' ensuing day the delegated band
Approach'd with oars the rough Chalybian land;
Whose sons ne'er yoke their oxen to the plough,
Nor healing plants, nor fruits delicious know: 1245
Nor aught delight they in th' irriguous mead,
Retir'd and still, their fleecy flocks to feed;
But they dig iron from the mountain's side,
And by this ore are nature's wants supply'd.
Devoid of toil ne'er beam'd Aurora's ray, 1250
And dust and smoke obscur'd the dismal day.

From thence they pass where Tibarenians till,
Sacred to Jove, the Genetæan hill.
Here, when the teeming wives are brought to bed,
Their groaning husbands hang the drooping head;
Equal attendance with their wives they claim; 1256
The same their diet, and their baths the same.

Next by the sacred hill their oars impel
Firm Argo, where the Mossynœcians dwell.

In towers they live, of solid timber fram'd, 1260
Moſſynes call'd, and thence the nation nam'd:
Of manners ſtrange; for they with care conceal
Thoſe deeds which others openly reveal;
And actions, that in ſecret ſhould be done,
Perform in public and before the ſun: 1265
For, like the monſters of the briſtly drove,
In public they perform the feats of love.
Exalted in his tower that mates the ſky,
The monarch here diſpenſes law from high:
But if his judgment err, this rigid ſtate 1270
Condemns their chief, and ſtarving is his fate.
Theſe nations paſt, with unremitting oar
They reach, Aretias, thy sea-girt ſhore.
Then ſunk the breezes with the cloſing day,
When down the ſky deſcending they ſurvey 1275
A winged monſter of enormous might,
Which toward the ſhip precipitates her flight.
Her wings ſhe ſhook, and from her pinions flung
A dart-like quill, which on Oïleus hung;
Down his left ſhoulder ſwift it fell: no more, 1280
Faint and enfeebled, could he hold his oar.
In ſilence long the Grecian heroes gaze,
And view the feathery javelin with amaze.

But

But Erybotes, foon approaching near,
Extracted from the chief the winged fpear; 1285
Then from his fide his pendent belt unbound,
And wrapp'd that bandage o'er the gaping wound.
When, lo! a fecond bird appear'd in view,
But ready Clytius firft had bent his yew;
By his keen fhaft the feather'd monfter flain 1290
Faft by the fhip fell headlong in the main.
Then thus Amphidamas: ' My friends, ye know,
' And thefe obfcene voracious fiends forefhow
' Aretias near: then lift to what I fay,
' Fruitlefs are fhafts to drive thefe pefts away; 1295
' But, would you here a fit reception find,
' Recall th' advice of Phineus to your mind.
' For when Alcides to Arcadia went
' Well arm'd with arrows, on his toils intent,
' From the Stymphalian lake he fail'd to fright 1300
' Thefe ravenous Harpies (I beheld the fight)
' But when he rung a cymbal with his fpear;
' The clanging cymbal fill'd the birds with fear:
' In wild confufion far away they fly,
' And with fhrill clamours pierce the diftant fky. 1305
' 'Tis ours to practife this expulfive art;
' But hear ye firft the counfel I impart:

K 3

' Let

' Let half our crew, in glittering armour drefs'd,
' Nod, as by turns they row, the high-plum'd creft;
' The reft bright fpears and fwords and fhields pro-
    vide,   1310
' And meet difpofe them round the veffel's fide.
' Then all at once your voices raife on high,
' And with loud pealing fhouts affail the fky;
' The deafening clamours, the protended fpears,
' And nodding crefts will fill the birds with fears. 1315
' And when Aretias' barren ifle ye gain,
' Ring your broad bucklers, and all fhout amain.'
He fpoke, the chiefs approv'd the wife defign;
High on their heads the brazen helmets fhine,
Whofe purple crefts wav'd dreadful in the wind; 1320
To thefe alternate were ftout oars affign'd;
The reft with care their veffel's fide conceal'd
With glittering fpears, and many a fhining fhield.
As when induftrious builders cover o'er
With tiles the walls their hands had rais'd before; 1325
In chequer'd fquares they decorate the roof,
And make it fair to view, and tempeft-proof;
Thus they with fhields, difpos'd in order due,
Shelter'd their veffel, and adorn'd it too.
As when embattled hofts their foes affail,   -   1330
Tumultuous fhouts, and martial founds prevail;

Book II.   APOLLONIUS RHODIUS.   135

So from the ship loud clamours pierc'd the sky;
No more the Greeks their feather'd foes descry:
Rattling their bucklers, near the land they drew,
And far away the winged furies flew.   1335
So when great Jove on close-throng'd cities pours
From hyperborean clouds his haily show'rs;
Within, the dwellers sit in peace profound,
Nor heed the rattling storms that rage around;
In vain the hail descends, the tempests roar,   1340
Their roofs from harm were well secur'd before:
Thus on their shields the furies shot their quills,
Then clamouring vanish'd to far distant hills.

Say, Muse, why Phineus counsel'd here to land,
On Mars's isle, this delegated band?   1345
And what advantage could the Grecians gain
From all the toils and perils of the main?

To fam'd Orchomenos, with favouring gale,
From Æa's walls the sons of Phrixus sail,
Their grandsire's vast inheritance to share,   1350
Who dying left this voyage to their care.
Near Mars's island on this signal day
The sons of Phrixus plough'd the liquid way.
But Jove ordain'd that Boreas' blasts should blow,
While moist Arcturus soak'd the vales below.   1355

First on the mountains, rising by degrees,
All day rough Boreas shook the trembling trees;
Then, night approaching, he with hideous sound
Roll'd the big wave, and heav'd the vast profound.
No stars appear translucent thro' the clouds,   1360
But gloomy darkness every object shrouds.
The sons of Phrixus, tost by whelming waves,
With horror shudder'd at the watery graves;
For the fierce blast, impell'd with might and main,
Tore all their canvass, split the ship in twain   1365
And dash'd to pieces; but by heaven's kind aid
On a large fragment of the wreck convey'd,
The winds and waves the trembling brothers bore
Aghast, and half expiring to the shore.
Instant in floods descended copious rain,   1370
Drench'd the whole island, and increas'd the main;
(These shores, the neighbouring coast, and sacred hill
The rude, the barbarous Mossynœcians till)
Borne on a broken plank, the forceful blast
The sons of Phrixus on this island cast,   1375
Who met the Grecians with the rising sun;
Ceas'd was the rain, and Argus thus begun:
' Adjur'd by Jove, whose circumspective ken
' Surveys the conduct and the cares of men,

' Whate'er

‘ Whate'er your name or race, our tale attend, 1380
‘ And to the wretched your affiftance lend.
‘ The raging ftorms that Neptune's empire fweep,
‘ Have wreck'd our lucklefs veffel in the deep ;
‘ To you we pray, if pity touch your heart,
‘ Some fcanty raiment for our wants impart; 1385
‘ The fons of mifery for mercy call;
‘ To one low level forrow finks us all.
‘ They who to proftrate fuppliants lend an ear,
‘ The laws of hofpitable Jove revere.
‘ All-prefent he hath liften'd to our pray'r, 1390
‘ And finking fav'd us with a parent's care.'
　　Then Æfon's fon (fulfilling Phineus' plan)
Thus queftion'd mild the miferable man;
" But firft, of truth obfervant, frankly tell,
" In what far region of the world ye dwell; 1395
" What bufinefs call'd you from your native coaft,
" What race ye fprung from, and what names ye boaft."
　　Then Argus thus: ‘ Ye, fure, have heard the fame
‘ Of Phrixus, who from Greece to Æa came.
‘ To great Æeta's citadel he fwam 1400
‘ Supported on the fhoulders of the ram,
‘ Whofe fleece now high-fufpended ye behold,
‘ By Hermes metamorphos'd into gold.
　　　　　　　　　　　　　　　　　　‘ On

' On the tall oak's high top it hangs in view,
' The ram to Jove, propitious, Phrixus flew.   1405
' The generous king receiv'd him as his gueft,
' And with undower'd Chalciope he blefs'd.
' From thefe we fprung; but Phrixus breathes no more,
' His bones lie buried on the Colchian fhore.
' We now to fam'd Orchomenos repair,   1410
' The wide domains of Athamas to fhare;
' Such were the laft injunctions of our fire:
' Our bufinefs this—if ye our names require,
' This Cytiforus, that will Phrontis claim,
' He furnam'd Melas, Argus is my name.'   1415
   He fpoke: the Argonauts with ftill amaze,
And fecret tranfport on the ftrangers gaze.
Then Jafon mark'd the much-enduring man,
And thus with mild benevolence began :
" Friends as ye are, and near relations too,   1420
" To us for fuccour not in vain ye fue.
" Cretheus and Athamas their fire the fame;
" And Cretheus was my honour'd grandfire's name:
" With thefe companions join'd, I fail from Greece
" To Colchos, famous for the golden fleece—   1425
" Some diftant day, at eafe may we relate
" Thefe ftrange events, and all our various fate.
                                         " Now

" Now shall warm robes to clothe your limbs be giv'n,
" We meet conducted by the hand of heav'n."
He said, and from the ship rich vestments sent; 1430
Then to the sacred fane of Mars they went.
From fleecy flocks they drain'd the life-warm blood,
And all devoutly round the altar stood;
This, of small stones compos'd, was plac'd before
The lofty temple's double-folding door :   1435
(Within the fane a stone of sable hue
Stood where the Amazons their victims slew;
Who held it lawless, when they sojourn'd here,
To slay the sheep, or sacrifice the steer;
Instead of these the full-fed, pamper'd steed   1440
Was doom'd, a victim at this fane, to bleed.)
These rites dispatch'd, and hunger's rage repress'd,
Thus Æson's son the listening host address'd :
 " Impartial Jove the race of man regards;
" The bad he punishes, the just rewards: 1445
" As from a bloody stepdame's rage of yore
" He sav'd your sire, and blest with ample store,
" So he preserv'd you from the whelming deep,
" And in this vessel will securely keep;
" Whether for Æa in our ship ye sail,   1450
" Or to far Phthia court the favouring gale.
                                           " For

" For this fam'd ſhip of Pelion's pines was made,
" And form'd by Argus, with Minerva's aid;
" But ſtorms had laſh'd her, ere, with hideous ſhock,
" She reach'd thoſe ſtraits, where rock encounters
    rock. 1455
" Then lend your aid to gain the golden fleece,
" And be our guides to bring it back to Greece.
" Jove ſeems incens'd, and we this voyage take,
" To ſooth his anger, and for Phrixus' ſake."

Ardent he ſpoke; but they deſpair'd to find, 1460
Æeta of ſo tractable a mind,
To yield the fleece: then Argus thus replies,
Alarm'd and troubled at their bold empriſe;
' Whate'er our powers can grant, or wiſhes gain,
' The ſons of Greece ſhall never aſk in vain. 1465
' But proud Æeta, cruel and ſevere,
' I loath the tyrant, and his power I fear;
' The Sun his ſire, ſo fame relates, he boaſts;
' Unnumber'd ſubjects guard his ample coaſts;
' For mighty ſtrength he ſtands renown'd afar, 1470
' And voice terrific as the God of war.
' The golden prize a monſtrous dragon keeps;
' Hard taſk to ſeize it, for he never ſleeps.
' Earth on rough Caucaſus a being gave
' To this fierce beaſt near Typhaonia's cave, 1475
                                          ' Where

' Where huge Typhœus, as old stories prove,
' Was struck by lightning from almighty Jove,
' When fierce in arms against heaven's king he stood;
' From his head issu'd warm corrupted blood;
' To Nysa's hills, to Nysa's plains he flies,   1480
' And now beneath Serbonian marshes lies.
   He said; distress'd so sad a tale to hear,
On every countenance sat pallid fear;
When Peleus thus with confidence reply'd,
And gave that courage which their fears deny'd: 1485
   " Despair not, friend; for we disdain to yield,
" Nor dread to meet Æeta in the field.
" We too are skill'd in war, and draw our line
" From godlike chiefs, and origin divine.
" Incens'd should he the fleecy gold detain,   1490
" He'll ask, I trust, the Colchians' aid in vain."
   Conversing thus the chiefs their thoughts express'd,
And sated with repast reclin'd to rest.
With rising morn the gently-breathing gales
Play'd round the pine, and fill'd the swelling sails; 1495
The swelling sails expanded by the wind
Soon left Aretias' barren shore behind;
And swiftly skimming o'er the watery vast,
The Philyræan isle at eve they past;
                                          Where

Where Saturn firſt fair Philyra ſurvey'd, 1500
When on Olympus he the Titans ſway'd,
(Nurs'd by the fierce Curetes, yet a child,
Young Jove was hid in Cretan caverns wild)
Unknown to Rhea he the maid compreſs'd;
But ſoon to Rhea was the crime confeſs'd; 1505
Detected Saturn left his bed with ſpeed,
And ſprung all-vigorous as a mane-crown'd ſteed.
Swift fled fair Philyra, abaſh'd with ſhame,
And to the hills of Theſſaly ſhe came:
Fam'd Chiron ſprung from this embrace ſo odd, 1510
Ambiguous, half a horſe, and half a God.
From thence they ſail by long Macronian ſtrands,
And where Bechira's ample coaſt expands;
Shores where Byzerians wander far and wide,
And fierce Sapirians, ſtigmatiz'd for pride; 1515
And favour'd by the ſoft impelling wind,
Leave numerous coaſts and lands unnam'd behind:
And, ſailing ſwiftly o'er the waves, ſurvey,
Far on the Pontic main, an opening bay;
Then, Caucaſus, thy hills were ſeen on high, 1520
That rear their rocky ſummits in the ſky;
Fix'd to theſe rocks Prometheus ſtill remains,
For ever bound in adamantine chains:

On

On the rude cliffs a ravenous eagle breeds,
That on the wretch's entrails ever feeds. 1525
The Grecians faw him, ere th' approach of night,
Soar high in air, loud hiffing in his flight:
Around the fhip he flew in airy rings,
The fails all fhivering as he fhook his wings:
Not as a light aerial bird he foars, 1530
But moves his pinions like well-polifh'd oars.
The ravenous bird now rufhing from the fkies,
Sudden, they heard Prometheus' piercing cries:
The heavens re-echoed to the doleful found,
While the fell eagle gnaw'd the recent wound. 1535
Till gorg'd with flefh the bird of Jove they fpy'd
Again defcending from the mountain's fide.

Night now approaching, near the land they drew,
And Argus well his native country knew;
For, Phafis, thy wide-fpreading flood they gain, 1540
And the laft limits of the Pontic main.
At length arriv'd, fo many dangers paft,
They furl the mainfail, and they lower the maft:
Their bending oars the mighty ftream divide;
The ftream receives them on his foaming tide. 1545
All on the left, in ancient rolls renown'd,
Rife Æa's walls with glittering turrets crown'd;

And

And on the right the field, not diſtant far,
And grove, both ſacred to the God of war;
Where on an oak the fleece, ſuſpended high,   1550
A dragon guards with ever-watchful eye.
Then Jaſon haſtes, impatient to conſign
To the pure ſtream the unpolluted wine,
And from a golden vaſe fulfils the rite divine,
Sacred to earth, to Gods that guard the coaſts,   1555
And ancient heroes' long-departed ghoſts:
For their protection he preferr'd his pray'r,
To keep the ſhip with tutelary care.
Then thus Ancæus: 'Numerous perils paſt,
' Colchos and Phaſis we behold at laſt;   1560
' Behoves you now your ſage advice to lend,
' Whether to treat Æeta as a friend,
' With ſpeech accordant, and compliance bland,
' Or in rough terms the golden prize demand.'
  Thus he; but Jaſon urg'd, at Argus' call,   1565
High up the ſedgy ſtream the ſhip to haul;
Which, undiſturb'd, might there at anchor ride
In the calm boſom of the peaceful tide:
There ſought the chiefs the bleſſings of repoſe,
And ſlept ſecure till grateful morning roſe.   1570

END OF THE SECOND BOOK.

THE
THIRD BOOK.

THE ARGUMENT.

Juno and Pallas intercede with Venus. They requeſt that ſhe would perſuade Cupid to inſpire Medea with love for Jaſon. Venus conſents; and the ſhafts of Cupid, at her ſuit, have their deſired effect. Jaſon, Augeas and Telamon proceed to the court of Æeta, where they are hoſpitably entertained. But, having heard the occaſion of their voyage, Æeta is incenſed, and refuſes to beſtow the Golden Fleece on Jaſon, unleſs on ſuch terms, as he preſumed he durſt not comply with. The paſſion of Medea for Jaſon is deſcribed with great ſimplicity and delicacy. Medea early in the morning repairs to the temple of Hecate: thither Jaſon, at the ſuggeſtion of Mopſus, follows her. The poet dwells particularly on their interview and conference. Medea inſtructs him how to ſubdue the brazen bulls and armies of giants. With Jaſon's combat, and the ſucceſs of it, the book concludes.

THE
ARGONAUTICS
OF
APOLLONIUS RHODIUS.

BOOK III.

COME, heavenly maid, thy timely fuccour bring,
And teach thy poet, Erato, to fing,
How Jafon, favour'd by the Colchian maid,
To Grecian realms the golden prize convey'd.
Thy fongs the rites of Cyprian blifs proclaim,   5
And in young virgins raife the melting flame;
For the foft paffion thy behefts approve,
And Erato's the kindred name of love.

   Conceal'd in fedges as the heroes lie,
Juno and Pallas mark'd them from the fky;   10
Apart from all the Gods their feats they took
In heaven's high hall, and thus Saturnia fpoke:
" Daughter of Jove, thy fage advice impart,
" By what nice fraud, what well-diffembled art,

L 2

" Thefe

148 *The* Argonautics *of* Book III.

" Thefe venturous chiefs fhall gain the golden fleece,
" And fafe convey it to the realms of Greece.   16.
" Say, fhall they call entreaties to their aid ?
" Will foft addrefs the wayward king perfuade,
" So fam'd for fierce barbarity and pride ?
" No art, no effort muft be left untry'd."   20
She faid ; and Pallas thus: ' O Queen, I find
' The fame ideas rifing in my mind :
' To lend affiftance to the Grecian train
' My heart is willing, but my counfel vain.'
  This faid, their minds on various projects ran, 25
On earth their eyes were fix'd, when Juno thus began:
" To Venus inftant let us fpeed our way,
" (Her foft perfuafions Cupid will obey)
" Intreat her that the wily God infpire
" Medea's foul with love's unconquer'd fire,   30
" Love for great Æfon's fon ; applauding Greece
" Will by her aid regain the glorious fleece."
  She faid ; Minerva patronis'd the plan,
And thus with mild benevolence began :
' I, who arofe from Jove's immortal brain,   35
' Stranger to love, his pleafure or his pain,
' Thy fage propofal from my foul approve ;
' Do thou explain it to the queen of love.'
                                        This

This said, with speed the two immortals came
To the grand mansion of the Cyprian dame, 40
Which crippled Vulcan rais'd, when first he led
The Paphian goddess to his nuptial bed.
The gate they pass, and to the dome retire
Where Venus oft regales the God of fire:
(He to his forge had gone at early day, 45
A floating isle contain'd it on the bay,
Here wondrous works by fire's fierce power he wrought,
And on his anvil to perfection brought.)
Fronting the door, all lovely and alone,
Sat Cytherea on a polish'd throne. 50
Adown the shoulders of the heavenly fair,
In easy ringlets flow'd her flaxen hair;
And with a golden comb, in matchless grace,
She taught each lock its most becoming place.
She saw the deities approach her dome, 55
And from her hand dismiss'd the golden comb;
Then rose respectful, all with beauty grac'd,
And on rich thrones the great immortals plac'd;
Resum'd her seat, and with a ready hand
Bound her loose ringlets, and thus question'd bland:
' What cause, ye visitants from heaven, relate, 61
' Has brought such guests to Cytherea's gate?

' Ye

'Ye who excel in high Olympus' sphere,
'Such mighty deities, and strangers here?'
Then thus Saturnia: "Wantonly you jest, 65
" When pressing grief sits heavy on our breast.
" Now in the Phasis, with his warlike train,
" Great Jason moors, the golden fleece to gain:
" For that fam'd chief, and for his martial host,
" Dire fears alarm us, but for Jason most: 70
" This potent arm, whate'er our prowess can,
" Shall snatch from misery the gallant man,
" Tho' far as hell he, rash adventurer! go,
" To free Ixion, link'd in chains of woe;
" Left Pelias proudly heaven's decrees deride, 75
" Who on my altars sacrifice deny'd.
" Nay more, young Jason claims my love and grace,
" Whom late I met returning from the chace,
" Returning met, as o'er the world I stray'd,
" And human kind, and human works survey'd; 80
" Hard by Araurus I beheld the man,
" Wide o'er its banks whose rapid currents ran;
" (From snow-clad hills, in torrents loud and strong,
" Roar'd the swoln streams the rugged rocks among.)
" He on his back, though like a crone I stood, 85
" Securely brought me o'er the foaming flood;

" This

" This won my love, a love for ever true,
" Nor will the haughty-minded Pelias rue
" His flagrant crimes, till you propitious deign
" To speed my Jason to his Greece again." 90
She spoke, and Venus stood amaz'd to find
The queen of heaven to humble prayer inclin'd;
Then thus familiar said: ' O wife of Jove,
' Basest of beings call the queen of love,
' Unless her every word and work conspire 95
' To give you all the succour you require:
' All that my hand, my feeble hand can do,
' Shall unrewarded be perform'd for you.'
Then Juno thus: " Not difficult the task;
" No mighty force, no strength of arm I ask. 100
" Bid gentle Love the Colchian maid inspire,
" And for my Jason fan the rising fire;
" If kind she prove, he gains the golden fleece,
" And by her subtle aid conducts it safe to Greece."
Love's queen replied: 'Cupid, ye powers divine, 105
' Will reverence your injunctions more than mine:
' Your looks will awe him, tho', devoid of shame,
' Of me the urchin makes eternal game,
' Oft he provokes my spleen, and then I vow,
' Enrag'd, I'll break his arrows and his bow: 110

L 4 " Restrain

" Reſtrain your ire," exclaims the ſneering elf,
" Leſt you find reaſon to upbraid yourſelf."
　At this the Powers with ſmiles each other view'd,
And Venus thus her woeful tale purſu'd :
' Others may ridicule the pains I feel, 115
' Nor boots it all my ſufferings to reveal.
' But ſince ye jointly importune my aid,
' Cupid ſhall yield, and Venus be obey'd.'
She ſaid ; and Juno preſs'd her hand and ſmil'd,
Then anſwered thus, benevolent and mild : 120
" O grant this boon ; do inſtant as you ſay ;
" Chide not the boy, and he will ſoon obey."
　This ſaid, both haſten'd to the realms above,
And left the manſions of the queen of love :
The Cyprian goddeſs o'er Olympus flies, 125
To find her ſon in every dale ſhe pries,
Through heaven's gay meads the queen purſu'd her
　　way,
And found him there with Ganymede at play.
Him Jove tranſlated to the bleſt abodes,
And, fam'd for beauty, plac'd among the Gods. 130
With golden dice, like boon compeers they play'd :
Love in his hollow hand ſome cubes convey'd,
Reſolv'd to cheat young Ganymede with thoſe,
While on his cheeks the conſcious crimſon roſe.

　　　　　　　　　　　　　　　　　　　The

The Phrygian boy was vanquifh'd to his coft, 135
Two dice alone remain'd, and thofe he loft.
Silent he fat in dull dejected ftate,
Enrag'd that Cupid fhould deride his fate:
His lofs increafing with protracted play,
He went a wretch with empty hands away, 140
Nor faw he Venus: fhe her Cupid took
Faft by the cheek, and thus upbraiding fpoke:
' And can you laugh, you fly, deceitful elf?
' Such tricks will bring a fcandal on yourfelf.
' But hafte, my Cupid, my commands obey, 145
' And a nice plaything fhall your toils repay,
' What once to Jove dear Adraftæa gave,
' When Jove was nourifh'd in the Cretan cave,
' A fweet round ball; oh! keep it for my fake,
' A finer ball not Vulcan's hands can make. 150
' Gold are the circles, beauteous to behold,
' And all the finifh'd feams are wrought in gold;
' But all fo clofe they fcarcely can be found:
' And the pale ivy winds its wreaths around.
' If high in air you fling this ball afar, 155
' It fhines and glimmers like a radiant ftar.
' This prize I'll give, if you propitious prove,
' And lure Medea to the toils of love;

' Fire

'Fire all her soul for Jason: haste, away;
'The favour is diminish'd by delay.' 160
She said, and Cupid listening long'd to hear,
For her sweet words are music to his ear.
He ceas'd his pastime, and with both his hands
Hangs on the Goddess, and the ball demands.
She kiss'd her boy, and press'd him to her cheek, 165
And fondly smiling thus she answer'd meek:
'By thee, my son, and by myself I swear,
'By all that's sacred, and by all that's dear,
'This ball I'll give thee, if thy fatal dart
'Thou fix unerring in Medea's heart.' 170
This said; he gather'd all his dice with haste,
And in his mother's splendid lap he plac'd.
Then snatch'd his bow and quiver from the ground,
And to his back with golden girdle bound.
From Jove's all-fertile plains he swift withdrew, 175
And thro' Olympus' golden portals flew.
Thence the descent is easy from the sky,
Where the two poles erect their heads on high,
Where the tall mountains their rough tops display,
And where the sun first gives the radiant day. 180
Hence you behold the fertile earth below,
The winding streams, the cliffs' aerial brow,

Cities

Cities extended on the diftant plain,
And thro' the vaſt expanſe the roaring main.
 On the broad Phaſis, in a ſedgy bay,   185
Stretch'd on the deck the Grecian heroes lay;
Till call'd to council roſe each godlike man,
And Jaſon thus the conference began:
" To you, my comrades, be my counſel known,
" 'Tis yours that counſel with ſucceſs to crown. 190
" One common cauſe our great empriſe is made;
" The common cauſe demands the common aid.
" He who unutter'd can his counſel keep,
" Stays our reſailing o'er the founding deep.
" I to Æeta's court will ſpeed my way,   195
" The reſt well-arm'd ſhall in the veſſel ſtay;
" With me ſhall go, the palace to explore,
" Phrixus' brave ſons, and two aſſociates more.
" Firſt will I prove the power of ſoft addreſs
" To gain the fleece; complacence wins ſucceſs. 200
" If in his arms he ſternly ſhould confide,
" And ſpurn our claims with inſolence and pride,
" Conſult we whether, when ſuch powers oppreſs,
" By arms or arts to free us from diſtreſs.
" Be force the laſt alternative we take,   205
" For ſoothing ſpeeches deep impreſſions make;
             " And

" And oft, where force and martial prowefs fail,
" The milder powers of eloquence prevail.
" Once king Æeta kind reception gave
" To blamelefs Phrixus, when efcap'd the wave 210
" He fled from Ino's unrelenting hate,
" And the dire altars that denounc'd his fate.
" Savage or focial, all alike approve
" The facred rites of hofpitable Jove."

He faid: the Greeks his fage advice rever'd; 215
No voice diffentient thro' the hoft was heard:
Augeas then, and Telamon attends,
And with them Phrixus' fons, his faithful friends;
Jafon they follow; he thy peaceful wand,
All-fapient Hermes, brandifh'd in his hand. 220
Soon from the fhip they gain the rifing ground,
Mount every fteep, and o'er the marfhes bound,
Till Circe's plain they reach; in many a row
Here humble fhrubs and lonely willows grow;
On whofe tall branches, wavering o'er the fen, 225
Sufpended hang the carcafes of men.
At Colchos ftill this barbarous rite prevails:
They never burn the bodies of the males,
Nor deep in earth their decent limbs compofe,
And with fepulchral duft the dead enclofe; 230

But

Book III.   APOLLONIUS RHODIUS.   157

But in raw hides they hang them high in air:
And yet, that earth may equal portions share,
Departed females to the grave they doom,
(Such are their rites) and clofe them in the tomb.

The chiefs advance; but friendly Juno shrouds   235
Her favourite heroes in a veil of clouds,
That none, too curious, might their steps delay,
While to the regal dome they bent their way:
But when unseen they pass'd the vulgar crowd,
The same kind deity dissolv'd the cloud.   240
Full in the court they stand with fix'd amaze,
On the proud gates, strong walls and columns gaze,
Which, rear'd in rows, erect their heads on high,
And lift the brazen cornice to the sky.
The portal past, young branching vines appear,   245
And high in air their verdant honours rear:
Beneath whose boughs, by matchless Vulcan made,
Four copious fountains in four currents play'd;
The first with milk, with wine the second glow'd,
Ambrosial oil the third, the fourth with water flow'd;
This, as by turns the Pleiads set or rose,   251
Dissolv'd in summer, and in winter froze.
Such were the wonders which the chiefs admire,
All highly finished by the God of fire.

With

With thefe were brafs-hoof'd bulls, of curious frame,
From brazen noftrils breathing living flame.   256
And, near, a plough of burnifh'd fteel was laid,
Which for the God of day great Vulcan made,
When Phœbus brought him in his friendly car,
Sore harrafs'd in the fierce Phlegræan war.   260
The midmoft court they reach; on either fide
Large folding doors the various rooms divide.
Two painted porticoes falute their eyes,
And high in air tranfverfe two turrets rife;
In this, which far in ftately height excels,   265
Æeta with his royal confort dwells:
Abfyrtus that contains, his royal heir,
Defcended from Afterode the fair,
A Scythian nymph, ere yet Æeta led
Idya, Ocean's daughter, to his bed.   270
Him Phaeton the youthful Colchians call,
For he in beauty far furpafs'd them all.
The proud apartments that remain'd contain
Chalciope, Medea and their train.
Ordain'd a prieftefs to the Stygian queen,   275
She at the palace now was feldom feen:
But artful Juno, on this fignal day,
Within the regal court decreed her ftay.

Here

Here now, from room to room, the penſive maid,
To find Chalciope her ſiſter, ſtray'd.   280
Soon as ſhe ſpied them in the ſpacious hall,
Aloud ſhe call'd, her ſiſter heard her call,
And with her maidens ſallied from the door;
Their growing webs were ſcatter'd on the floor.
Well-pleas'd her ſons ſhe ſees, and raptur'd ſtands, 285
While high to heaven ſhe rears her greeting hands;
With equal joy to her embrace they fly.
Then thus Chalciope with plaintive cry:
' Here tho' you left me, heedleſs of my cries,
' See! fate hath frown'd upon your bold empriſe; 290
' Hath check'd your voyage o'er the diſtant main,
' And ſoon reſtor'd you to theſe arms again.
' Wretch that I was, when by your ſire's command,
' Ye ſought in evil hour the Grecian land!
' Sad was the taſk your dying ſire enjoin'd,   295
' Sad and diſtreſsful to a mother's mind.
' Ah! whence the wiſh Orchomenos to ſee,
' His city viſit, and abandon me?
' Yes, Athamas's fancied wealth to gain,
' Ye left me ſorrowing, and ye ſought the main.' 300
    Rous'd by her cries, at length Æeta came,
And to the hall repair'd his royal dame.   •

With

160   *The* ARGONAUTICS *of*   Book III.

With bufy crowds the fpacious hall is fill'd;
The fteer is chofen, and the victim kill'd.
Some heat the baths, fome cleave the knotty wood, 305
And all attentive round their monarch ftood.

 Cupid mean time, thro' liquid air ferene,
Speeds to the Colchian court his flight unfeen;
Like that large fly, which breefe the fhepherds call,
That haftes to fting the heifers in the ftall. 310
The nimble God, unfeen, the porch afcends,
And there his bow behind a pillar bends;
A fatal arrow from his quiver took,
And quick advancing with infidious look,
Behind great Æfon's fon, conceal'd from fight, 315
He fits the arrow, fatal in its flight;
Bends the tough bow with all his ftrength and art,
And deep he hides it in Medea's heart.
A fudden tranfport feiz'd the melting maid:
The God, exulting now, no longer ftaid. 320
The glowing fhaft the virgin's heart infpires,
And in her bofom kindles amorous fires.
On Jafon beam'd the fplendor of her eyes;
Her fwoln breaft heav'd with unremitting fighs:
The frantic maid had all remembrance loft, 325
And the foft pain her fickening foul engrofs'd.

           As

As some good housewife, who, to labour born,
Fresh to her loom must rise with early morn;
Studious to gain what human wants require,
In embers heap'd preserves the seeds of fire ;   330
Renew'd by these the brand rekindling burns,
And all the glowing heap to ashes turns:
Thus, kindling slow, love's secret flames invade,
And torture, as they rise, the troubled maid:
Her changeful cheeks the heart-felt anguish show, 335
Now pale they turn, now like the ruby glow.

 The rich repast by seneschals prepar'd,
Fresh from their baths return'd, the strangers shar'd;
And when the rage of hunger was suppress'd,
His grandsons thus the Colchian king addrefs'd: 340

 ' Sons of my child, and Phrixus, honour'd most
' Of all the guests that reach'd the Colchian coast,
' Say, why so soon return'd ? what loss constrains
' This speedy visit to your native plains ?
' In vain, with terrors for your safety fraught,   345
' I urg'd the distance of the climes ye sought;
' Warn'd, since of old my sire's bright chariot bore
' Me and fair Circe to Hesperia's shore,
' Where now o'er Tuscan realms my sister reigns,
' A long, long distance from the Colchian plains. 350

    M   ' But

'But what of this? come now, the caufe declare
'That brought you back, and who thefe heroes are.'
Then Argus, anxious for the Grecian band,
By birthright eldeft, rofe and anfwer'd bland:
"Our fhip, O king, by nightly tempefts toft, 355
"On Mars's ifle, a dreary coaft, was loft;
"We, on the wreck by furious furges driv'n,
"Were fav'd at laft by kind protecting heav'n.
"Nor did thofe birds then defolate the fhore,
"Dire Harpies, that infefted it before; 360
"For thefe brave warriors, the preceding day,
"Had driven the curft, infernal fiends away.
"Sure to our prayer fome God inclin'd his ear;
"For when of Phrixus and your name they hear,
"Food for our wants, and raiment they convey, 365
"And to your city now they bend their way.
"But would you know, I'll tell their purpos'd plan:
"Lo! fprung from Æolus the godlike man,
"Whom a fierce tyrant's ftern decree conftrains
"To quit his country and his rich domains: 370
"Nor can he fcape Jove's rage, unlefs the fleece,
"Bafe theft of Phrixus, be reftor'd to Greece.
"Their fhip was fafhion'd by Minerva's aid;
"How different are the Colchian veffels made!

"Ours,

" Ours, far the worſt that ever rear'd a maſt,   375
" Split with the tempeſt's defolating blaſt;
" Theirs, firm-compacted, and of fitteſt wood,
" Defied each ſtorm that heav'd the troubled flood:
" With equal ſpeed their nimble veſſel ſails,
" Impell'd by oars alone, or favouring gales.   380
" In this their chief, with choſen Greeks, explores
" Unnumber'd ſeas, and towns, and wide-extended
 ſhores.
" And now he ſues the golden fleece to gain;
" But that as beſt your princely will ordain—
" Nor hoſtile comes he; as a friend he brings   385
" Large gifts proportion'd to the ſtate of kings.
" Inform'd the fierce Sarmatians waſte your lands,
" He vows deſtruction to their barbarous bands.
" Their names and lineage ſhould you wiſh to hear,
" Lend to my narrative a liſtening ear.   390
" He, in whoſe cauſe the Grecian chiefs conſpire,
" Is valiant Jaſon, Æſon is his ſire,
" The ſon of Cretheus: thus are we ally'd
" By blood, relations on the father's ſide:
" The ſons of Æolus were Cretheus fam'd,   395
" And Athemas, whoſe heir was Phrixus nam'd.
" 'Mid yon brave chiefs, Augeas you ſurvey,
" Illuſtrious offspring of the God of day,

M 2   " And

" And Telamon, who high his birth can prove,
" His fire is Æacus, his grandfire Jove: 400
" The reft, that vifit your auguft abodes,
" Are all the fons or grandfons of the Gods."
   This faid, the King with indignation fwell'd,
But chief enrag'd his grandfons he beheld;
Thro' them he deem'd the Greeks to Colchos came: 405
His eye-balls redden'd with avenging flame,
While thus he fpoke: ' Hence from my fight away,
' Nor longer, traitors, in my kingdom ftay:
' Back, back to Greece your fpeedy courfe purfue,
' Nor idly hope the golden fleece to view.   410
' Not for that fleece (vain pretext ye muft own)
' But for my fceptre came ye, and my crown.
' Had ye not firft my feaft partook to-day,
' Your tongues and hands, torn out and lopp'd away,
' Should for your bold atrocious crimes atone: 415
' My juft revenge had fpar'd your feet alone,
' To bear you haftily to Greece again,
' Dreading to vifit more my juft domain,
' And with your perjuries the Gods profane.'
  He faid: bold Telamon with fury burn'd,   420
And to the King ftern anfwer had return'd,
But Jafon check'd his warmth, and mild reply'd:
" Let not Æeta falfly thus decide.

                             " Nor

" Nor crowns, nor empires come we here to gain;
" Who for such wealth would measure half the
    main? 425
" But fate, and Pelias' more severe command,
" Have forc'd the suppliant on your friendly land.
" Aid us, and Greece your praises shall record,
" And thank you, sovereign, with their conquering
    sword;
" Whether the fierce Sarmatians to inthrall, 430
" Or realms more barbarous for your vengeance call."
While Jason thus in gentlest terms reply'd,
The tyrant's breast distracting thoughts divide,
Whether with vengeance on the foe to fly,
Or in the field of Mars his courage try. 435
On this resolv'd, ' What need (he thus begun)
' With tedious tales my harrass'd ears to stun?
' For whether from immortals ye descend,
' Or match'd in might ye dare with me contend,
' Soon will I prove; that proof must thou display; 440
' Then, if victorious, bear the fleece away;
' Nor shall my hand the golden prize withold:
' Like your proud lord, I envy not the bold.
' This nervous arm shall now sustain the fight,
' Which calls to speedy proof thy boasted might. 445

' Two bulls in Mars's field your wonder claim,
' Their hoofs of brass, their nostrils breathing flame.
' These oft I seize, and to the yoke constrain
' To plough four acres of the stubborn plain.
' No seeds I sow, but scatter o'er the land   450
' A dragon's teeth; when, lo! an armed band
' Of chiefs spring up: but soon as they appear,
' I slay th' embattled squadrons with my spear.
' Each morn I yoke the bulls, at eve resign:
' Perform this labour, and the fleece is thine.   455
' These are the terms; on these the prize I quit:
' The weaker to the stronger must submit.'
He said; and Jason, sunk in thought profound,
Sat mute, his eyes fast fix'd upon the ground;
Long time he ponder'd o'er the vast design,   460
Nor dar'd with confidence the battle join.
So hard the task, he stood embarrass'd long,
At last these words dropp'd cautious from his tongue:
" Cruel thy terms, but just: my strength I'll try
" In this dread conflict, though ordain'd to die. 465
" For, say, what law so rigorous can there be,
" As the hard law of fix'd necessity?
" That law which forc'd me from my native home,
" And bad me thus in search of dangers roam?"

Perplex'd

Perplex'd he spoke: then thus the king in rage, 470
' Rejoin thy comrades, since thou dar'st engage.
' But if the bulls constrain thy heart to yield,
' Or the dread dangers of the martial field,
' Be mine the toil; that hence the coward-slave
.' May dread to combat with the bold and brave.' 475
Imperious thus the haughty king replies:
And from their seats incens'd the heroes rise.
To warn his brothers here, at home, to wait,
Argus stopp'd short awhile: then rush'd they thro'
    the gate.
Far o'er the rest, in grace unmatch'd alone, 480
And charms superior youthful Jason shone.
Him thro' her veil the love-distracted maid
With melting eyes, and glance oblique survey'd:
Her mind, as in a dream, bewilder'd ran,
And trac'd the footsteps of the godlike man. 485
Sorrowing they went: to shun the monarch's ire,
With fond Chalciope her sons retire;
Medea follow'd, but with cares opprefs'd;
Such cares as love had rais'd within her breast.
His graceful image in her mind she bore, 490
His gait, his manner, and the robe he wore,
His pointed words: thro' earth's remotest bound
No prince she deem'd with such perfections crown'd.

His

His tuneful voice still, still she seems to hear,
Still the sweet accents charm her listening ear. 495
The bulls and wrathful king excite her dread:
She mourns his fate, as if already dead.
From her bright eyes the shower of anguish breaks,
And thus, o'erwhelm'd with woe, Medea speaks:
  " Why fall the tears of sorrow from my eyes, 500
" Tho' he the first or last of heroes dies?
" Perish the man!—no, safely let him sail;
" And may my prayer, kind Hecate, prevail!
" Safe sail he home: but, ah! if doom'd to bleed,
" Teach him, that I rejoice not in the deed." 505
   Thus mourn'd the maid: meantime to join their
     train,
The chiefs pursue their course along the plain;
Then Argus thus: 'Though, Jason, you may blame,
' And spurn the counsel which I now proclaim;
' Yet sure for us, with threatening dangers press'd,
' To try some safe expedient must be best. 511
' A maid there is whose wondrous art excels,
' Long taught by Hecate, in magic spells:
' If she propitious to our wishes yield,
' Thou com'st victorious from the martial field: 515
' But if Chalciope decline her aid,
' Be mine with tenderest motives to persuade.

' Instant

' Inftant I'll go, on her for fuccour call;
' For, lo! one general ruin threatens all.'
Humane he fpoke, and Jafon thus rejoin'd; 520
" Much I admire the purpofe of thy mind.
" Go, friend, to thy Chalciope repair,
" Sue her with foft entreaty and with pray'r:
" But, ah! vain hopes our vacant minds muft fill,
" Who truft for conqueft to a woman's fkill." 525
He faid; and foon they join'd their focial train,
Rejoic'd to meet their princely peers again.
Then Jafon thus began his mournful tale:
" With proud Æeta foft entreaties fail;
" Our purpos'd end unable to attain, 530
" Vain are my words, and your enquiries vain.
" Two monftrous bulls the tyrant bids me tame;
" Their hoofs of brafs, their noftrils breathing flame;
" Thefe muft my prowefs to the yoke conftrain,
" To plough four acres of the ftubborn plain; 535
" My feed a dragon's teeth, to fow the land;
" When lo! up fprings a formidable band
" Of bright-arm'd giants; foon as they appear,
" Poiz'd by this arm, my well-directed fpear
" Muft pierce the foe: intrepid I accede 540
" To the hard terms, nor future dangers heed."
He faid: they deem'd it all a defperate deed;

Silent

Silent they stood, with sad dejected look
Each gaz'd on other, till bold Peleus spoke:
' Time calls for our resolves; our safety stands 545
' No more in counsel, but in strength of hands.
' If, Jason, eager of the honour, thou
' Wilt yoke these fiery monsters to the plough,
' Haste to the charge; but if thy soul relent,
' Sunk in sad bodings of the dire event, 550
' Nor dar'st thou go; then go not, nor look round,
' If haply here some fitter man be found;
' Myself will go, and risk my dearest breath;
' No greater evil can befall than death.'

He spoke; and Telamon with rage inspir'd 555
Starts up, and Idas with like fury fir'd; —
Next the twin-race of Tyndarus arise;
Last Oeneus' son, who with the bravest vies;
Tho' o'er his cheeks scarce spreads the callow down,
His heart beats high for honour and renown. 560
And while the rest in mute attention stand,
Argus bespeaks the emulative band:
" Tho' hard the task, O chiefs, I still portend
" My parent will assist, and prove a friend.
" Still in your ship awhile with patience wait; 565
" For rashness will accelerate your fate.

" Know,

" Know, at Æeta's court a maiden dwells,
" Deep fkill'd by Hecate in magic fpells:
" All plants fhe knows that grow on mountains fteep,
" On vales, or meads, or in the boundlefs deep; 570
" By thefe fhe quells the fire's relentlefs force,
" Stops the mad torrent in its headlong courfe,
" Retards the planets as they roll on high,
" And draws the moon reluctant from the fky.
" As from the palace o'er the plain we came 575
" We mention'd oft my mother's honour'd name;
" If fhe perchance her fifter could perfuade,
" And fix our intereft in the magic maid.
" Back, if you bid, my ready fteps I bend;
" Fortune may fmile, and fair fuccefs attend." 580
He faid; when, lo! this fignal of their love,
Was kindly given them by the Powers above;
For, by the falcon chas'd, a trembling dove,
Far from his foe, to Jafon's bofom flies;
Stunn'd on the deck the felon falcon lies. 585
Then Mopfus thus divin'd: 'The Powers of heav'n,
' They, they alone this gracious fign have giv'n.
' Be then the maid in mildeft terms addrefs'd;
' She'll liften friendly to our joint requeft,
' I ween fhe will; if Phineus could foreknow 590
' That we to Venus muft our fafety owe.

' For,

'For, lo! her bird efcapes: oh! may we prove
'With fafety crown'd, like her aufpicious dove.
'Entreat we now for Cytherea's aid,
'And let th' advice of Argus be obey'd.'   595
    Thus he; the chiefs approv'd, remembering well
What Phineus deign'd prophetic to foretell:
Idas alone with indignation burn'd,
And with loud voice thus infolent return'd:
'Gods! what a crew hath Argo wafted o'er!   600
'Women, not heroes throng the hoftile fhore.
'Women, who ftill to Venus' altars fly,
'Nor dare but only on her aid rely.
'No warlike deeds your daftard fouls inflame:
'To you is Mars an unregarded name.   605
'As doves or falcons but direct your flight,
'You flinch at danger, and you dread the fight.
'Go; and all manly, martial toils forbear,
'Sue to weak women, and deceive the fair.'
    Furious he fpoke; a general murmur ran   610
Thro' the whole train; yet none oppos'd the man:
Indignant then he fat. Of dauntlefs breaft
Thus Æfon's fon the liftening train addrefs'd:
" This inftant Argus to the town I fend,
" For thus the general fuffrages intend: 615
                            " Meanwhile

" Meanwhile approach we nearer to the land,
" And fix, in fight, our halfers to the ftrand:
" Ill fuits us longer thus to lie conceal'd;
" We neither fhun, nor dread the fighting field."
He faid, and Argus went without delay, 620
And to the city backward fped his way;
At Jafon's call they ply the labouring oar,
And land their beds and couches on the fhore.

Meantime the king a council call'd, and fat,
(So were they wont) without the palace-gate. 625
Affembled there, unceafing toils they plann'd,
And wiles deftructive to the Grecian band.
Thus he ordain'd, that when the bulls had flain
And ftretch'd this dauntlefs hero on the plain,
Himfelf would lay the lofty foreft low, 630
And for the funeral-pile prepare the bough:
Their boafted fhip fhould be confum'd with fire,
And every traitor in the flames expire.
No hofpitable rites had Phrixus fhar'd,
Though much he wifh'd and merited regard, 635
Had not Jove haften'd Hermes from above
To win his favour and befpeak his love.
Were thefe invaders of his native foil
To thrive unpunifh'd by rapacious fpoil,

Soon

Soon would they make his lowing herds a prey, 640
And drive the shepherds and their flocks away.
But Phrixus' sons, who join'd the lawless crew,
He vow'd with double vengeance to pursue:
Base plunderers! come to spoil him of his crown,
So had the Sun, his sapient sire, foreshown: 645
Who warn'd him to suspect his faithless race,
And dread from them destruction and disgrace.
Therefore dismiss'd he, by his sire's command,
The youths far distant, ev'n to Grecian land.
His daughters gave him no perplexing care, 650
Nor young Absyrtus, his adopted heir;
But from Chalciope's detested race
He look'd for injuries, and fear'd disgrace.
Thus stern denouncing, as with rage he swells,
Death on each daring subject that rebels, 655
His guards he charg'd, and threaten'd vengeance due,
If either 'scap'd, the vessel or the crew.

Swift to the palace Argus now repairs,
And to his pitying mother pours his pray'rs,
That she might importune Medea's aid; 660
Nor had the queen her son's request delay'd,
But boding fears her willing mind restrain,
Lest all her fond entreaties should be vain;

And

And should the project be disclos'd to view,
Her father's ire the magic maid must rue. 665
As on her couch reclin'd the virgin lay,
Soft slumbers chas'd her anxious cares away;
But frantic dreams, which love-sick minds infest,
Present false terrors, and disturb her rest.
Her hero seem'd the task to undertake, 670
But not for honour, or the fleece's sake;
For her alone he risk'd the glorious strife,
To gain her love, and win her for his wife.
She then in dreams her utmost succour lends,
And with the bulls herself in fight contends. 675
Her parents she, in fancied rage, aver'd
False and regardless of their promis'd word,
Who Jason doom'd the brazen bulls to foil,
But made not her a partner of the toil.
Then warm disputes and fierce contentions reign 680
Between Æeta and the Grecian train:
On her decision both the parties wait,
And deem what she determines to be fate.
In spite of parents, the fond maid express'd
Her choice in favour of her godlike guest. 685
Rage wrung their souls, and grief, and dire dismay,
Till the loud clamour chas'd her sleep away.

Trembling

Trembling she starts; pale fears confus'd her look;
Her soul reviv'd, and thus the virgin spoke:
' Alas! what frightful dreams alarm my breast 690
' For these fam'd chiefs, but most the royal guest?
' I fear, some mighty mischief will ensue
' From this bold leader and his gallant crew.
' Yes, let him wed far off some Grecian dame;
' Be mine my parents' house, my virgin's fame. 695
' If from my headstrong purpose I refrain,
' My sister's counsel might relieve my pain:
' Oh! for her sons would she my aid implore,
' My griefs would cease, my sorrows be no more!'
She said, and rose, nor longer deign'd to wait, 700
But past the threshold of her sister's gate,
Barefoot, undrest; long time she there remain'd,
(For modest fears her passing step restrain'd;)
Then back retreats; new courage soon acquires;
Again advances, and again retires: 705
Passions so various sway'd the virgin's breast,
That when fierce love impell'd her, fear reprefs'd:
Thrice she essay'd, and thrice retreating fled;
Then on the pillow sunk her drooping head:
As some young damsel, whom her friends had join'd
In marriage to the darling of her mind, 711
Conceal'd

Conceal'd in secret, mourns her blooming mate
Snatch'd from her arms by some untimely fate,
Ere yet kind heaven indulg'd them to employ
The golden moments in connubial joy: 715
In silence she, tho' stung with torturing grief,
Seeks on the widow'd bed the wish'd relief;
Looks eager round, then sheds the trembling tear,
Screen'd from the female eye, and tongue severe.
Thus mourn'd Medea, not unseen; her pain 720
Was mark'd by one, the youngest of her train;
Who told Chalciope Medea's grief;
And the sad tale exceeded her belief:
Her sons consulting, she with them essay'd
To sooth the sorrows of the love-sick maid. 725
Instant she rose, and trembling with dismay
Came to the chamber where her sister lay;
Torn were her cheeks, the tears her grief confess'd;
And thus Chalciope the maid address'd:

' Say, why those tears that thus incessant fall? 730
' What mighty ills your feeble mind appal?
' Say, does some heaven-sent woe your grief inspire?
' Or in your bosom dwells Æeta's ire,
' My sons and I the cause? Oh! far from home,
' On the world's utmost limits may I roam, 735

' Nor

' Nor see my parents, nor my native shore,
' Nor hear the hated name of Colchos more!'
    She said: Medea's cheeks the crimson stain'd;
She strove to speak, but shame her words restrain'd.
Now on her lips the ready accents hung,   740
Now stifled in her breast: her faltering tongue
Long time the purpose of her soul withheld,
Artful at length she spoke, by love impell'd:
    " Dire fears, Chalciope, my soul dismay,
" Lest with these guests my sire thy children slay, 745
" My frightful dreams such horrid scenes present;
" May some kind deity these woes prevent!
" Lest for thy sons the tears eternal flow:"
Thus spoke the maid, inquisitive in woe,
If haply, for her children's fate afraid,   750
Chalciope might first solicit aid.
Mix'd grief and terror all the mother shook,
At last, impassion'd, thus she trembling spoke:
    ' 'Tis for their sakes I now before thee stand;
' Lend me, O lend thy salutary hand!   755
' But swear by earth and heaven what I unfold
' Rests in thy bosom, never to be told:
' By the great Gods, and all that's dear I call,
' Swear thou wilt never see my children fall,

' Lest

Book III. APOLLONIUS RHODIUS.

' Left I too perish, and in fell despight   760
' Rise a dread fury from the shades of night.'
Earnest she spoke, and tears inceffant shed,
Then on her sister's breast reclin'd her head,
And mix'd their mutual sighs; groan answer'd groan,
And the wide palace echo'd to their moan.   765
Medea thus in mournful terms replies:
" Alas! what succour can my thoughts devise,
" Thus with thy cruel menaces opprefs'd?
" Oh, still uninjur'd may thine offspring rest!
" By heaven above I swear, and earth below,   770
" Earth, the great mother of the Gods, I vow,
" (If aught my power can do, or words persuade)
" To give thee counsel, and to lend my aid."
Thus spoke the maid; and thus Chalciope;
' Perhaps, in favour of my sons and me,   775
' Thy mind, to save the hero, might impart
' Some secret counsel, some mysterious art.
' From Jason Argus comes, imploring aid;
' They rest their safety on the magic maid.'
Thus she; with joy exults the virgin's heart, 780
And rising blushes rosy charms impart;
But soon o'ercast with grief she thus reply'd:
" To serve thee, sister, be no art untry'd.

N 2   " Ne'er

" Ne'er may I fee with pleafurable eyes
" In yon bright orient cheerful morning rife, 785
" If aught on earth be half fo dear to me
" As is the welfare of thy fons and thee.
" As brethren they my fond regard engage,
" By blood related, and the fame our age.
" My fifter, moft efteem'd, and ever dear, · 790
" Thee with a daughter's love I ftill revere.
" For with thy children, nurs'd by thee, I fhar'd
" (So fame reports) a mother's fond regard.
" Go then, and from my prying parents hide
" The means of fuccour which I now provide. 795
" All-potent fpells will I, at dawn of day,
" To Hecate's myfterious fhrine convey."
Pleas'd with the tale, Chalciope departs,
And with the proffer'd aid tranfports her children's hearts.
Fear mix'd with fhame now feiz'd the lonely maid, 800
Who dare, her fire reluctant, lend her aid.
  Now rifing fhades a folemn fcene difplay
O'er the wide earth, and o'er th' etherial way;
All night the failor marks the northern team,
And golden circlet of Orion's beam: 805
A deep repofe the weary watchman fhares, .
· And the faint wanderer fleeps away his cares;

Ev'n

Ev'n the fond maid, while yet all breathless lies
Her child of love, in slumber seals her eyes:
No sound of village-dog, no noise invades   810
The death-like silence of the midnight shades;
Alone Medea wakes: to love a prey,
Restless she rolls, and groans the night away:
For lovely Jason cares on cares succeed,
Lest vanquish'd by the bulls her hero bleed;   815
In sad review dire scenes of horrors rise,
Quick beats her heart, from thought to thought she
    flies:
As from the stream-stor'd vase with dubious ray
The sun-beams dancing from the surface play;
Now here, now there the trembling radiance falls; 820
Alternate flashing round th' illumin'd walls:
Thus fluttering bounds the trembling virgin's blood,
And from her eyes descends a pearly flood.
Now raving with resistless flames she glows,
Now sick with love she melts with softer woes: 825
The tyrant God, of every thought possess'd,
Beats in each pulse, and stings and racks her breast:
Now she resolves the magic to betray—
To tame the bulls—now yield him up a prey.
Again the drugs disdaining to supply,   830
She loaths the light, and meditates to die:

Anon, repelling with a brave difdain
The coward thought; fhe nourifhes the pain.
Then paufing thus: " Ah wretched me! fhe cries,
" Where'er I turn what varied forrows rife! 835
" Toft in a giddy whirl of ftrong defire,
" I glow, I burn, yet blefs the pleafing fire:
" Oh! had this fpirit from its prifon fled,
" By Dian fent to wander with the dead,
" Ere the proud Grecians view'd the Colchian fkies,
" Ere Jafon, lovely Jafon, met thefe eyes! 841
" Hell gave the fhining mifchief to our coaft,
" Medea faw him, and Medea's loft---
" But why thefe forrows? if the powers on high
" His death decree,---die, wretched Jafon, die! 845
" Shall I elude my fire? my art betray?
" Ah me! what words fhall purge the guilt away!
" But could I yield------O whither muft I run
" To find the chief---whom virtue bids me fhun?
" Shall I, all loft to fhame, to Jafon fly? 850
" And yet I muft------if Jafon bleeds I die!
" Honour farewell! adieu for ever fhame!
" Hail black difgrace! and branded be my fame!
" Live, Jafon, live! enjoy the vital air!
" Live thro' my aid! and fly where winds can bear. 855
" But

" But when he flies, cords, poisons lend your pow'rs;
" That day Medea treads th' infernal shores!
" Yet what reproach will after death be cast?
" The maids of Colchos will my honour blast---
" I hear them cry---the false Medea's dead, 860
" Thro' guilty passion for a stranger's bed;
" Medea, careless of her virgin fame,
" Preferr'd a stranger to a father's name!
" O may I rather yield this vital breath,
" Than bear that base dishonour worse than death!"
Thus wail'd the fair, and seiz'd, with horrid joy, 866
Drugs foes to life, and potent to destroy;
A magazine of death! again she pours
From her swoln eye-lids tears in shining show'rs.
With grief insatiate, comfortless she stands, 870
And opes the casket, but with trembling hands.
A sudden fear her labouring soul invades,
Struck with the horrors of th' infernal shades:
She stands deep-musing with a faded brow,
Absorb'd in thought, a monument of woe! 875
While all the comforts that on life attend,
The cheerful converse, and the faithful friend,
By thought deep-imag'd in her bosom play,
Endearing life, and charm despair away.

Enlivening

Enlivening funs with fweeter light arife, 880
And every object brightens to her eyes.
Then from her hand the baneful drugs fhe throws,
Confents to live, recover'd from her woes;
Refolv'd the magic virtue to betray,
She waits the dawn, and calls the lazy day: 885
Time feems to ftand, or backward drive his wheels;
The hours fhe chides, and eyes the eaftern hills:
At length the morn difplays her rofy light,
And the whole town ftands pictur'd to her fight.
Back to the fhip (his brothers left behind 890
To mark the motions of Medea's mind)
Argus return'd; meanwhile her golden hair,
That flow'd diffufive in the wanton air,
The virgin binds; then wipes the tears away,
And from her eyes bids living lightning play; 895
On every limb refrefhing unguents pours,
Unguents, that breathe of heaven, in copious fhow'rs.
Her robe fhe next affumes; bright clafps of gold
Clofe to the leffening waift the robe infold:
Down from her fwelling loins the reft unbound 900
Floats in rich waves redundant o'er the ground:
Then takes her veil, and ftately treads the room
With graceful eafe, regardlefs of her doom.

Thus

Thus forward moves the faireſt of her kind,
Blind to the future, to the preſent blind. 905
Twelve maids, attendants on her virgin bow'r,
Alike unconſcious of the bridal hour,
Join to the car her mules; dire rites to pay,
To Hecate's fair fane ſhe bends her way.
A juice ſhe bears, whoſe magic virtue tames 910
(Thro' fell Perſephone) the rage of flames;
For one whole day it gives the hero might,
To ſtand ſecure of harms in mortal fight;
It mocks the ſword; the ſword without a wound
Leaps as from marble ſhiver'd to the ground. 915
This plant, which rough Caucaſean mountains bore,
Sprung from the venom of Prometheus' gore,
(While on the wretch the ſavage eagle ſtorm'd)
In colour like Corycian crocus form'd:
On two tall ſtems up-ſprings the flowery ſhoot, 920
A cubit high; like red raw fleſh its root.
From this root's juice, as black as that diſtill'd
From mountain beeches, the fair maid had fill'd
A Caſpian conch; but firſt, as beſt beſeems,
Array'd in black ſeven times in living ſtreams 925
She bath'd; and call'd ſeven times on Brimo's name,
At midnight hour, the ghoſt-compelling dame.

She

She pluck'd the root, earth murmur'd from below,
And sad Prometheus groan'd with agonizing woe.
This root the Colchian maid selecting plac'd   930
In the rich zone that bound her slender waist:
Then issuing mounts the car, but not alone,
On either side two lovely damsels shone:
Her hand with skill th' embroider'd rein controuls,
Back fly the streets as swift the chariot rolls.   935
Along the wheel-worn road they speed their way,
The domes retreat, the sinking towers decay:
Bare to the knee succinct a damsel-train
Close throng behind them, hastening to the plain.

As when her limbs divine, Diana laves   940
In fair Parthenius, or th' Amnesian waves,
Sublime in royal state the bounding roes
Whirl her bright car along the mountain brows:
Swift to some sacred feast the goddess moves,
The nymphs attend that haunt the shady groves; 945
Th' Amnesian fount, or silver-streaming rills,
Nymphs of the vales, or Oreads of the hills:
The fawning beasts before the goddess play,
Or, trembling, savage adoration pay:

Thus on her car sublime the nymph appears, 950
The croud falls back, and, as she moves, reveres:

Swift

Swift to the fane aloft her course she bends,
The fane she reaches, and on earth descends;
Then to her train------ " Ah me! I fear we stray,
" Misled by folly to this lonely way !   955
" Alas ! should Jason with his Greeks appear,
" Where should we fly ? I fear, alas, I fear!
" No more the Colchian youths, and virgin train,
" Haunt the cool shade, or tread in dance the plain.
" But since alone---with sports beguile your hours, 960
" Collect sweet herbs, and pluck the fairest flow'rs:
" If due attention to my words ye pay,
" With richest spoils ye shall return to-day.
" For Argus and Chalciope require,
" (But sacred keep this secret from my sire)   965
" That for large presents, for my succour paid,
" To this rash stranger I should lend my aid.
" I pass'd my word, and soon without his train
" The Grecian will attend me at the fane:
" In equal portions we the spoil will share---   970
" For him a dose more fatal I prepare---
" But when he comes, ye nymphs, retire apart."
She spoke; the nymphs approv'd the virgin's art.
When Argus heard the maid with early day
To Hecate's fair fane would speed her way,   975
He

He beckon'd Jason from his bold compeers
Apart, and Mopsus most renown'd of seers;
For prescient Mopsus every omen knew
Of birds that parting or approaching flew.
No mortal ever of the first-born race   980
Display'd like Jason such superior grace,
Whether from demigods he trac'd his line,
Or Jove himself immortal and divine,
As grac'd by Juno, Jove's imperial queen,
With soft addrefs, and dignity of mien.   985
His comrades gaz'd with wonder as he went;
Mopsus foresaw and hail'd the blest event.
Hard by the path, and near the temple, stands
A poplar tall that wide its arms expands;
Here frequent rooks their airy paftime take, 990
And on the boughs their fpray-form'd mansions make;
One shook its pinions, (louder than the rest)
And croaking, thus Saturnia's mind exprefs'd:
' Vain seer! whose divinations fail to tell
' Those plain events which children know so well; 995
' That maids will not, with comrades in the train,
' Tell the soft love-tale to their favour'd swain.
' False prophet, hence! for thee nor love inspires,
' Nor Venus gratifies with soft desires.'

    3   Then

Then Mopfus laugh'd, as fcoffing thus fhe fpoke, 1000
To hear the bird her dark predictions croak;
And thus: " Hence, Jafon, to the fane, and find
" The maiden to thy warmeft wifhes kind;
" Venus approves, and fortune will enfue,
" If what prophetic Phineus faid prove true. 1005
" Myfelf and Argus here will wait apart,
" Go and unfold the fecrets of thy heart;
" Be every mode of foft perfuafion try'd."
He counfel'd wifely, and the chief comply'd.

Meanwhile the maid her fecret thoughts enjoy'd,
And one dear object all her foul employ'd: 1011
Her train's gay fports no pleafure can reftore,
Vain was the dance, and mufic charm'd no more;
She hates each object, every face offends,
In every wifh her foul to Jafon fends; 1015
With fharpen'd eyes the diftant lawn explores,
To find the hero whom her foul adores;
At every whifper of the paffing air,
She ftarts, fhe turns, and hopes her Jafon there;
Again fhe fondly looks, nor looks in vain, 1020
He comes, her Jafon fhines along the plain.
As when, emerging from the watery way,
Refulgent Sirius lifts his golden ray,

He

He shines terrific! for his burning breath
Taints the red air with fevers, plagues and death;
Such to the nymph approaching Jason shows,   1026
Bright author of unutterable woes;
Before her eyes a swimming darkness spread,
Her flush'd cheeks glow'd, her very heart was dead:
No more her knees their wonted office knew,   1030
Fix'd, without motion, as to earth they grew.
Her train recedes---the meeting lovers gaze
In silent wonder, and in still amaze.
As two fair cedars on the mountain's brow,
Pride of the groves! with roots adjoining grow;   1035
Erect and motionless the stately trees
Short time remain, while sleeps each fanning breeze,
Till from th' Æolian caves a blast unbound
Bends their proud tops, and bids their boughs resound:
Thus gazing they; till by the breath of love,   1040
Strongly at last inspir'd, they speak, they move;
With smiles the love-sick virgin he survey'd,
And fondly thus address'd the blooming maid:

'Dismiss, my fair, my love, thy virgin fear;
'Tis Jason speaks, no enemy is here!   1045
'Dread not in me a haughty heart to find,
'In Greece I bore no proud inhuman mind.

'Whom

' Whom would'ft thou fly? ftay, lovely virgin, ftay!
' Speak every thought! far hence be fears away!
' Speak! and be truth in every accent found! 1050
' Scorn to deceive! we tread on hallow'd ground.
' By the ftern power who guards this facred place,
' By the fam'd authors of thy royal race;
' By Jove, to whom the ftranger's caufe belongs,
' To whom the fuppliant, and who feels their wrongs;
' O guard me, fave me, in the needful hour! 1056
' Without thy aid thy Jafon is no more.
' To thee a fuppliant, in diftrefs I bend,
' To thee a ftranger, one who wants a friend!
' Then, when between us feas and mountains rife, 1060
' Medea's name fhall found in diftant fkies;
' All Greece to thee fhall owe her heroes' fates,
' And blefs Medea thro' her hundred ftates.
' The mother and the wife, who now in vain
' Roll their fad eyes faft-ftreaming o'er the main, 1065
' Shall ftay their tears: the mother, and the wife,
' Shall blefs thee for a fon's or hufband's life!
' Fair Ariadne, fprung from Minos' bed,
' Sav'd valiant Thefeus, and with Thefeus fled,
' Forfook her father, and her native plain, 1070
' And ftem'd the tumults of the furging main;

' Ye

' Yet the stern fire relented, and forgave
' The maid, whose only crime it was to save;
' Ev'n the just Gods forgave: and now on high
' A star she shines, and beautifies the sky: 1075
' What blessings then shall righteous heaven decree
' For all our heroes sav'd, and sav'd by thee?
' Heaven gave thee not to kill, so soft an air;
' And cruelty sure never look'd so fair!'
    He ceas'd, but left so charming on her ear 1080
His voice, that listening still she seem'd to hear;
Her eyes to earth she bends with modest grace,
And heaven in smiles is open'd on her face.
A look she steals; but rosy blushes spread
O'er her fair cheek, and then she hangs her head. 1085
A thousand words at once to speak she tries;
In vain---but speaks a thousand with her eyes;
Trembling the shining casket she expands,
Then gives the magic virtue to his hands;
And had the power been granted to convey 1090
Her heart---had given her very heart away.
For Jason beam'd in beauty's charms so bright,
The maid admiring languish'd with delight.
Thus, when the rising sun appears in view,
On the fair rose dissolves the radiant dew. 1095
                                        Now

Book III. APOLLONIUS RHODIUS.

Now on the ground both cast their bashful eyes,
Both view each other now with wild surprize.
The rosy smiles now dimpling on their cheeks,
The fair at length in faltering accents speaks:
" Observant thou to my advice attend,   1100
" And hear what succour I propose to lend.
" Soon as my sire Æeta shall bestow
" The dragon's teeth in Mars's field to sow,
" The following night in equal shares divide;
" Bathe well thy limbs in some perennial tide; 1105
" Then all retir'd, thyself in black array,
" Dig the round foss, and there a victim slay,
" A female lamb; the carcase place entire
" Above the foss, then light the sacred pyre,
" And Perseus' daughter, Hecate, appease   1110
" With honey, sweetest labour of the bees;
" This done, retreat, nor, while the relicks burn,
" Let howling dogs provoke thee to return,
" Nor human footsteps; lest thou render vain
" The charm, and with dishonour join thy train. 1115
" Next morn, the whole enchantment to fulfil,
" This magic unguent on thy limbs distil:
" Then thou with ease wilt strong, and graceful move,
" Not like a mortal, but the Gods above.

O " Forget

" Forget not with this unguent to befmear   1120
" Thy fword, thy buckler, and tremendous fpear:
" No giant's falchions then can harm thy frame,
" Nor the fell rage of bulls expiring flame.
" One day, nor longer, wilt thou keep the field;
" Nor thou to perils, nor to labour yield.   1125
" But mark my words; when thou, with ceafelefs toil,
" Haft yok'd the bulls and plough'd the ftubborn foil;
" And feeft up-fpringing on the teeth-fown land
" Of giant foes a formidable band,
" Hurl flily 'midft their ranks a rough hard ftone,
" And they, like dogs contending for a bone,   1131
" Will flay each other: thou with fpeed renew
" The glowing fight, and conqueft will enfue.
" Thus fhalt thou bear from Æa's realms to Greece,
" If fuch thy fix'd refolve, the Golden Fleece." 1135
  This faid, her eyes were fix'd upon the ground,
And her fair cheeks with ftreaming forrows drown'd;
Defponding anguifh feiz'd her gentle mind,
Left he fhould leave her comfortlefs behind.
Imbolden'd thus, him by the hand fhe prefs'd,   1140
And in the language of her foul addrefs'd;
" If fafely hence thou fail'ft, O, think of me!
" As I for ever fhall remember thee!

" And

" And freely tell me, to relieve my pain,
" Where lies thy home beyond the boundlefs main ?
" Say, is Orchomenos thy native foil ? 1146
" Or dwell'ft thou nearer on th' Æaean ifle ?
" Let me that far-fam'd virgin's name inquire,
" Who boafts the fame high lineage with my fire."
She faid; her tears his foft compaffion won, 1150
And thus the chief, by Love infpir'd, begun :
' While on my fancy bright ideas play,
' Thy image never from my foul fhall ftray,
' If fafe I fail, preferv'd by thee, to Greece,
' Nor heavier labours interrupt my peace. 1155
' But if the diftant country where I dwell
' Thy will demands, my ready tongue fhall tell.
' A land there is which lofty hills furround,
' For fertile paftures and rich herds renown'd,
' Where from Prometheus good Deucalion came,
' His royal heir, Hæmonia is the name. 1161
' Deucalion here the firft foundations laid
' Of towns, built fanes, and men by empire fway'd ;
' There my Iolcos ftands, and many more
' Fair ample cities, that adorn the fhore. 1165
' What time, as rumour'd by the voice of fame,
' Æolian Minyas to that country came,

O 2 ' He

' He built, close bordering on the Theban ground,
' Orchomenos, a city far renown'd.
' But why your wonder should I vainly raise? 1170
' My birth-place tell, and Ariadne's praise?
' For this the virgin's name you now inquire,
' A lovely maid, and Minos is her sire.
' Oh! may, like hers, your sire propitious prove,
' Who honour'd Theseus with his daughter's love!"
Complacent thus he sooth'd her sorrowing soul;
Yet anxious cares within her bosom roll.
" Perchance in Greece" (the pensive maid rejoin'd)
" Oaths are rever'd, and solemn compacts bind.
" But Minos greatly differs from my sire, 1180
" Nor I to Ariadne's charms aspire.
" Then mention hospitality no more;
" But, safe conducted to thy native shore,
" Grant this, 'tis all I ask, Oh! think of me,
" As I for ever shall remember thee, 1185
" In my great sire, the Colchian king's despite:
" But if thy pride my ardent passion slight,
" Fame, or some bird the hateful news will bring;
" Then will I chace thee on the tempest's wing,
" Brand thy false heart, thy curs'd familiar be, 1190
" And prove thou ow'st thy life, thy all to me."

Medea thus, and tears abundant shed;
And mildly thus the son of Æson said:
' In vain, dear nymph, thy missive bird shall soar
' Thro' air sublime, in vain the tempest roar.   1195
' But if towards Greece thou deign'st thy course to
         bear,
' Immortal honours shall attend thee there;
' There husbands, brothers, sons, so long deplor'd,
' Safe to their native land by thee restor'd,
' Shall as a Goddess reverence thy name,   1200
' And pay thee rites which only Gods can claim.
' But would'st thou grace my bed with bridal state,
' Our love can only be dissolv'd by fate.'

His words with raptures all her soul subdue;
Yet gloomy objects rise before her view,   1205
Ordain'd, ere long, Thessalia's realms to see;
For such was Juno's absolute decree,
That soon to Greece the Colchian maid should go,
To Pelias source of unremitting woe.

Meanwhile apart her anxious handmaids stay, 1210
In silence waiting till the close of day:
Such pleasing transports in her bosom roll,
His form, his words so captivate her soul,
On feather'd feet the hours unheeded fled,
Which warn'd her home: ' Hence (cautious Jason said)

O 3   ' Hence

'Hence let us haften unperceiv'd away, 1216
' And here enraptur'd pafs fome future day.'
Thus the bleft hours in converfe fweet they fpent,
And both unwilling from the temple went;
He to his comrades bordering on the main, 1220
The fair Medea to her virgin train.
Her train approach'd, but ftood unnotic'd by;
Her foul fublime expatiates in the fky.
Her rapid car fhe mounts; this hand fuftains
The polifh'd thong, and that the flowing reins. 1225
Fleet o'er the plain the nimble mules convey'd
To Æa's walls the love-tranfported maid.
Meanwhile Chalciope aftonifh'd ftands,
And inftant tidings of her fons demands;
In vain: fad cares had clos'd Medea's ears, 1230
No anfwers gives fhe, and no queftions hears;
But on a footftool low, befide her bed,
All bath'd in tears fhe fits; her hand fuftains her head.
There fits fhe pondering, in a penfive ftate,
What dire diftreffes on her counfels wait. 1235
But Jafon, eager to return, withdrew
With his two friends, and join'd his focial crew,
Who throng'd impatient round, while he difplay'd
The fecret counfels of the Colchian maid,

And

Book III. APOLLONIUS RHODIUS.

And show'd the potent herbs: Idas apart   1240
Conceal'd the choler rankling in his heart.
Meanwhile the rest, when glimmering day-light clos'd,
Wrapp'd in the mantle of the night repos'd.
Next morn they sent Æthalides the son
Of Mercury, and valiant Telamon,   1245
(For thus in council had the Greeks decreed)
Of fierce Æeta to demand the seed,
The serpent's teeth, whose ever-wakeful sight
Watch'd o'er the fountain of the God of fight.
This baneful monster was by Cadmus slain,   1250
Seeking Europa o'er the Theban plain;
An heifer to his seat of regal sway,
So will'd prophetic Phœbus, led the way.
These teeth Minerva from the monster rent,
And part to Cadmus and Æeta sent: 1255
Sow'd on Bœotia's ample plains, from those
A hardy race of earth-born giants rose.
To Jason these he gave, a precious spoil;
Nor, tho' his matchless arm the bulls might foil,
Deem'd he, that victory would crown his toil. 1260
The sun now sinking with a feeble ray
To distant Ethiopians slop'd his way;
Night yok'd her steeds: the Grecian heroes spread
Around the halsers and the sails their bed.

The

The northern Bear was funk beneath the hills, 1265
And all the air a folemn filence fills:
Jafon to lonely haunts purfu'd his way;
(All rites adjufted the preceding day.)
'Twas Argus' care a lambkin to provide,
And milk, the reft the ready fhip fupply'd.   1270
A fweet fequefter'd fpot the hero found,
Where filence reigns, and welling ftreams abound;
And here, obfervant of due rites, he laves,
His limbs immerging in the cleanfing waves;
Then o'er his fhoulders, pledge of favours paft, 1275
The gift of fair Hypfipyla he caft,
A fable robe: a deep round fofs he made,
And on the kindling wood the victim laid:
The mix'd libation pouring o'er the flame,
Loud he invok'd infernal Brimo's name;   1280
Then back retires: his call her ears invades,
And up fhe rifes from the land of fhades:
Snakes, wreath'd in oaken boughs, curl'd round her hair,
And gleaming torches caft a difmal glare.
To guard their queen the hideous dogs of hell 1285
Rend the dark welkin with inceffant yell;
The heaving ground beneath her footfteps fhakes;
Loud fhriek the Naiads of the neighbouring lakes;

And

And all the fountain-nymphs aftonifh'd ftood
Where Amaranthine Phafis rolls his flood. 1290
Fear feiz'd the chief, yet backward he withdrew,
Nor, till he join'd his comrades, turn'd his view.

And now on Caucafus, with fnow o'erfpread,
The rifing morn her filver radiance fhed,
When proud Æeta, earlier than the reft, 1295
The fencing corflet buckled to his breaft,
The fpoils of Mimas of gigantic race,
Whom Mars had vanquifh'd on the plains of Thrace:
His golden helmet to his head he bound,
With four fair crefts of glittering plumage crown'd,
Bright as the fun new rifing from the main; 1301
His nervous arms a mighty fpear fuftain :
From his broad fhoulder beams his fevenfold fhield,
Which not a chief of all the Greeks could wield,
Since great Alcides, of his friend bereft, 1305
Was (fad mifchance !) on Myfia's borders left.
His fon hard by with ready chariot ftands;
The king afcends; the reins adorn his hands;
Fierce to the field he haftes in regal ftate,
And crouds of Colchians round their monarch wait.
  As ocean's god, when drawn by rapid fteeds, 1311
To Ifthmian games, or Calaureia fpeeds,

To

To Tænarus, or rocky Petra roves,
Or where Geræftus boafts her oaken groves,
Oncheftus' woods, or Lerna's limpid fpring; 1315
So to the combat drives the Colchian king.

Meanwhile, inftructed by the magic maid,
The chief his fhield, his fpear and trenchant blade
With unguents fmear'd: the Greeks approaching nigh
In vain their efforts on his armour try; 1320
But chief the fpear fuch magic charms attend,
No force can break it, and no onfet bend.
Idas enrag'd deals many a furious wound,
But, as hard hammers from an anvil bound,
So from the fpear his fword recoiling fprung: 1325
The diftant vales with loud applaufes rung...
Next, with the potent charm the chief anoints
His well-turn'd limbs, and fupples all his joints.
And, lo! new powers invigorate his hands,
And arm'd with ftrength intrepidly he ftands. 1330

As the proud fteed, exulting in his might,
Erects his ears, impatient for the fight,
And pawing fnuffs the battle from afar;
So pants the hero for the promis'd war.
Firmly he moves, incapable of fear; 1335
One hand his fhield fuftains, and one the fpear.

                                            Thus,

Thus, when black clouds obscure the darkening day,
And rains descend, the living lightnings play.

And now the fight draws near; the Grecian train
Sail up the Phasis to the martial plain;   1340
From which as far the towers of Æa stand,
As when the chieftains, who the games command
For some dead king, the bounding barriers place
For steeds or men contending in the race.
Æeta there they found, of mind elate;   1345
On Phasis' banks his chariot rolls in state.
On the Caucasian summits, that command
The field of Mars, the crowded Colchians stand.
Now Argo moor'd, the prince invades the field,
Arm'd with his magic spear, and ample shield;   1350
With serpents' teeth his brazen helm was stor'd,
And cross his shoulder gleam'd his glittering sword:
Like Mars the chief enormous power display'd,
Or Phœbus brandishing his golden blade.
O'er the rough tilth he cast his eyes around,   1355
And soon the plough of adamant he found,
And yokes of brass: his helm (approaching near)
He plac'd on earth, and upright fix'd his spear.
To find the bulls he farther went afield,
And trac'd their steps, arm'd only with his shield.   1360

In a dark cave which smoky mists surround,
Horrid and huge their safe retreat he found.
With rage impetuous forth the monsters came,
And from their nostrils issued streams of flame.
Fear seiz'd the Greeks, but he their fury braves; 1365
Firm as a rock, defies the roaring waves;
Screen'd by his shield, intrepidly he scorns
The bulls loud-bellowing, and their butting horns;
Collected firm he wards each threatening blow.
As at the forge where melting metals glow, 1370
While now the bellows heave, now sink by turns,
The flame subsides, or with fresh fury burns;
Stirr'd to the bottom roars the raging fire:
So roar the bulls, and living flame respire,
That fierce as lightning round the hero play'd, 1375
In vain, now shelter'd by the magic maid.
One bull he seiz'd, that aim'd a deadly stroke,
Seiz'd by his horns, and dragg'd him to the yoke;
Then hurl'd the roaring monster on the ground;
An equal fate his fellow-captive found, 1380
Loos'd from his arm he flung his shield aside,
And the two monsters manfully he ply'd,
Dragg'd on their knees his fiery foes o'ercame,
And shifting artfully escap'd the flame.

Æeta

Æeta view'd him with aftonifh'd eyes; 1285
When lo! the fons of Tyndarus arife,
As erft it was decreed, and from the land
Heav'd the ftrong yokes and gave them to his hand:
Thefe o'er the bulls' low-bended necks he flung;
The brazen beam by rings fufpended hung. 1390
The youths retreating from the burning field,
The chief refum'd his loaded helm, his fhield
Behind him thrown; then grafp'd his maffy fpear,
(Thus arm'd the hinds of Theffaly appear,
With long fharp goads to prick their bullocks' fides)
And the firm plough of adamant he guides. 1396
The reftiff bulls with indignation fir'd,
From their broad noftrils living flames expir'd,
Loud as the blafts when wintry winds prevail,
And trembling failors furl the folding fail. 1400
Urg'd by his fpear the bulls their tafk fulfil,
Prove their own prowefs, and the ploughman's fkill.
As the fharp coulter cleft the clodded ground,
The roughen'd ridges fent a rattling found.
Firm oe'r the field undaunted Jafon treads, 1405
And fcattering wide the ferpent's teeth he fpreads;
Yet oft looks back, fufpecting he fhould find
A legion rifing up in arms behind:

Unwearied

Unwearied ſtill the bulls their toil purſue;
Their brazen hoofs the ſtubborn ſoil ſubdue.   1410
   When now three portions of the day were ſpent,
And weary hinds at evening homeward went,
The chief had till'd four acres of the ſoil;
He then releas'd the monſters from their toil.
Away they ſcamper'd wildly o'er the plain;   1415
Himſelf rejoin'd his delegated train,
Till on the field his earth-born foes appear:
The Greeks their animated hero cheer.
He in his helm, repleniſh'd at the ſprings,
To ſlake his burning thirſt freſh water brings.   1420
His limbs renew'd with forceful vigour play,
His heart beats boldly and demands the fray.
Thus the fell boar diſdains the hunter-bands,
Foams, whets his tuſks, and in defiance ſtands.
Now roſe th' embattled ſquadron in the field,   1425
In glittering helms array'd, with ſpear and ſhield,
Bright o'er the Martial plain the ſplendors riſe,
And dart in ſtreams of radiance to the ſkies.
Thus, when thick ſnow the face of nature ſhrouds,
And nightly winds diſpel the wintry clouds,   1430
The ſtars again their ſplendid beams diſplay;
So ſhone the warriours in the face of day.

                                                        But

But Jason, mindful of the maid's command,
Seiz'd a vaft rock, and rais'd it from the land : 1434
Not four ftout youths, for ftrength of limbs renown'd,
Could lift a weight fo ponderous from the ground :
This 'midft his foes, embattled on the field,
He hurl'd, and fafe retir'd behind his fhield.
The Colchians fhout, as when the raging main
Roars round tremendous rocks, but roars in vain. 1440
In filence fix'd, Æeta ftands aghaft
To fee the fragment with fuch fury caft.
The hoft, like dogs contending o'er their prey,
With curs'd ferocity their comrades flay,
Then leave on earth their mangled trunks behind,
Like pines or oaks uprooted by the wind. 1446
As fhoots a ftar from heaven's etherial brow,
Portending vengeance to the world below,
Who thro' dark clouds defcry its radiant light :
Thus Jason rufh'd, in glittering armour bright. 1450
His brandifh'd falchion fell'd the rifing foes :
Succinct in arms, fome half their lengths difclofe,
Some fcarce their fhoulders ; other feebly ftand,
While others, treading firm, the fight demand.

As on the bounds which feparate hoftile ftates, 1455
Eternal fource of battle and debates,

The

The cautious hind the cruel spoiler fears,
And reaps his wheat with yet unripen'd ears;
Ere yet the spikes their wonted growth attain,
Ere yet the sun-beams have matur'd the grain :   1460
So Jason's arms the rising squadrons mow'd;
Their blood profusely in the furrows flow'd.
Some sidelong fall on earth, and some supine,
Some prone lie groveling and their lives resign,
Like whales incumbent on the buoyant main :   1465
Some wounded perish ere they tread the plain;
As late in air they held their heads on high,
So lowly humbled in the dust they lie.
Thus tender plants, by copious torrents drown'd,
Strew their fresh leaves, uprooted from the ground;
The tiller views with heart-corroding pain   1471
His fostering care, and all his labours vain.
Æeta thus with wild vexation burn'd,
And with his Colchians to the town return'd,
Some weightier task revolving in his mind :   1475
Thus clos'd the combat, and the day declin'd.

END OF THE THIRD BOOK.

THE
FOURTH BOOK.

THE ARGUMENT.

Jason obtains the Golden Fleece by the assistance of Medea. She embarks with the Argonauts for Greece. Æeta pursues them. Having crossed the Euxine sea, they sail up the Ister; and by an arm of that river enter the Adriatic. Absyrtus is treacherously murdered by Jason. They sail into the Sardinian sea by the way of the Eridanus and the Rhone. The murder of Absyrtus is expiated by Circe, at whose island they land. Thetis and her nymphs conduct the heroes through the straits of Scylla and Charybdis. They sail by the island infested with the Syrens, from whose enchantments Orpheus delivers them. At Corcyra, once called Drepane, they meet with the Colchians that pursued them through the Symplegades; who request Alcinous, king of the island, to deliver up Medea. He agrees to send her back to her father, if unmarried; but if married to Jason, he refuses to separate them. Upon this determination her nuptials are immediately celebrated. They again put to sea, and are driven upon the quicksands of Africa. The tutelary Deities of the country extricate them from their distresses. They bear Argo on their shoulders as far as the lake Tritonis. The Hesperides, who were bewailing the death of the serpent, slain the preceding day by Hercules, give some account of that hero. The death of Canthus and Mopsus, two of their comrades, is related. Triton, whose figure is particularly described, gives them directions about their voyage. They sail near Crete. The story of Talus. At Hippuris they sacrifice to Phœbus, who, standing on the top of an hill, enlightens their way. The clod of earth, given by Triton to Euphemus, becomes an island, called Calliste. They anchor at Ægina; and loosing from thence, arrive, without further interruption at Thessaly.

T H.E

THE
ARGONAUTICS
OF
APOLLONIUS RHODIUS.

BOOK IV.

O Goddess, daughter of th' eternal king,
Medea's various cares and counsels sing:
Far from my mind the sad suspense remove,
Whether to celebrate her lawless love,
Or whether her base flight from Colchis' bay,　　5
Best claims the tribute of my tuneful lay.
　In solemn council to his faithful chiefs
The vengeful king disclos'd his bosom-griefs:
Sore disconcerted at the recent fight,
He spent in long debate the doleful night;　　10
Mistrusting still, these schemes, so deeply laid,
Were all conducted by his daughters' aid.
Meanwhile th' imperial queen of heaven had shed
O'er the fair virgin's breast despondent dread.

P 2　　　　　　　　　　　　She

She starts, she trembles, as, pursu'd by hounds,   15
The fawn light skipping o'er the meadow bounds.
She fears the secrets of her soul betray'd,
And her sire's vengeance for her proffer'd aid,
Her handmaids, conscious of her crimes, she fears;
Her eyes fierce flames emit, loud murmurs fill her
    ears.   20
Her death she meditates in wild despair,
And, sadly sighing, tears her golden hair.
Now fate imbibing from the poison'd bowl,
Soon had she freed her voluntary soul,
And Juno's projects all been render'd vain,   25
But, kindly pitying a lover's pain,
The Goddess urg'd with Phrixus' sons her flight,
And eas'd her bosom of its sorrow's weight.
Forth from her casket every drug she pours,
And to her lap consigns the magic stores.   30
Then with a parting kiss her bed she press'd,
Clung round each door, and ev'n the walls caress'd.
A lock she tore of loosely-flowing hair,
And safe consign'd it to her mother's care,
The sacred relick of her virgin-fame;   35
And, wailing thus, invok'd Idya's name:

' This lock, O mother, at my hand receive,
' Which I, far-distant roaming, with thee leave.
                                          ' Farewell,

'Farewell, Chalclope; far hence I roam!
'And thou farewell, my firſt, my deareſt home! 40
'Oh! hadſt thou, ſtranger, in deep ocean drown'd,
'Periſh'd, and never trod on Colchian ground!'
 She ſpoke, and tears her heart-felt woe betray'd;
Then fled ſhe inſtant. Thus the captive maid,
When, from her friends and country baniſh'd far, 45
She ſhares the miſerable fate of war,
Difus'd to toil beneath a tyrant's ſway,
Flies from oppreſſion's rod with ſpeed away.
With ſpeed like her's the weeping fair withdrew:
The doors ſpontaneous open'd as ſhe flew, 50
Shook by her magic ſong; barefoot ſhe ſtrays
Thro' winding paths and unfrequented ways.
Before her face one hand her veſture holds,
And one confines its border's flowing folds.
Beyond the city-walls with trembling haſte, 55
Unſeen of all the centinels, ſhe paſs'd,
Then by accuſtom'd paths explor'd the fane,
Where ſpectres riſe, and plants diffuſe their bane;
(Thus practiſe magic maids their myſtic art)
Fears ill portending flutter round her heart. 60
Her frenzy Cynthia, riſing bright, ſurvey'd,
And this ſoliloquy in triumph made:

P 3 'Yes,

' Yes, with Endymion's heavenly charms o'ercome,
' I to the cave at Latmos once could roam,
' Of love regardful, when your potent lay   65
' Had from the starry spheres seduc'd my ray,
' That you, protected by the gloom of night,
' Might celebrate unseen the mystic rite,
' Your lov'd employ: now Cupid's shafts subdue,
' Not Cynthia only, but, fair sorceress, you.   70
' For you his toils the wily god hath wove,
' And all your heart inflam'd with Jason's love.
' Come then, those pangs which love ordains endure,
' And bear with courage what you cannot cure.'
She said: impetuous hastening to the flood,   75
Soon on its lofty banks Medea stood.
A fire, which midnight's deadly gloom dispell'd,
Signal of conquest gain'd, she here beheld.
Involv'd in shade, the solitary dame
Rais'd her shrill voice, and call'd on Phrontis' name. 80
Known was her voice to Phrixus' sons, who bear
The grateful tidings to their leader's ear.
The truth discover'd, the confederate host
All silent stood, in wild amazement lost.
Loud call'd she thrice; and with responsive cries, 85
His friends requesting, Phrontis thrice replies.

Quick

Book IV. APOLLONIUS RHODIUS. 215

Quick at her call they ply the bending oar;
Nor were their halfers faften'd to the fhore,
When Æfon's fon at one decifive bound
Leaps from the lofty deck upon the ground; 90
Phrontis and Argus haften to her aid,
Whofe knees embracing, thus Medea pray'd:
' Oh! fave me, friends, from my offended fire,
' Oh! fave yourfelves from dread Æeta's ire.
' Known are our projects: fail we hence afar, 95
' Ere Æa's monarch mounts his rapid car.
' My magic charms fhall clofe the dragon's eyes,
' And foon reward you with the golden prize.
' But thou, lov'd gueft, continue faithful ftill,
' And fwear whate'er thou promis'dft to fulfil: 100
' Ah! leave me not to infamy a fcorn,
' By all my friends abandon'd and forlorn.'
Plaintive fhe fpoke: his arms around her waift
Rapturous he threw, then rais'd her and embrac'd,
And folac'd thus in terms of tendereft love: 105
" By heaven's high king I fwear, Olympian Jove,
" By Juno, goddefs of the nuptial rite,
" Soon as my native land tranfports my fight,
" Thou, lovely virgin, fhalt be duly led,
" Adorn'd with honours, to my bridal bed." 110

P 4   This

This said, in her's he clos'd his plighted hand:
To Mars's grove Medea gave command,
Spite of her fire, the veffel to convey,
And bear by night the golden fleece away.
Swift at the word they fprung; the Colchian maid 115
Embark'd, and inftant was their anchor weigh'd.
Their crafhing oars refound: fhe oft to land
Reverts her eye, and waves her trembling hand:
But Æfon's fon his ready aid affords,
And fooths her forrows with confoling words. 120

 Wak'd by their hounds, what time the huntfmen rife,
And fhake the balm of flumber from their eyes,
At twilight, ere Aurora's dreaded ray
Efface the tracks, and waft the fcent away:
Jafon, then landing with the fair, attains, 125
With flowers diverfified, the verdant plains,
Where firft the ram, with Phrixus' weight opprefs'd,
His wearied knee inclin'd, and funk to reft.
Hard by, an altar's ftately ftructure ftands,
To favouring Jove firft rais'd by Phrixus' hands, 130
Where he the golden monfter doom'd to bleed;
So his conductor Hermes had decreed.
Here, as by Argus taught, the chiefs withdrew,
While their lone courfe the regal pair purfue

Book IV. APOLLONIUS RHODIUS. 217

Thro' the thick grove, impatient to behold   135
The spreading beech that bears the fleecy gold.
Suspended here, it darts a beamy blaze,
Like a cloud tipp'd with Phœbus' orient rays.
With high-arch'd neck, in front the dragon lies,
And towards the strangers turns his sleepless eyes; 140
Aloud he hisses: the wide woods around,
And Phasis' banks return the doleful sound.
Colchians, far distant from Titanus' shore,
Heard ev'n to Lycus' streams the hideous roar;
Lycus, who, sever'd from Araxis' tides,   145
A boisterous flood, with gentle Phasis glides:
One common course their streams united keep,
And roll united to the Caspian deep.
The mother, starting from her bed of rest,
Fears for her babe reclining on her breast,   150
And closely clasping to her fondling arms,
Protects her trembling infant from alarms.

As from some wood, involv'd in raging fires,
Clouds following clouds ascend in curling spires;
The smoky wreaths in long succession climb,   155
And from the bottom rise in air sublime;
The dragon thus his scaly volumes roll'd,
Wreath'd his huge length, and gather'd fold in fold.

Him,

Him, winding flow, beheld the magic dame,
And Sleep invok'd the monster's rage to tame. 160
With potent song the drowsy God she sway'd
To summon all his succour to her aid;
And Hecate from Pluto's coasts she drew,
To lull the dauntless monster, and subdue.
Jason advanc'd with awe, with awe beheld 165
The dreaded dragon by her magic quell'd.
Lifeless he lay, each languid fold unbound,
And his vast spine extended on the ground.
Thus, when the boisterous wave forbears to roar,
It sinks recumbent on the peaceful shore. 170
Still strove the monster his huge head to heave,
And in his deadly jaws his foe receive.
A branch of juniper the maid applies,
Steep'd in a baneful potion, to his eyes:
Its odours strong the branch diffus'd around, 175
And sunk th' enormous beast in sleep profound.
Supine he sunk; his jaws forgot to move,
And his unnumber'd folds are spread o'er half the
    grove.
Then Jason to the beech his hand applies,
And grasps, at her command, the golden prize. 180
Still she persists to ply the potent spell,
And the last vigour of the monster quell,

Till

Till he advis'd her to rejoin the crew;
Then from the grove of Mars the maid withdrew.
  As some fair dame, when Cynthia rises bright, 185
Beholds the beamy splendors with delight,
Which from her vestment strong-reflected rise;
Thus gloried Jason in the glistering prize.
The flaming rays, that from its surface flow'd,
Beam'd on his cheeks, and on his forehead glow'd. 190
Large as the heifer's hide, or as the hind's,
Which in Achaia's plains the hunter finds,
Shone the thick, ponderous fleece, whose golden rays
Far o'er the land diffus'd a beamy blaze.
He on his shoulders, now, the spoil suspends, 195
Low at his feet the flowing train descends;
Collecting, now, within its ponderous folds,
His grasping hand the costly capture holds.'
Fearful he moves, with circumspect survey,
Lest men or gods should snatch the prize away. 200
  Now as returning morn illumes the land,
The royal pair rejoin the gallant band.
The gallant band beheld with wondering eyes,
Fierce as Jove's fiery bolt, the radiant prize.
Their hands extending as they flock around, 205
All wish to heave the trophy from the ground.

But

But Jason interdicting singly threw
O'er the broad fleece a covering rich and new;
Then in the ship he plac'd the virgin-guest,
And thus the listening demigods addrefs'd: 210
' No longer doubt ye, comrades, to regain
' Far o'er a length of seas your lov'd domain.
' For see, the end of all our glorious toil,
' Won by Medea's aid, this precious spoil!
' Her, not reluctant, I to Greece will bear, 215
' And with connubial honours crown her there.
' Guard your fair patroness, ye gallant crew,
' Who sav'd your country when she succour'd you.
' Soon will Æeta with his Colchian train
' Preclude, I ween, our passage to the main. 220
' Some with your oars resume your destin'd seat;
' Some with your shields secure your wish'd retreat;
' This rampire forming, we their darts defy,
' Nor, home returning, unreveng'd will die.
' Lo! on our prowess all we love depends, 225
' Our children, parents, country and our friends.
' Greece, as we speed, thro' future times shall boast
' Her empire fix'd, or wail her glory lost.'
He said, and arm'd; the heroes shout applause:
Then from its pendent sheath his sword he draws, 230

Severs

Severs the halfer, and, in arms array'd,
His station fixes near the magic maid,
And where Ancæus' hand the pilot's art difplay'd.
Keen emulation fir'd the labouring crew,
As down the stream of Phasis Argo flew.   235
  Medea's flight now reach'd Æeta's ear,
And all her crimes in all their guilt appear.
To council call'd, in arms the Colchian train
Rush thick as billows on the roaring main,
Thick as the leaves that flutter from above,   240
When blasting autumn strips the faded grove;
So thick the shouting Colchians rush to war,
Led by Æeta in his splendid car,
Glorying in Phœbus' gifts, his rapid steeds,
Whose swiftness far the speed of winds exceeds.   245
His left a buckler's wide circumference rais'd;
In his extended right a flambeau blaz'd;
His girded belt a mighty spear sustains;
His son Abfyrtus grasps the flowing reins.
Now by tough oars impell'd and prosperous tides,   250
The vessel glibly down the river glides.
Th' indignant king invok'd the powers above,
His parent Phœbus, and almighty Jove,
His wrongs to witness: and to sudden fate
Doom'd in his fury the devoted state.   255
                                          Who

Who dar'd delay the guilty maid to bring,
From land or ocean, to their injur'd king,
On their rebellious heads his wrath should fall,
And vengeance merited o'ertake them all.

Thus menac'd he; and, lo! the Colchian train 260
Launch'd on that day their veffels in the main;
Swift, on that day, unfurl'd their bellying fails,
And all embarking caught the balmy gales.
Nor deem ye this a well-train'd naval hoft;
Like flocks of birds they fcream around the coaft. 265
Juno, propitious to her favourite-crew,
Infpir'd the breezes that ferenely blew,
That foon on Grecian land the fair might tread,
And pour deftruction down on Pelias' head.
With the third morn, on Paphlagonia's fhore, 270
Where Halys rolls his ftream, the heroes moor.
Medea here ordain'd a folemn rite
To Hecate, the magic queen of night.
But what, or how fhe form'd the potent fpell,
Let none enquire, nor fhall my numbers tell: 275
Fear holds me filent. Here the pious band
Erect a facred temple on the ftrand,
Sacred to Hecate, night's awful queen;
And ftill befide the beach the holy fane is feen.

And

And now the words of Phineus, old and blind, 280
Recurr'd to Jason, and each hero's mind.
From Æa he advis'd them to purſue
A different courſe, a courſe no pilot knew,
Which Argos thus delineates to the crew :
' When towards Orchomenos our courſe we bent, 285
' We took that route th' inſtructive prophet meant.
' For in times paſt a different road was known,
' And this thy prieſts, Ægyptian Thebes, have ſhewn.
' Before the ſtars adorn'd the ſaphire-ſphere,
' Or Danaus' race had reach'd th' enquirer's ear; 290
' In Greece the bold Arcadians reign'd alone,
' And, ere bright Cynthia deck'd her ſilver throne,
' On acorns liv'd, the food of ſavage man;
' Before Deucalion's ſons their reign began;
' With harveſts, then, was fertile Ægypt crown'd, 295
' Mother of mighty chiefs, of old renown'd;
' Then the broad Triton, beauteous to behold,
' His ſtreams prolific o'er the country roll'd.
' For Jove deſcends not there in bounteous rains,
' But inundations fertilize the plains.   300
' Hence roſe the matchleſs chief (if fame ſays true)
' Who conquer'd Europe's realms and Aſia's too;
' His hardy troops embattled at his ſide,
' He on his valour and thoſe troops rely'd.

' Who

'He built and peopled with fuperior fkill 305
'Unnumber'd cities, fome remaining ftill.
'Though many ages now have pafs'd away,
'Yet Æa ftands, nor haftens to decay;
'Peopled at firft by his adventurous train,
'Whofe long-continued race ev'n now remain. 310
'With care they ftill recording tablets keep
'Of all the limits of the land and deep,
'Wherever rivers flow, or ftorms prevail,
'Wherever men can march, or fhips can fail.
'A river, ftately-winding, deep and wide, 315
'From far, far diftant mountains rolls its tide;
'Where fhips of burden fure protection claim:
'Long is its courfe and Ifter is its name.
'Far, o'er Riphæan hills, where Boreas reigns,
'He undivided flows thro' various plains; 320
'But when thro' Thrace and Scythian climes he glides,
'In two broad ftreams his rapid flood divides:
'This to th' Ionian fea its circuit fweeps,
'That wider ftretches to Trinacria's deeps,
'Whofe lofty fhores your Grecian coaft command,
'If Achelöus flow through Grecian land.' 326
He faid: a favouring fign the Goddefs gave,
Which with new courage animates the brave.

Celeftial

Celestial fires emit a living ray,
And beams of glory point the certain way. 330
Here, leaving Lycus' valiant son behind,
They spread with joy their canvass to the wind.
Afar the Paphlagonian hills appear;
And from Carambis' cape remote they steer,
Led by the heavenly light and kindly gales, 335
Till in broad Ister's flood the vessel sails.

Where the Cyanean rocks o'erlook the main,
Part of the Colchians steer their course in vain;
While they, whose counsels sage Absyrtus guides,
Cut through the mouth call'd Calon Ister's tides. 340
Outsailing thus yon' tardy ships, they sweep
With skilful oars the wide Ionian deep.
An isle, which Ister's branching streams comprise,
Peuce, triangular, before them lies:
Wide o'er the beach its ample base extends, 345
And in the flood its pointed angle ends.
The two broad streams, that round the island flow,
They by Arecos' name and Calon know.
Below this isle Absyrtus and his crew
Through the wide Calon their swift course pursue: 350
Above it sailing Jason's comrades stray,
And through Arecos wind their distant way.

Q   Such

Such naval force dismay'd the neighbouring swains;
They left their fleecy flocks and verdant plains:
The ships in view, with terrour struck they stood, 355
And deem'd them monsters rising from the flood:
Never beheld they from their native shore
Ships proudly sailing on the seas before.
For the fierce Scythians and Sigynnian race
Maintain'd no commerce with the sons of Thrace: 360
Nor Sindians e'er, who roam the desert plain,
Nor e'er Graucenians crofs'd the seas for gain.
When Argo's crew the mount Angurus pafs'd,
And reach'd the rock Cauliacus at last,
(Ifter near which his stately stream divides 365
And mingles with the deep his sever'd tides;)
And distant left the wide Talaurian plain,
Then had the Colchians plough'd the Chronian main.
Here, left the vessel scape, they cautious stay,
And strive to intercept her in her way. 370
At length appears to their expecting view
On Ifter's flood the enterprising crew.
Two lovely sea-girt isles their notice claim'd,
Dear to Diana, and the Brugi nam'd.
Superb in one a sacred temple rose, 375
And one secur'd them from their Colchian foes.

Her

Her power revering whom thefe ifles obey,
The foe had quitted them without delay.
Each ifle befide was throng'd with Colchian hofts,
Who, guarding every pafs, protect the coafts.   380
For troops of enemies embattled ftood,
Far ev'n as Neftis and Salango's flood.

Their numbers few, the Mynian chiefs forbear
To wage with numerous foes unequal war.
Preventive of debate, this truce was feal'd;   385
That, fince the king propos'd the Fleece to yield,
Whether by open force, or arts unknown,
Conqueft the daring combatant might crown,
He, though reluctant, muft refign his right,
And the contefted prize the victor's toil requite.   390
That, from the crowd with fecrecy convey'd,
Diana's fane fhould guard the magic maid,
Till mid' the fceptred princes one arofe
To fix their vague opinions, and propofe,
Or to reftore her to her fire's embrace,   395
Or in Orchomenos's city place;
Or freely grant her to embark in peace,
And with the Grecian heroes vifit Greece.

When now, long pondering, the fufpicious maid
Had learn'd, and all their fecret counfels weigh'd,   400

Tormenting

Tormenting cares difturb'd her mind's repofe,
And keen reflection added woes to woes.
Afide fhe then, from all th' affembled crew,
With cautious fecrecy her Jafon drew :
Him, thus withdrawn, th' impaffion'd maid addrefs'd,
And told the fecret forrows of her breaft : 406
' Say, what the caufe that hoftile hofts are join'd,
' And leagues, deftructive of my peace, combin'd ?
' Say, have thefe charms, with rapture once explor'd,
' Lull'd to forgetfulnefs my faithlefs lord ? 410
' Hath time effac'd the promifes he made,
' When in the needful hour he afk'd mine aid ?
' Where now thine oaths, prefer'd to mighty Jove ?
' Where now thy tenders of unalter'd love ?
' Curs'd oaths! which bade me all I love difclaim, 415
' Friends, parents, country, every honour'd name !
' Forlorn and vex'd left thou fhould'ft toil in vain,
' I with the plaintive halcyon fought the main.
' I follow'd but to fhield thee from alarms,
' When bulls breath'd fire, and giants rofe in arms. 420
' Now is the Fleece, for which ye fail'd, poffefs'd,
' And by my foolifh fondnefs thou art blefs'd.
' Blefs'd thou ; but me what fecret forrows vex,
' Whofe deeds reflect difhonour on my fex !

' Me

Book IV. Apollonius Rhodius. 229

' Me as thy daughter, sister, wife they brand, 425
' Who dare attend thee to a distant land.
' But stay, protect me, ease my weight of woe,
' Nor to my royal sire without me go.
' Oh! think on justice, and revere thine oath,
' Which both consented to, which bound us both: 430
' Or instant, should'st thou every tie evade,
' In this frail bosom plunge the pointed blade.
' Thus frantic love its due desert shall see,
' And death come grateful to a wretch like me.
' Think, should the king exert his sovereign sway, 435
' And with my brother destine me to stay,
' (That king with whom ye both with treacherous aim
' Have form'd a league, subversive of my fame;)
' Oh! how shall I behold my father's face?
' With courage I! not shrinking at disgrace!   440
' No; stung by conscience, I forestall my fate,
' And feel the horrours which my crimes create.
' Back o'er the seas, mid' raging tempests borne,
' Long may'st thou wander joyless and forlorn.
' Ne'er may thy boasted patroness and friend, 445
' Juno, to thee her wonted aid extend.
' Stern fate may still severer toils ordain,
' And thou, false wretch, remember me in vain.

Q 3   ' Oh!

'Oh! may the Fleece deceive thy ravish'd sight,
'And, like a vision, vanish into night.   450
'Rise may my Furies, vengeance to demand,
'And distant drive thee from thy native land.
'From thee, their guilty source, my sorrows flow:
'Share now thy part, and suffer woe for woe.
'Thine oaths no more a slighted maid shall wrong,
'Nor this perfidious truce protect thee long.'   456
  Stung with despair, she utter'd thus her grief,
Thus to her angry spirit gave relief.
To burn the ship forth rush'd th' impetuous dame,
And wrap its heaven-built sides in sudden flame; 460
Resolv'd in thought, as now the vessel blaz'd,
To perish dauntless in the flame she rais'd:
But Jason thus, with boding fears impress'd,
Sooth'd the mad tumults of Medea's breast:
  " Cease, heavenly maid, nor wound a lover's ear 465
" With words unwelcome, and unfit to hear,
" The common safety bids us all unite
" To gain a timely respite from the fight.
" See, fair protectress, to restore thee lost,
" What clouds of enemies surround the coast.   470
" The country arms thy brother's cause to aid,
" And bear thee to thy sire a captive maid.

" Against

" Againſt ſuch force ſhould we our arms oppoſe,
" Periſh might all our hoſt, o'erpower'd by foes:
" Then, ſad to think! if, every hero ſlain,   475
" In long captivity muſt thou remain.
" Our arts perfidious will this truce conceal,
" Whoſe baneful influence muſt thy brother feel.
" Bereav'd of him, the Colchians' cauſe to aid,
" And to recover thee, a captive maid,   480
" No more the neighbouring forces will unite:
" Inſtant will I renew the deſperate fight,
" Secure my wiſh'd return, and vindicate my right."
  Thus ſpoke he mild: the miſchief-brooding maid
Told her dark purpoſe, and, 'O think,' ſhe ſaid, 485
' Think, Jaſon, now: oppoſe we, as beſeems,
' To their deſtructive deeds deſtructive ſchemes.
' Urg'd firſt by Love, in errour's maze I ſtray'd,
' And through that God is every luſt obey'd.
' Decline the fight, till I the youth betray,   490
' And to your hands conſign, an eaſy prey.
' With preſents be the heedleſs ſtripling lur'd:
' Heralds, of faith approv'd, by me procur'd,
' Ere long a ſecret audience ſhall obtain,
' And to my purpoſes Abſyrtus gain.   495
' My plan (I reck not) if it pleaſe, purſue:
' Go, ſlay my brother, and the fight renew.'

Such were the snares the treacherous lovers laid;
And by large presents was the prince betray'd.
The heralds with these specious presents bore 500
The veil Hypsipyle so lately wore.
Each Grace in Naxos' isle, with art divine,
Wrought the rich raiment for the God of wine;
He gave it Thoas, his illustrious heir,
And Thoas to Hypsipyle the fair; 505
She gave it Jason: wondering you behold,
And with new transport trace th' embroider'd gold.
What time with large nectareous draughts oppress'd,
On the soft vesture Bacchus sunk to rest,
Close by his side the Cretan maid reclin'd, 510
At Naxos' isle whom Theseus left behind;
From that bless'd hour the robe, with odours fill'd,
Ambrosial fragrance wide around distill'd.

Her guileful purposes the magic maid
In order thus before the heralds laid: 515
That, soon as night her sable shade had spread,
And to the temple was Medea led,
Thither Absyrtus should repair, and hear
A project pleasing to a brother's ear:
How she, the Golden Fleece in triumph borne, 520
Would to Æeta speed her wish'd return;

How

How Phrixus' treacherous fons prolong'd her ſtay,
And her to cruel foes confign'd a prey.
Then far ſhe flung her potent ſpells in air,
Which lur'd the diſtant ſavage from his lair.   525
Curſe of mankind! from thee contentions flow,
Diſaſtrous Love! and every heart-felt woe:
Thy darts the children of thy foes infeſt,
As now they rankle in Medea's breaſt.
How, vanquiſh'd by her wiles, Abſyrtus fell,   530
In ſeemly order now my Muſe muſt tell.

Medea now ſecur'd in Dian's fane,
The Colchians haſten to their ſhips again.
Jaſon meanwhile lies in cloſe ambuſh, bent
Abſyrtus and his friends to circumvent.   535
Him, yet unpraƈtis'd in his ſiſter's guile,
His ready ſhip had wafted to the iſle:
Conceal'd in night they tugg'd their toilſome oars,
Till in the bay ſecure the veſſel moors.
Alone, in confidence, the ſtripling came,   540
And at Diana's porch approach'd the dame,
(She like a torrent look'd, when ſwoln with rain,
Which foaming terrifies the village-ſwain;)
To learn what ſnare her wily art could lay,
To drive theſe bold adventurers away.   545

And

And all was plann'd; when from his ambufcade
Sprung Æfon's fon, and fhook his lifted blade.
The confcious fifter, ftung with fecret dread,
Left her own eyes fhould view Abfyrtus dead,
Turn'd from the murderous fcene afide diftrefs'd, 550
And veil'd her guilty face beneath her veft.
As falls an ox beneath the ftriker's blow,
So was Abfyrtus laid by Jafon low.
Near that bright fane the neighbouring Brugi built,
He eyes his victim, and completes his guilt. 555
Here funk he low; and to his bleeding fide,
Compreffing both his hands, the hero died.
Medea's veil receiv'd the purple flood,
And her fair vefture blufh'd with brother's blood.
Hell's blackeft Fury the dire fcene furvey'd, 560
And mark'd with fidelong eye the reeking blade.
The pious rite for blood in fecret fpilt,
Jafon fulfils, and expiates his guilt.
The fkin he rafes from the body flain,
Thrice licks the blood, thrice fpits it out again. 565
Then with collected earth the corfe he prefs'd;
And ftill his bones with Abfyrteans reft.

 When in full profpect the bright flambeau blaz'd,
Which to conduct the chiefs Medea rais'd,

Elate

Book IV.   APOLLONIUS RHODIUS.   235

Elate with hope the radiant guide they view,   570
And near the Colchian veffel Argo drew.
As lions fierce the timorous flocks difmay,
Leap o'er the folds, and drive them far away;
As trembling doves before the kite retreat,
So before Argo flies the Colchian fleet.   575
Furious as flame, on all the hoft they prey'd,
And low in death was each affailant laid.
Jafon at length, to aid his valiant crew,
Who little need his aid, appear'd in view.
For not a fear their gallant hearts opprefs'd,   580
Save what their Jafon's fafety might fuggeft.
The chiefs affembled with Medea fat,
And on their future voyage thus debate;
Peleus began: ' Now, ere Aurora rife,
' A fpeedy embarkation I advife: 585
' A different courfe with caution let us choofe,
' From that far different which the foe purfues.
' For (fuch my fanguine hope) when morning-light
' Yon flaughter'd heaps difclofes to their fight,
' No words will win them to purfue us far,   590
' No tongue entice them to renew the war.
' Sedition foon, their prince Abfyrtus dead,
' Will, like a peft, o'er all their navy fpread:

' Secure

' Secure and free shall we recross the main,
' Their forces scatter'd, and their sovereign slain.' 595
   He said; the chiefs consented, and with haste
Re-enter'd Argo, and their oars embrac'd.
Hard by Electris, last of isles, they row,
Near which, Eridanus, thy waters flow.
   Soon as their leader's fate the Colchians knew, 600
They vow'd destruction to the Grecian crew;
And, eager to o'ertake the Mynian train,
Had travers'd in their wrath the boundless main,
But Juno, as her thunder awful roll'd,
Presag'd her vengeance, and their pride control'd. 605.
Dreading Æeta's ire, the vanquish'd host
Far distant voyag'd from the Colchian coast.
Unnumber'd ports the scatter'd fleet explor'd:
Some to those isles repair'd where Jason moor'd,
Nam'd from Absyrtus: some, where stately flows 610
The flood Illyricum, expect repose;
Beside whose bank a lofty tower they rear'd,
Where Cadmus' and Harmonia's tomb appear'd;
Here with the natives dwell they. Others roam
Till midst Ceraunian rocks they find a home; 615
Ceraunian nam'd, since Jove's red thunder tore
Their ships that anchor'd on the neighbouring shore.

But

But towards th' Hyllean port the heroes bear,
And, fortune smiling, fix their halsers there.
For many an isle projected o'er the tide,   620
Near which no vessel could with safety ride.
No hostile arts th' Hylleans now devise:
They teach the Mynians where their voyage lies;
And for their friendly intercourse obtain
The largest tripod from Apollo's fane.   625
For, doubtful of the Fleece, when Jason came
To hear responses from the Pythian dame,
Enrich'd, and honour'd from the shrine he trod
With two bright tripods, given by Delphi's God.
'Twas doom'd no power should lay the country waste,
Within whose confines were these tripods plac'd.   631
Hid, for this cause, in earth the sumptuous prize
Hard by the fair Hyllean city lies;
Deep, deep it lies, with ponderous earth oppress'd,
That there unseen it might for ever rest.   635
King Hyllus, whom in fam'd Phœacia's shore
Fair Melite to great Alcides bore,
To mortal view was manifest no more.
Nausithoüs, to youthful Hyllus kind,
The heedless stripling in his courts confin'd;   640
(For, when to Macris' isle Alcides fled,
That far-fam'd isle, which infant Bacchus fed,

To

To expiate his guilt, and wash the stain
Of blood yet streaming from his children slain,
Here, as beside his favourite-beach he rov'd,   645
The naiad Melite he saw and lov'd,
The daughter of Ægeus, fair and young,
From whose caresses hopeful Hyllus sprung.)
But he, to manhood ripening, wish'd to roam
Far from his sovereign's eye and regal home :   650
The native islanders augment his train,
And with their leader tempt the Chronian main.
Nausithoüs complied with each demand,
And Hyllus settled on th' Illyric strand:
But, as he strove his scatter'd herd to shield,   655
A boor's rude weapon stretch'd him on the field.

How crofs these seas, how round th' Ausonian shores,
And the Ligurian isles they plied their oars,
Ye Muses, tell : what tokens still remain
Of Argo's voyage, what her feats, explain :   660
Say, to what end, by what impelling gales
She o'er remotest seas unfurl'd her sails.

All-seeing Jove their perfidy discern'd,
And for Absyrtus slain with anger burn'd.
By Circe's mystic rites heaven's sire decreed   665
The guilt to expiate of so base a deed.

To

To fufferings dire, but what no mortal knew,
He, ere they fafe return'd, foredoom'd the crew.
 Beyond th' Hyllean land their courfe they fteer'd:
Remote the vaft Liburnian ifles appear'd,   670
Late fill'd with Colchians; Pityëa fair,
And rocky Iffa, are the names they bear.
 Thefe iflands paft, Cercyra's cliffs they greet,
Where dwelt (for here had Neptune chofe her feat)
Cercyra: he, by tender paffions fway'd,   675
From diftant Phliuns fetch'd the black-ey'd maid;
Melaine her admiring failors name,
As through dark groves they view the fwarthy dame.
Fleet as the veffel fails before the wind,
Ceroffus, Melite they leave behind.   680
Soon on Nymphæa, though remote, fhe gains,
Where Atlas' daughter, queen Calypfo, reigns:
The crew conjectur'd, through far diftant fkies
They faw the tall Ceraunian mountains rife.
 And now Jove's purpofes and vengeful rage   685
Propitious Juno's anxious thoughts engage.
That every toil with glory might be crown'd,
And no difaftrous rocks their fhip furround,
She wak'd the brifker gales in Argo's aid,
Till in Electris' ifle fhe rode embay'd: 690

        Sudden,

Sudden, the veffel, as fhe fail'd along;
Spoke, wondrous portent! as with human tongue:
Her fturdy keel of Dodonean oak,
By Pallas vocal made, prophetic fpoke.
This folemn voice fhook every heart with fear : 695
They deem'd the Thunderer's threaten'd vengeance
near.
' Expect,' fays Argo, ' ftorms and wintry feas,
' 'Till Circe's rites the wrath of Jove appeafe.
' Ye guardian twins, who aid our great defign,
' By humble prayer the heavenly powers incline 700
' To fteer me fafe to each Aufonian bay,
' And to the haunts of Circe point my way.'
Thus Argo fpoke, as night her fhades difplay'd :
The fons of Leda liften'd and obey'd.
Before th' immortal Powers their hands they fpread; 705
All, fave thefe chiefs, were ftruck with filent dread.
The canvafs wide-diftended by the gales,
Swift down Eridanus the galley fails.
Here Jove's dread bolt transfix'd the ftripling's fide,
Who greatly dar'd the car of Phœbus guide. 710
This flood receiv'd him ; and the flaming wound
Still fteams, and fpreads offenfive vapours round.
The feathery race, as o'er the flood they fly,
Wrapp'd in fulphureous exhalations die.

The

The poplar's winding bark around them spread, 715
Apollo's daughters wail their brother dead.
Down their fair cheeks bright tears of amber run,
Sink in the sand, and harden by the sun.
When boisterous winds the troubled waters urge,
And o'er its bank ascends the swelling surge, 720
These amber gems, swept by the tide away,
Their pearly tribute to the river pay.
But, down the stream, as Celtic legends tell,
The tears of Phœbus floated as they fell
In amber drops, what time from angry Jove 725
The God withdrew, and left the realms above:
To the far Hyperborean race he fled,
Griev'd for his favourite Æsculapius dead.
From fair Coronis sprung this godlike son,
Where Amyros' streams near Lacerea run. 730

Strangers to mirth, the pensive Mynians muse
On their hard lot, and strengthening food refuse.
Loathing the stench these putrid streams emit,
Sickening and spiritless whole days they sit;
Whole nights they hear the sorrowing sisters tell, 735
How by the bolts of Jove their brother fell.
Their mingled tears, as o'er the stream they weep,
Like drops of oil float down the rapid deep.

The Rhone's broad channel Argo's keel divides,
Which mingles with Eridanus its tides: 740
There, where the confluent floods unite their force,
Boisterous they foam. The Rhone derives its source
From caverns deep, which, far from mortal sight,
Lead to the portals, and the realms of night.
One stream its tribute to th' Ionian pays,   745
One to the wide Sardinian ocean strays;
Thro' seven wide mouths it disembogues its tides,
Where foaming to the sea its stream divides.
This winding stream transmits th' adventurous train
To lakes that delug'd all the Celtic plain.   750
Disastrous fate had here their labour foil'd,
And of her boasted prowess Argo spoil'd,
(For through a creek to ocean's depths convey'd,
To sure destruction had the heroes stray'd;)
But Juno hasten'd from on high, and stood   755
On a tall rock, and shouted o'er the flood.
All heard, and all with sudden terrour shook;
For loud around them bursts of thunder broke.
Admonish'd thus, submissive they return,
And steering back their better course discern.   760
Mid' Celtæ and Ligurians long they stray'd,
But reach'd the sea-beat shore by Juno's aid:

O'er

O'er them each day her cloudy veil she drew,
And thus from human sight conceal'd the crew;
Whose ship had now the broad, mid channel pass'd, 765
And rode amidst the Stœchades at last:
For Jove's twin sons had pray'd, nor pray'd in vain.
Hence rear they altars, and due rites ordain
To these kind Powers, whose influential aid
Not only Argo's bold adventurers sway'd; 770
But later voyagers, by Jove's decree,
Have own'd their happy influence o'er the sea.

The Stœchades now lessening from their view,
Swift to Æthalia's isle the vessel flew.
With chalks, that, as they cover'd, ting'd the shore, 775
The heroes rubb'd their wearied bodies o'er.
Here are their quoits and wondrous armour fram'd,
Here is their port display'd, Argoüs nam'd.
Hence sailing, they the Tyrrhene shores survey,
As through Ausonia's deeps they cleave their liquid
    way. 780
Æea's celebrated port they reach,
And fasten here their halsers to the beach.
Here saw they Circe, as in ocean's bed,
Dismay'd with nightly dreams, she plung'd her head.
For thus the sorceress dream'd; that blood and gore
Had smear'd her walls, and flow'd around her floor: 786

That all her treasur'd stores were wrapp'd in flame,
With which she lur'd each passenger that came;
That copious streams of blood her hand apply'd,
And her fears vanish'd as the flames subside. 790
For this the magic dame, as morning rose,
Wash'd in the cleansing wave her locks and clothes.
Monsters, unlike the savage, bestial race,
Unlike to humankind in gait or face,
Limbs not their own support whose hideous frame, 795
As sheep their shepherd follow, these their dame.
Such monsters once the pregnant earth disclos'd,
Of heterogeneous shapes and limbs compos'd:
No drying winds had then the soil condens'd,
No solar rays their genial warmth dispens'd; 800
But time perfection to each creature gave:
Monsters like these were seen in Circe's cave.
All, stedfast gazing on her form and face,
Pronounc'd the sorceress of Æeta's race.
Those terrors vanish'd, which her dream inspir'd, 805
Back to her gloomy cell the dame retir'd.
Close in her guileful hand she grasp'd each guest,
And bade them follow where her footsteps press'd.
The crowd aloof at Jason's mandate stay'd,
While he accompanied the Colchian maid. 810

Together

Book IV. APOLLONIUS RHODIUS. 245

Together thus they Circe's steps pursue,
Till her enchanting cave arose in view.
  Their visit's cause her troubled mind distress'd;
On downy seats she plac'd each princely guest.
They round her hearth sat motionless and mute: 815
(With plaintive suppliants such manners suit)
Her folded hands her blushing face conceal;
Deep in the ground he fix'd the murderous steel;
Nor dare they once, in equal sorrow drown'd,
Lift their dejected eyelids from the ground. 820
Circe beheld their guilt: she saw they fled
From vengeance hanging o'er the murderer's head.
The holy rites, approv'd of Jove, she pays:
(Jove, thus appeas'd, his hasty vengeance stays)
These rites from guilty stains the culprits clear, 825
Who lowly suppliant at her cell appear.
To expiate their crime in order due,
First to her shrine a sucking pig she drew,
Whose nipples from its birth distended stood:
Its neck she struck, and bath'd their hands in blood.
Next with libations meet and prayer she ply'd 831
Jove, who acquits the suppliant homicide.
Without her door a train of Naiads stand,
Administering whate'er her rites demand;

R 3   Within,

Within, the flames, that round the hearth arife, 835
Wafte, as fhe prays, the kneaded facrifice:
That thus the Furies' vengeful wrath might ceafe,
And Jove appeas'd difmifs them both in peace,
Whether they came to expiate the guilt
Of friends' or ftrangers' blood by treachery fpilt. 840
 Circe arofe, her myftic rites complete,
And plac'd the princes on a fplendid feat.
Near them fhe fat, and urg'd them to explain
Their plan and progrefs o'er the dangerous main:
Whence rofe the wifh to vifit Circe's ifle, 845
And thus beneath her roof converfe awhile.
For ftill on every thought the vifion prefs'd,
And its remembrance ftill difturb'd her reft.
Soon as the forcerefs faw Medea raife
From earth thofe eyes which fhot a beamy blaze, 850
Anxious fhe wifh'd to hear her native tongue,
Conjecturing from her features whence fhe fprung.
For all Sol's race are beauteous as their fire;
Their radiant eyes emit celeftial fire.
The willing maid complied with each demand, 855
And in the language of her native land
Her ftory told; each ftrange event declar'd,
What countries they had feen, what dangers fhar'd,
Her

Her sister's counsels how they sway'd her breast,
How with the sons of Phrixus she transgress'd; 860
How from her father fled, his threats disdain'd:
But still untold her brother's fate remain'd.
His fate th' enchantress knew; no arts could hide
The murderous deed: she pitied and reply'd:
 ' Ah! wretch, dire mischiefs thy return await. 865
' Hope not to shun thy father's vengeful hate;
' Resolv'd on right, he to the realms of Greece
' Will close pursue thee, nor his fury cease,
' Till he avenge the murder of his son:
' For deeds of blackest darkness hast thou done. 870
' But go, at once my kin and suppliant, free,
' Nor fear additional distress from me.
' Thy lover hence, far hence thyself remove,
' Who scorn'dst a father's for a vagrant's love.
' Here supplicate no more: my heart disclaims 875
' Thy guilty wanderings and sinister aims.'
 She spoke: the maid lamented; o'er her head
Her veil she cast, and many a tear she shed.
Her trembling hand the hero rais'd with speed,
And from the cave of Circe both recede. 880
 By watchful Iris taught, Saturnia knew
What time from Circe's cave they both withdrew.

To mark their steps commission'd Iris staid,
On whom these fresh injunctions Juno laid:
' Haste, Iris, now; thy pinions wide expand, 885
' And bear once more Saturnia's dread command.
' Go, Thetis rouze from ocean's dark retreat;
' Her potent aid my projects will complete.
' Spread then towards Vulcan's shores thy speedy
  wing,
' Where round his anvils ceaseless hammers ring. 890
' Bid him no more his boisterous bellows ply,
' Till heaven-built Argo sail securely by.
' Then to the Deity, whose sovereign sway
' Controls the winds, whom raging storms obey,
' Haste; and request that every rising gale ' 895
' Be hush'd, and silence o'er the seas prevail:
' That round the waves sereneft zephyrs play,
' Till Argo anchors in Phæacia's bay.'
 She said: and Iris, poiz'd on airy wings,
From the bright summit of Olympus springs: 900
Descends impetuous down th' Ægean deeps,
Where in his watery caverns Nereus sleeps.
To Thetis first repairs the winged maid;
Solicits and obtains her potent aid.
Vulcan she next in humble prayer address'd; 905
The God of fire complied with her request:

His

His bellows heave their windy fides no more,
Nor his fhrill anvils fhake the diftant fhore.
Her wants to Æolus fhe next difclos'd:
And while her wearied limbs fhe here repos'd, 910
Thetis from all her Naiad-train withdrew,
And from her Nereus to Olympus flew.
Juno with tranfport hail'd her fea-born gueft,
Whom near her throne fhe feated, and addrefs'd:
' O, hear my tale, bright Goddefs of the main: 915
' Thou know'ft my care for Jafon and his train;
' Thou know'ft how Juno's arm alone upheld,
' And through the jutting rocks their fhip impell'd;
' Around whofe fides fierce, fiery tempefts rave,
' And the huge crag is whiten'd by the wave.   920
' Now muft they fail near Scylla's awful height,
' And where the rock Charybdis forms a ftreight.
' Thee yet an infant in my arms I prefs'd,
' And more than all thy fifter-nymphs carefs'd.
' Revering me, the wife of fovereign Jove,   925
' Thou fcorn'dft the tenders of his lawlefs love.
' (For him a mortal beauty now inflames,
' And now he revels with celeftial dames.)
' And Jove, in vengeance for his flighted bed,
' Swore, not a Deity fhould Thetis wed.   930
' Nor

'Nor could the fervour of his love abate,
' Till Themis thus disclos'd the will of fate;
' That from thy womb in future times should spring,
' Superior to his sire, an infant-king.
' Dreading th' event, left in some future day   935
' This infant-king should claim celestial sway,
' Thee Jove abandon'd to secure his throne,
' And reign unrival'd ever and alone.
' But, lo! I gave, thy bridal bed to grace,
' A mortal husband worthy thy embrace;   940
' I made thee mother of a happy line,
' And to thy nuptials call'd the Powers divine.
' Myself, in honour to the godlike pair,
' Deign'd on that day the bridal torch to bear.
' Soon as thy son (believe the truths you hear)   945
' Shall in Elysium's blissful plains appear,
' Whom kindly now the fostering Naiads guard
' In Chiron's mansion, of thy milk debarr'd,
' In Hymen's silken chains the hero led,
' Must share the honours of Medea's bed.   950
' Oh! be a mother's tenderest care display'd,
' Succour thy Peleus, and thy daughter aid.
' Hath he transgrefs'd? thy rising wrath subdue;
' For Ate's dire effects th' immortals rue.

' Vulcan,

' Vulcan, I ween, obsequious to my will, 955
' His fires will stifle, and his bellows still;
' His boisterous waves will Æolus restrain,
' And zephyrs only fan the curling main,
' Till Argo anchors in Phæacia's bay.
' But shelves and stormy seas obstruct her way; 960
' These, these I dread: but, with thy train expert,
' Be thine the care these mischiefs to avert.
' Safe from Charybdis' gulf the vessel guide,
' Safe from loud Scylla's all-absorbing tide;
' Scylla, the terrour of Ausonia's shore, 965
' Whom Phorcuns to infernal Hecat bore,
' Cratæis nam'd. Oh! summon all thy pow'r,
' Lest her voracious jaws my chiefs devour.
' Hope's cheerly dawn if haply thou discern,
' Snatch from the watery grave the sinking stern.' 970
" If 'tis resolv'd," replies th' assenting queen,
" Tempests to curb, and oceans to serene,
" Fear not; but in my proffer'd aid confide:
" This arm shall convoy Argo o'er the tide.
" The surge subsiding shall confess my sway, 975
" While harmless zephyrs round the canvass play.
" Now must I traverse the wide fields of air,
" And to my sisters' crystal grots repair;
                            " Request

" Requeſt their aid, and haſten to the ſhores,
" Where anchor'd Argo unmoleſted moors : 980
" That each brave comrade, at the dawn of day,
" With heart elate may cleave the liquid way."
 She ſpoke, and through th' aërial regions ſped,
Then in the pools of ocean plung'd her head.
At Thetis' call the ſiſter Nereids came, 985
And flock'd obedient round their oozy dame.
Juno's commands ſhe bade the ſiſters heed,
And to th' Auſonian deep deſcend with ſpeed.
 Swifter than lightning, or than Phœbus' beams,
The Goddeſs darted thro' the yielding ſtreams; 990
Till, gliding ſmooth beſide the Tyrrhene ſtrand,
Her ſpeedy footſtep preſs'd th' Ææan land.
Along the winding beach the Mynians ſtray,
And while with quoits and darts their hours away.
Here Thetis ſingled from the gallant band 995
Peleus her ſpouſe, and preſs'd the hero's hand :
Unſeen by all the hoſt, his hand ſhe preſs'd ;
By all, ſave Peleus, whom ſhe thus addreſs'd :
 ' Loiter not here; but with returning light
' Unfurl your ſails, nor Juno's counſels ſlight. 1000
' Safe thro' th' Erratic rocks your ſhip to guide,
' Which frown tremendous o'er the toſſing tide,
            ' For

' For this the sea-green sisters join their force,
' And smooth through dangerous seas your destin'd
    course.
' My form, what time we urge the foaming keel, 1005
' By you not unobserv'd, to none reveal;
' Left, as before, your folly I chastise,
' And to more desperate heights my vengeance rise.'
    She said, and vanish'd to the deeps below.
The wondering chief was pierc'd with keenest woe.
For since the dame, with indignation fir'd,   1011
Had from her Peleus' hated bed retir'd,
Unseen till now she lurk'd: the strife begun
From this unweeting cause, her infant-son.
For, soon as night diffus'd its darkest shade,   1015
Her young Achilles o'er the flame she laid,
And, at return of day, with ceaseless toil
Applied to all his limbs ambrosial oil,
That youth might triumph o'er th' attacks of time,
Nor creeping age impair his vigorous prime.   1020
The father saw, as from his bed he rose,
Fierce, ambient flames his infant's limbs enclose;
And, as he gaz'd, his rueful cries confess'd
The boding sorrows of a parent's breast.
Fool! for his queen, who heard her lord deplore, 1025
Dash'd in a rage her infant on the floor.

Then

Then fleet as air, or like a dream of night,
She vanish'd sudden from his odious sight;
Plung'd in her fury down the whelming main,
Nor e'er emerg'd she from the waves again.   1030
For this he sorrow'd: but each sage command
Which Thetis gave, he told his gallant band.
They heard, and from their sports retir'd in haste;
Then shar'd, recumbent, in a short repast.
Sated, they catch the comforts of repose,   1035
Till, every toil renewing, morn arose.

   Soon as her radiant light illumin'd heav'n,
And to their wish were breezy zephyrs giv'n,
Quitting the land, they climb with nimble feet
The lofty decks, and reassume their seat.   1040
Each to his toil returns alert and bold:
They tear the griping anchor from its hold;
They hoist the yard, their bracing ropes unbind,
And give the flapping canvas to the wind.
Swift sails the ship: soon to th' expecting crew,   1045
Anthemoessa's isle arose in view.
The Syrens here, from Acheloüs sprung,
Allure the loitering sailors with their tongue,
Who, fastening to the beach the corded stay,
Neglect their voyage, and attend the lay.   1050

                                           What

Book IV. APOLLONIUS RHODIUS.

What time to Acheloüs' longing arms
The Mufe Terpfichore refign'd her charms,
Their mutual love thefe wily fongfters crown'd;
Who lur'd, in times remote, with tempting found
Ceres' fair daughter, and fallacious fhew   1055
A virgin-face, while wing'd like fowls they flew.
On a bright eminence the charmers ftand,
And watch the veffels as they tug to land.
Full many a mariner their fongs betray,
Who lifts and lingers till he pines away.   1060
As Argo fail'd they rais'd their tuneful tongue;
And here their halfers had the heroes hung,
But Thracian Orpheus wak'd his wonted fire,
And fung refponfive to his heavenly lyre;
That each refounding chord might pierce their ear,
And none the mufic of the Syrens hear.   1066
Yet ftill they fung: ftill brifkly, with the breeze,
The veffel tilted o'er the curling feas.
Butes alone became an eafy prey,
Who all enraptur'd liften'd to their lay.   1070
Erect, above the rowing chiefs, he ftood,
And frantic fprung into the faithlefs flood.
His helplefs hands he rais'd, the fhip to gain,
And, but for Venus' aid, had rais'd in vain:

She,

She, Eryx' honour'd queen, the wretch defcry'd, 1075
And fnatch'd him floundering from the foaming tide,
His kind protectrefs, as her courfe fhe bends
Where Lilybœum's ample cape extends.
This dire mifhap difhearten'd all the band,
Who row with vigour from the traiterous ftrand. 1080
   But other pefts, more fatal to their freight,
Threaten their progrefs to that dangerous ftreight,
Where Scylla's rock projects its wave-worn fide,
And where Charybdis' gulf abforbs the tide.
Dafh'd by the driven waves the Planctæ roar'd, 1085
From whofe cleft fummits flames fulphureous pour'd,
Thick, dufky clouds involve the darken'd fkies,
And hid are Phœbus' fplendours from their eyes.
Though Vulcan ceas'd from his affiduous toils,
The fires flafh thick, and fervid ocean boils.   1090
Here o'er the failing pine the nymphs prefide,
While Thetis' forceful hands the rudder guide.
As oft in fhoals the fportive dolphins throng,
Circling the veffel as fhe fails along,
Whofe playful gambols round the prow and ftern 1095
The much-delighted mariners difcern;
Round Argo thus the toiling nymphs attend,
And, led by Thetis, their affiftance lend.

O'erhanging

O'erhanging black th' rocks' bleak brow they see,
And gird their azure vestures to their knee. 1100
Now here, now there, as danger warns, they glide,
And stem mid' crushing crags the troubled tide.
Pendent on mountain-waves the veffel hung,
That pierc'd her folid planks, and foam'd the rocks
  among.
Above thefe rocks, here now the Nereids rife, 1105
And float on billows hid amidft the fkies ;
Defcending now to ocean's fecret bed,
They in his gulphy deeps conceal their head.

As when along the beach, fuccinét for play,
To tofs the flying ball the Nereids ftray, 1110
From hand to hand the fphere unerring flies,
Nor ever on the ground inglorious lies ;
The fifters thus, with coadjutant force,
High o'er the furge impel the veffel's courfe:
From fecret fhelves her wave-dafh'd fides they fhove,
Tho' fturdy billows ftrong againft them ftrove. 1115
On a tall fragment that o'erlook'd the flood,
His fhoulder refting on his hammer, ftood
The footy God: and from her ftarry fkies
Juno beheld the fcene with ftedfaft eyes. 1120
Her hand around Minerva's neck fhe threw ;
For much Saturnia trembled at the view.

S Long

Long as the vernal suns protract the light,
So long in Argo's cause the nymphs unite.
Propitious to their labours sprung the breeze,   1125
And the free vessel shot across the seas.
Trinacria's verdant meads they soon survey,
Where graze thy herds, illustrious God of day.
Juno's commands obey'd, the watery train,
Like diving mews, explore the deeps again.   1130
Coasting along, the bleating flocks they hear,
And herds loud bellowing strike their listening ear.
Sol's youngest daughter, Phaëthusa, leads
The bleating flocks along the dewy meads;
Propp'd on her silver crook the maid reclin'd: 1135
A stouter staff, with brazen ringlets join'd,
Lampetie takes; whose herds the heroes see
Slunk to the brook, or browsing on the lea.
Of sable hue no cattle you behold;
Milkwhite are all, and tipp'd their horns with gold.
They pass'd these meads by day; at day's decline   1141
They brush'd with pliant oars the yielding brine.
At length Aurora's all-reviving ray
Redden'd the waves, and shew their certain way.

 A fertile isle towers o'er th' Ionian tide,   1145
Ceraunia nam'd; the land two bays divide.

           Fame

Book IV. APOLLONIUS RHODIUS. 259

Fame says, (forgive me, Muse, while I unveil,
Reluctant too, a legendary tale;)
A sickle lies conceal'd within this land,
With which rash Saturn's mutilating hand, 1150
His father castrated: for Ceres' aid
Others assert this rural sickle made.
For Ceres once, with love of Macris fir'd,
To this fam'd isle, her favourite seat, retir'd.
The Titans here she taught her arms to wield, 1155
And crop the bearded harvest of the field.
This island hence, nurse of Phœacian swains,
Th' expressive name of Drepane obtains.
From mangled Uranus's blood they trace
The source inglorious of Phœacia's race. 1160
  Trinacria left, and numerous perils past,
Here heaven-protected Argo moors at last.
The heroes disembark'd Alcinoüs hails,
And at their festive sacrifice regales.
Mirth unremitted through the city runs, 1165
As though they welcom'd home their darling sons.
The godlike guests their social part sustain,
Joyous as though they press'd Hæmonia's plain:
But ere that distant plain delights their view,
The chiefs must buckle on their arms anew. 1170

S 2   For,

For, lo! those Colchians who adventurous stray'd
Through deeps unknown, and enter'd undismay'd
The dire Cyanean rocks, here throng the coast,
And wait th' arrival of the Grecian host.
The forfeit maid should Argo's crew refuse,   1175
War in each sad, disastrous shape ensues.
Arm'd and resolv'd they threaten instant fight,
And future fleets t' assert their monarch's right.
But king Alcinoüs interpos'd his aid,
And, ere they rush'd to fight, their wrath allay'd. 1180
Arete's knee the suppliant virgin press'd,
And thus th' associate band and queen address'd:
  ' O queen,' exclaim'd she, ' lend thy timely aid
' To save from Colchian hands a suffering maid.
' With ruffian rage to bear me hence they come, 1185
' And to my wrathful sire conduct me home.
' Thou know'st, if one, like me, of humankind,
' How prone to err is man's unstable mind.
' Deem me no slave to lust's usurping pow'r;
' Prudence forsook me in the needful hour.   1190
' Be witness, Sun, and thou, whose every rite
' Is wrapp'd, dire Hecate, in sable night,
' How I reluctant left my native home,
' And with rude foreigners abhor'd to roam.
                  2   ' Fear

' Fear wing'd my flight; and, having once tranfgrefs'd,
' To flee I judg'd my laft refource and beft.   1196
' Still have I liv'd, as with my father, chafte,
' My fpotlefs zone faft girded to my waift.
' Oh! may my tale, fair princefs, claim thy tears ;
' Oh! teach thy lord compaffion as he hears.   1200
' On thee may all th' immortal Gods beftow
' Beauty and life, exempt from age and woe ;
' Cities, that need no bold invaders dread,
' And a fair progeny to crown thy bed.'
In tears fhe fpoke: then to each gallant chief 1205
Told in thefe plaintive ftrains her tale of grief:
' Low at your feet, ye warriours, fuppliant view
' A princefs doom'd to wretchednefs for you.
' Yok'd were the bulls, and, defperate as they rofe,
' Crufh'd by my aid were hofts of giant-foes.   1210
' Yes, foon Hæmonia the rich prize will fee,
' And boaft of conquefts which fhe owes to me.
' My country I, my parents, palace left,
' To pine through life, of all its joys bereft ;
' But gave to you, a bafe, ungrateful train,   1215
' To fee your country and your friends again.
' Spoil'd of my beauty's bloom by fate fevere,
' In endlefs exile muft I languifh here.

S 3 ' Revere

' Revere your oaths ; Erynnis' vengeance dread,
' Who heaps her curses on the perjur'd head : 1220
' Dread heaven's sure wrath, if, to my sire restor'd,
' My shame or ruin wait his desperate word.
' No sheltering shrine, no fortress near, I fly
' To you alone, on your defence rely.
' Yet why on you ? who, merciless and mute, 1225
' Have heard my cries, nor seconded my suit ;
' Unmov'd have seen me lift my suppliant hand
' To the kind princess of this foreign land.
' Elate with hope the Golden Fleece to gain,
' Colchos oppos'd you, and her king in vain : 1230
' But fearful now the battle to renew,
' Ye dread detachments, nor will fight with few.'

She said ; and all, who heard her suppliant moan,
Cheer'd her sad heart, and check'd the rising groan.
Each gallant man his brandish'd spear display'd, 1235
And vow'd assistance to the suffering maid,
Shook his drawn sword, a prelude to the fight,
Resolv'd on vengeance, and resolv'd on right.

Night now dispers'd the faint remains of day,
And all the slumbering world confess'd its sway : 1240
Grateful its gloom to men with toils oppress'd ;
Grateful to all but her, with sleep unbless'd.

She,

She, haplefs fair, her painful vigils kept;
Revolving ftill her griefs, fhe watch'd and wept.
 As at the diftaff toils th' induftrious dame, 1245
Whofe frequent tears her orphan children claim.
All night fhe toils, while clinging round they ftand,
Wail their loft fire, and his return demand.
Swift down her cheek defcends the filent tear:
So hard the lot fate deftines her to bear! 1250
Like her's Medea's copious tears defcend,
Such agonizing griefs her tortur'd bofom rend.
The royal pair retir'd with wonted ftate
From the throng'd city to their palace-gate.
On their foft couch reclin'd, at evening's clofe, 1255
Long conference held they on Medea's woes.
Thus to Alcinöus the queen exprefs'd
The kind fuggeftions of her pitying breaft:
 ' Oh! may the Minyans, prince, thy favours fhare;
' Oh! fhield from Colchian foes an injur'd fair, 1260
' Not diftant far Hæmonia's plains extend,
' And near our ifland Argos' frontiers end,
' But far remote Æeta reigns; his name
' Unknown to us, or faintly known by fame.
' She, in whofe forrows now I bear a part, 1265
' Hath, to redrefs them, open'd all my heart,
    S 4   ' Let

' Let no rude Colchian bear her hence away,
' To her fire's vengeance a devoted prey.
' Her error this: the fiery bulls to quell,
' Fond and officious she prepar'd the spell. 1270
' Augmenting then (as oft offenders will)
' Her firſt with future errors, ill with ill,
' Far from her native home, impreſs'd with dread,
' Far from her angry fire the damſel fled.
' But bound is Jaſon by ſtrong ties, ſays fame, 1275
' To wed the wanderer, and retrieve from ſhame.
' Urge him not then, with many an added threat,
' His faith to violate, his oaths forget;
' Nor ſtimulate Æeta's wrath to riſe:
' Their daughters parents rigorouſly chaſtiſe. 1280
' Thus Pyƈteus, with parental zeal o'ercome,
' Compell'd his child Antiope to roam.
' Thus Danaë, by her wrathful fire ſecur'd,
' Toſs'd in the troubled deep diſtreſs endur'd.
' Nor long ſince Echetus, a wretch accurs'd, 1285
' With brazen pins his daughter's eye-balls pierc'd:
' Pent in a dungeon's awful gloom ſhe pin'd,
' Doom'd by her ſavage fire obdurate braſs to grind.'
  She ſaid: ſoft pity touch'd the ſovereign's breaſt,
Who thus his ſupplicating queen addreſs'd: 1290

" In

"In me, O queen, these heroes should descry,
" For the fair sufferer's sake, a firm ally;
" Soon should my arms the Colchian foes remove,
" But I revere the just decrees of Jove.
" Unsafe I deem Æeta to deride,   1295
" Who sways the sceptre with a monarch's pride;
" Able, though distant, if averse from peace,
" To scatter discord through the realms of Greece.
" Hear my proposal then; which you, I trust,
" And all who hear it, will applaud as just: 1300
" If still a virgin's spotless name she bear,
" Safe to her sire's domains conduct the fair:
" But if one bed the wedded pair contain,
" I will not sever Hymen's silken chain.
" Forbid it, heaven! that I in wrath expose   1305
" Her sinless offspring to insulting foes."
  He said, and sunk to rest: his sage resolves
Anxious and oft the wakeful queen revolves.
She rose: their princess' footstep heard, arise
Her female train, and each her wants supplies. 1310
  ' Go,' to her page apart Arete said,
' Bid Æson's valiant son the virgin wed.
' Bid him no more Alcinoüs' ears assail
' With long entreaties and a well-known tale.

            ' Himself,

' Himself, unask'd, his advocate will go, 1315
' And tender these conditions to the foe:
' If still the fair a spotless maid remain,
' Soon shall she view her father's courts again;
' But, if a matron's honour'd name she bear,
' He will not separate the wedded pair.' 1320
  She said: her herald, eager to convey
The royal message, sped without delay;
To Æson's son he told Arete's word,
And the kind counsels of her sovereign lord.
Hard by their ship, in glistering arms array'd, 1325
Deep in the port of Hyllicus embay'd,
He spies the chiefs, his embassy repeats,
And every gallant heart with transport beats.
They crown the goblets to the Powers divine,
And drag th' accustom'd victims to the shrine: 1330
Then for the pensive fair officious spread
In a sequester'd grot the bridal bed.
Hither, in days of yore, fair Macris came,
Daughter of Aristæus, honour'd name!
He taught mankind the virtues and the use 1335
Of the bee's labours, and the olive's juice.
For, know, when Hermes infant-Bacchus bore,
Snatch'd from the flames, to fair Eubœa's shore,

Macris

Macris embrac'd him with a mother's love,
And there, awhile, she nurs'd the seed of Jove, 1340
And there with honey fed; till Juno's spite
Far from Eubœa's isle compell'd her flight.
At length, of this Phœacian grot possess'd,
She with vast opulence the natives bless'd.

To deck with honours due the bridal bed, 1345
Around it wide the Golden Fleece was spread.
With sweetest flowers, that deck or dale or hill,
Th' assiduous nymphs their snowy bosoms fill.
The Golden Fleece emits so bright a ray,
They shone all radiant as the star of day, 1350
Inspiring love: the prize though strong desire
Prompts them to touch, with reverence they retire.
These are the daughters of the Ægeän flood,
Those, Meletæum, haunt thy lofty wood.
From groves, from streams, at Juno's call they ran,
To grace the nuptials of this godlike man. 1356
The sacred grot, recorded still by fame,
Bears to this day Medea's honour'd name:
For here the nymphs, their veils around them spread,
To nuptial joys the happy lovers led: 1360
And every chief, to guard the blissful spot,
Clad in bright armour, stood before the grot,

3 Left

Left hostile troops, with rude tumultuous noise,
Should force an entrance, and distract their joys.
Thus station'd, they protect the hallow'd ground, 1365
Their festive brows with leafy chaplets crown'd.
As Orpheus struck his tuneful lyre, they sung,
And Hymeneals round the grotto rung.
But in Alcinoüs' court the fair to wed,
O'er Jason's anxious mind disquiet spread: 1370
Full oft he wish'd Iolcos' coast to gain,
And wed the virgin in his sire's domain;
Such too Medea's wish: but fate severe
Forc'd him to celebrate his nuptials here.
For pleasure unalloy'd we look in vain; 1375
Pleasure to suffering man is mix'd with pain.
Whether the Colchian foe had scorn'd or clos'd
With the just terms Phœacia's prince propos'd,
Of this they doubted: mid' the mirthful scene
Fears, which these doubts suggested, intervene. 1380
  Aurora now her orient beams display'd,
And pierc'd the sullen night's surrounding shade.
The circling shores and dew-bespangled ground
Reflect her rays: the streets with noise resound.
The citizens and Colchians, who possess'd 1385
The distant coast, awake from balmy rest.

Impatient

Impatient now his purpofe to difclofe,
To plead Medea's caufe the monarch rofe:
His hand fuftain'd a fceptre's maffy gold,
Which kings, deciding right, were wont to hold. 1390
Around their prince, in gliftering arms array'd,
Phœacia's peers a feemly pomp difplay'd.
Eager on each adventurous chief to gaze,
A female troop beyond the city ftrays.
In feftive bands the diftant fwains unite: 1395
(For Juno had divulg'd the nuptial rite)
One from his fold a ram felected brought,
An heifer one, to feel the yoke untaught;
Flagons of wine fome for libation bear:
The fmoke of victims blacken'd all the air. 1400
As women wont, the female train felect
Their coftly veils, with gay embroidery deck'd:
Such golden toys, fuch trinkets they provide,
As on a nuptial day adorn the bride.
The comely chiefs their admiration won; 1405
But more than all Æager's tuneful fon,
As lightly to the lyre's melodious found
Tripp'd the brifk dancer o'er the meafur'd ground.
In concert full the virgin-choir prolong
The happy day with Hymeneal fong. 1410
Here

Here a fair band, collected in a ring,
Praises to thee, auspicious Juno, sing.
By thee inspir'd, disclos'd the royal dame
The friendly terms her prince was pleas'd to name.
Nor are the terms Alcinoüs nam'd disown'd: 1415
(For now their faithful loves hath Hymen crown'd)
True to his oath, he heard with fix'd disdain
And deem'd Æeta's vengeful fury vain.

Soon as the Colchians saw their purpose cross'd,
Defeated all their schemes, their labour lost; 1420
That to the sovereign's terms they must accede,
Or quit his ports, and sail away with speed;
Dreading the monarch's wrath, submiss they try
To win his friendship, and commence ally.
Settling at last, long time the Colchian host 1425
Dwelt with the natives on Phœacia's coast:
Till Bacchus' hated race from Corinth fled,
Exil'd these Colchians, and the isle o'erspread.
They sought the neighbouring shores: in times to come
Their sons emigrating explor'd a home, 1430
Where far and wide extends th' Illyric coast,
And the Ceraunian hills in clouds are lost.
But these events, which now my Muse engage,
Were late fulfill'd in some succeeding age.

Yet

Yet ftill, in Phœbus' fane, uninjur'd ftand   1435
The altars rais'd by fair Medea's hand:
Some to the fates are pil'd with victims due,
Some to the nymphs their annual rites renew.
Towards the parting train the royal pair
Their generous love by coftly gifts declare.   1440
Twelve fair Phœacians, at the queen's command,
Conduct Medea to the fea-beat ftrand.

On the feventh morn with gently-breathing gales
Propitious Jove expanded Argo's fails;
Argo, decreed frefh dangers to fuftain,   1445
Ere Greece beholds her gallant fons again.
Ambracia's bay had open'd to their view,
Befide Curetes' land the galley flew,
The cluftering ifles, Echidanes, they pafs'd,
And Pelops' diftant realm beheld at laft.   1450
Nine tedious nights and days the veffel fweeps
The troubled furface of the Libyan deeps;
Till, driven by rapid tides and ftorms aftray,
She near the Syrtes' quickfands plough'd her way:
Whirl'd in whofe gulphy pools, their deftin'd grave,
Nor fails nor oars the finking galleys fave.   1456
Burft from its black abyfs, the boiling flood
Up-heaves its fhaggy weeds, involv'd in fhelves of mud.

With

With the far-spreading spray the sands arise;
But nought discern they here that creeps or flies. 1460
The tide (which now retreats into the main,
And now returns upon the beach again;)
Far o'er the shore, impell'd with fury, shew
All Argo's slimy keel expos'd to view.
They disembark, and gaze with aching eyes 1465
On ridgy mountains loft amid the skies.
No grateful streams, no beaten paths appear,
No rural cot discern they, far or near;
A death-like silence reign'd around: dismay'd
His comrade each interrogating said: 1470

' What country this? on what bleak clime at last
' Have the rude tempests heaven-built Argo cast?
' Oh! had we dar'd, devoid of vulgar fear,
' Our course undaunted through those fragments steer,
' Like heroes then (though Jove success deny'd) 1475
' We in the bold attempt had bravely died.
' What can our skill devise? the least delay
' Is fatal here; the winds forbid our stay.
' How bleak and barren is the coast we tread!
' And what a desert waste is wide around us spread!'
He said; and, joining in the loud lament, 1481
Ancæus thus foreboded the event:

' What

Book IV. APOLLONIUS RHODIUS. 273

' What dire mishaps our gallant host befall!
' Thus by stern fate's decree we perish all!
' What woes await us, on this desert cast, 1485.
' If from the land awakes the furious blast!
' For slimy seas my sight far off commands,
' And whitening billows bursting o'er the sands.
' And dreadfully had Argo's yawning sides,
' Remote from shore, receiv'd the gushing tides, 1490
' Had not the surge, which lifted her to heav'n,
' Full on the pebbly beach the vessel driv'n.
' But now the tide retiring quits the strand,
' And waves unfaithful skim the levell'd sand.
' Our projects baffled, and hope's cheerly dawn 1495
' From our expecting sight thus soon withdrawn,
' Let other hands the pilot's art display,
' And they who fear not danger steer the way.
' But our joint labours Jove decrees to foil,
' Nor will our native home reward our toil.' 1500
He said; and all, renown'd for naval skill,
Close with his words, and wait th' impending ill.
From every heart the vital motion fled,
O'er every face a deadly paleness spread.
As when from street to street, in wild dismay, 1505
Affrighted mortals, like pale spectres, stray;

T Expecting

Expecting wars, or plagues, or burſting rains,
That deluge all the harveſt of the plains:
Or, as when ſtatues drops of blood diſtil,
And fancied bellowings the temples fill;   1510
The noon-day ſun eclips'd involves in night
Th' aſtoniſh'd world, and ſtars emit their light:
Thus on the beach they ſtalk'd, a heartleſs clan!
Like ſweating ſtatues, or like ſpectres wan.
His feeble arm each round his comrade caſt,   1515
Then ſunk into the ſand to breathe his laſt,
Reſolv'd, as now the ſtar of Heſper roſe,
To ſhare the ſolace of united woes.
Some here, ſome there ſelect their clay-cold bed,
And round their ſhivering limbs their garments ſpread:
Reſign'd to death, in midnight's ſullen ſhade   1521
And at mid-day, here languiſhing they laid.
Remote, Medea's fair attendants moan,
Cling round their queen, and groan return for groan.
    As when a neſt, ſurcharg'd with callow young,   1525
Falls from the lofty cliff to which it clung,
Th' unfeather'd brood by ſhrilleſt cries atteſt
Their far-flown mother, and their ruin'd neſt:
As on the banks Pactolus' ſtreams bedew,
Melodious ſwans their dying notes renew;   1530

                                                        The

The rivers, gliding the rich vales among,
Bear on their filver ftreams the foothing fong:
Thus they, their golden locks befmear'd with gore,
All night in plaintive elegies deplore.
Their toils yet incomplete, the godlike band   1535
Had now ignobly perifh'd on the fand,
But the bold heroines, who guard the coaft,
Beheld with pitying eye the drooping hoft:
Thofe nymphs, who, when in gliftering arms array'd,
Rufh'd from the Thunderer's brain the martial maid,
In needful hour their kind affiftance gave,   1541
And cleans'd her infant-limbs in Triton's wave.

'Twas noon: o'er Libya's fands the God of day
Darted the fplendouts of his fierceft ray.
Full before Jafon ftood the nymphs confefs'd,   1545
And gently from his head withdrew the veft.
Sudden he ftarts, imprefs'd with filent dread,
And from his fair protectors turns his head.
They in compaffion's mild addrefs began
To free from terrours vain the hopelefs man: 1550
' Why griev'ft thou thus? Oh! bid thy forrows
    ceafe:
' We know thy coming's caufe, the Golden Fleece.
' We know the various toils by land you bore;
' How tofs'd on ocean, how diftrefs'd on fhore.

' Terreftrial

' Terreſtrial Powers, for acts of friendſhip known, 1555
' We make the ſhepherd's rural cares our own.
' We, Libya's daughters and avengers, boaſt
' Our ſway extended o'er the Libyan coaſt.
' Ariſe, nor ſink beneath thy ſorrow's weight;
' But rouze thy fellows from their drooping ſtate. 1560
' When Amphitrite with officious ſpeed
' Unreins from Neptune's car the fiery ſteed,
' Thy mother then with duteous care repay,
' Whoſe womb hath borne thee many a toilſome day.
' Diſcharge this duty, and reſail to Greece, 1565
' Safe and triumphant with the Golden Fleece.'

They ſpoke, and vaniſh'd: from his ſandy bed
Jaſon aroſe, and looking round he ſaid;
' Ye godlike Powers, thé deſert plains who rove,
' Ye fair, who tend the flocks, propitious prove. 1570
' Thoſe dark myſterious truths your tongues foretold,
' I go, if haply can my friends unfold.
' Conven'd, may they ſome prudent ſcheme deviſe,
' For in th' advice of numbers ſafety lies.'

He ſaid: and, wading thro' the driven ſand, 1575
Rouz'd with loud voice the ſad, deſponding band.
Thus, while the lion his loſt mate explores,
The foreſts ring, earth trembles as he roars:

Herdſmen

Herdsmen and herds, o'erwhelm'd with equal fear,
All mute and trembling deem destruction near. 1580
But grateful to the host was Jason's call;
No fears it cherish'd, but gave hope to all.
Yet with dejected looks the heroes meet.
Beside the female train to each his seat
He, near the shore, assign'd; in order due 1585
His wondrous tale relates, and cheers the pensive crew:

' Attend, my friends: three virgin-forms, who claim
' From heaven their race, to sooth my sorrows came.
' Their shoulders round were shaggy goat-skins cast,
' Which, low descending, girt their slender waist. 1590
' High o'er my head they stood; with gentle hand
' My vesture rais'd, and gave this dread command:
' That I with speed my piteous bed forsake,
' And, risen, haste my comrades to awake.
' That mindful we our mother's cares repay, 1595
' Whose womb sustain'd us many a toilsome day,
' When Amphitrite with officious speed
' Unreins from Neptune's car the fiery steed.
' Long have I sought this wonder to explain,
' And, still revolving, I revolve in vain. 1600

T 3 ' In

'In the bold name of heroines they boaſt,
'Daughters and guardians they of Libya's coaſt.
'Known to theſe nymphs are all the toils we bore
'On the rough ocean, and the faithleſs ſhore.
'Nor ſtaid they long; but, ſudden, from my view 1605
'Their radiant forms an ambient cloud withdrew.'
He ſaid: on every face ſat boding fears;
When, lo! a portent, greater far, appears.
Fierce from the foamy deep, of wondrous ſize,
Springs an huge horſe; his mane expanded flies. 1610
From his ſtrong ſides he ſhakes th' adherent ſpray,
Then towards the coaſt directs his rapid way.
Skill'd in whate'er this prodigy portends,
With pleaſure Peleus thus conſoles his friends:
  'Now by his conſort's hand releas'd I ſee 1615
'The car of Neptune, and his horſes free.
'A mother's name (or I predict in vain)
'Argo may boaſt; ſhe feels a mother's pain.
'Her pregnant womb a troop of heroes bears,
'And endleſs perils for their ſafety ſhares. 1620
'Come, let us now our boaſted ſtrength diſplay,
'And on our ſhoulders bear our ſhip away.
'Steer we through depths of ſand our dangerous courſe,
'Led by the ſteps of this portentous horſe.

'His

'His steps reluctant press the dusty plain, 1625
'But rapid bear him to his kindred main;
'Thither attend his flight.' Thus spoke the seer:
His pleasing counsels gratified their ear.
    This wondrous tale the tuneful Nine recite,
And as the Muses dictate must I write. 1630
This have I heard, and this as truth proclaim,
That you, O princely peers, of deathless fame,
By the joint efforts of united hands,
Twelve days and nights, through Libya's burning
    sands,
High on your shoulders rais'd the vessel's weight, 1635
All that its womb contain'd, a mighty freight!
What woes o'ertook them, and what toils befell,
No verse can celebrate, no tongue can tell.
Such brave exploits proclaim'd their godlike line,
For, as their lineage, were their deeds, divine. 1640
But when Tritonis' lake the chiefs attain,
They eas'd their shoulders, and embark'd again.
Doom'd to acuter griefs they now are curs'd
With all the miseries of burning thirst;
Like dogs they run its fury to assuage, 1645
And at a fountain's head suppress its rage.
Nor wander'd they in vain; but soon explor'd
The sacred spot with golden apples stor'd,

T 4

In Atlas' realm: the ferpent's wakeful eyes
Watch'd, till but yefterday, the golden prize. 1650
The fair Hefperides with kind furvey
Tended the ferpent as they tun'd their lay.
But, lo! the monfter, by Alcides flain,
Beneath a branching pear-tree prefs'd the plain.
His tail ftill vibrates, though his ghaftly head 1655
And fpine immenfe lie motionlefs and dead.
Flies in thick fwarms his gory fides furround,
Drink his black blood, and dry the dripping wound,
Made by the darts, whofe poifon'd tips detain
The deadly venom of the Hydra flain. 1660
As Ladon's fate the penfive maids deplore,
Their hands they wrung, their golden locks they tore;
But, fudden, as the heroes haften'd near,
They to the duft defcend, and difappear.
Struck with the prodigy his eyes furvey'd, 1665
Thus to the nymphs obfervant Orpheus pray'd:

' Ye Goddeffes, with blooming beauty blefs'd,
' Look with benevolence on men diftrefs'd.
' Whether ye grace the fplendid courts of Jove,
' Or on this humbler earth aufpicious move; 1670
' Whether to flowery paftures ye repair,
' And the lov'd name of fhepherdeffes bear;

' Illuftrious

' Illuftrious nymphs, from Ocean fprung, arife,
' Blefs with a recent view our longing eyes.
' Bid from the thirfty foil a torrent burft,   1675
' Or open fome hard rock to flake our thirft.
' Should we again our tatter'd fails expand,
' And greet at laft the dear Achaian land,
' Grateful we then thefe favours will repay,
' And choiceft offerings on your altars lay: 1680
' No Goddefs, who frequents the courts of Jove,
' Shall greater honour fhare, or greater love.'
    Thus Orpheus pray'd, with feeble voice and low:
The liftening nymphs commiferate their woe.
Firft tender grafs they bade the foil difclofe;   1685
Then high above it verdant branches rofe.
Erect and ftrong, the fpreading boughs difplay'd
Wide o'er the barren foil an ample fhade.
A poplar's trunk fair Hefpera receives,
And in a weeping willow Ægle grieves.   1690
But Erytheïs in an elm remains:
Each in her tree her proper fhape retains;
Stupendous fight! firft Ægle filence broke,
And kindly thus the fuppliant band befpoke:
    ' Hither fome lawlefs plunderer came of late, 1695
' Who will reverfe the colour of your fate.
                                        ' Yon

' Yon beast he slew, for whom we sorrow now,
' And tore the golden apples from their bough.
' But yesterday the desperate giant came;
' From his black eye-brows flash'd the livid flame:
' A lion's shaggy skin, besmear'd with gore,   1701
' Wide o'er his shoulders spread, the monster wore.
' On his stout staff his fearless step rely'd,
' And by his deadly dart the serpent died.
' He, like a sturdy traveller, stalk'd along,   1705
' Seeking some fount to cool his fiery tongue.
' With eager haste he trod the dusty plain,
' And still for water look'd, but look'd in vain.
' To this tall rock, hard by Tritonis' lake,
' Some God conducted him, his thirst to slake. 1710
' Struck by his heel, its deep foundations shook,
' And from the yawning clefts a torrent broke.
' Prone on the ground the limpid streams he swills,
' And, groveling like a beast, his belly fills.'

Elated with the tale, they speed their course, 1715
To find, as Ægle told, the fountain's source.

As when assembled ants with joint essay
Strive in some chink their lifted grain to lay:
Or as when flies some liquid sweet explore,
They hang in clusters round the honied store; 1720

Like

Like them the Mynians: such their numbers seem,
And such their haste to gather round the stream.
Conjecturing thus some grateful hero said,
As from the rill refresh'd he rais'd his head:
' Ye Gods! though absent, great Alcides gives   1725
' These limpid streams; by him each hero lives.
' Come, haste we now the country to explore,
' And the lost wanderer to our host restore.'
Instant to council rose th' associate band,
Selecting heroes to explore the land.   1730
For nightly winds disperfing o'er the plains
The light, loose sands, no step impress'd remains.
Boreas' fleet sons, who wing their airy flight,
Sagacious Lynceus bless'd with keenest sight,
Euphemus swift of foot, and Cantheus speed: 1735
Him his brave spirit urg'd and heaven decreed
To ask Alcides, on what fatal coast
He left his comrade, Polyphemus lost.
When this bold chief had rear'd on Mysian ground,
And fenc'd with circling walls a city round,   1740
Wide o'er the country, Argo's fate to learn,
He roam'd, with Argo anxious to return.
Scarce had his feet Calybian frontiers press'd,
Ere fate consign'd him to eternal rest.

Along

Along the beach, with stately poplars spread, 1745
They rear'd a tomb in honour of the dead.
But Lynceus deems, that, o'er the distant lands
His sight the long-lost Hercules commands.
Thus sees the clown, or thinks he can descry
The new moon breaking through a cloudy sky. 1750
Back to his comrades hastes the joyous chief,
Precludes their further search, and gives their mind
  relief.
Euphemus soon, and Boreas' sons, his friends,
Whose search in empty expectation ends,
Rejoin'd the host: but thee, brave Canthus, slain 1755
Stern fate foredoom'd to press the Libyan plain.
To feast his comrades with the grateful prey,
He forc'd through scatter'd flocks his desperate way.
Sudden, his flock to guard, the shepherd flew,
And with a rock's huge fragment Canthus slew. 1760
This sturdy villager, Caphaurus nam'd,
His lofty lineage from Apollo claim'd,
And Acacallis: conscious of his might,
He fear'd no rival, nor declin'd the fight.
Minos, her sire, to Libya's coast remov'd 1765
Fair Acacallis, by the God belov'd.
To Phœbus here a hopeful son she gave,
Amphithemis or Garamans the brave.

Thy

Thy love, Amphithemis, Tritonis crown'd,
And grac'd thy bed with Nafamon renown'd,   1770
And bold Caphaurus; whofe decifive blow
Tranfmitted Canthus to the fhades below.
The bloody deed divulg'd to all the hoft,
Not long his conqueft could Caphaurus boaft.
They to its fepulchre the corfe convey,   1775
Weeping; and make the fhepherd's flocks their prey.
   To Pluto's realms prophetic Mopfus fled,
And join'd, on that fad day, the mighty dead.
With fate's decrees muft mortal man comply,
And the wife feer, in fpite of prefcience, die.   1780
For, fhelter'd from the fierce meridian ray,
Beneath a fandy bank a ferpent lay.
Innoxious till incens'd, he ne'er annoy'd,
But ftrove th' affrighted traveller to avoid.
But all, whome'er the foodful earth contains,   1785
Who feel his darted venom in their veins,
Nor long, nor diftant deem the dreary road,
That leads direct to Pluto's dark abode.
His fangs infix'd when once the wretches feel,
In vain would medicine's God attempt to heal.   1790
For when brave Perfeus (this her godlike fon
His mother oftener nam'd Eurymedon)
                                            O'er

O'er Libya flew, the Gorgon's head to bring,
Fresh-slain and dripping, to th' expecting king,
From every drop, that dyed the soil with blood, 1795
A serpent sprung, and thus encreas'd the brood.
The monster's spiry tail rash Mopsus press'd
With his unheeding foot: his tortur'd breast
Upward he turn'd, and writh'd his spires around,
Then with his venom'd fang infix'd a deadly wound.
Medea trembled and her female train: 1801
Fearless he bathes the wound, nor heeds the pain.
But now, lost wretch! each sense is clos'd and dead,
And o'er his sinking eyes death's gloomy shade is
 spread.
Prone to the dust he falls: his cold remains 1805
Press with unwieldy weight the desert plains.
His faithful friends, and Jason with the rest,
Weep o'er the corse, with heart-felt grief impress'd.
His flesh all putrid from the taint within,
And hanging round him loose his flabby skin, 1810
The burning sun unable long to bear,
His busy comrades, with officious care,
Deep in the soil conceal their delving spade,
And soon a decent sepulchre was made.
Men, matrons, all, as round the grave they flock, 1815
Lamenting loud select the sacred lock:

His

His corfe the bright-arm'd heroes thrice furround,
And raife in feemly form the hallow'd mound,
Then haften to their fhip: the fouthern breeze
Curl'd, as it blew, the furface of the feas.   1820
   In fad fufpenfe, ftill wifhing to forfake,
And crofs with favouring gales Tritonis' lake,
They loiter long, and wafte the ufeful day
In idle conteft and in vain delay.
   A ferpent thus, long fcorch'd with fummer's heat,
Winds to fome fecret chink, his cool retreat.   1826
Enrag'd he hiffes, rears his creft on high,
And furious darts his fire-emitting eye,
Till haply he the wifh'd-for chink pervade,
And in its cool recefs fecure a fhade.   1830
Uncertain thus, the fhip explor'd in vain
The lake's wide mouth that open'd to the main.
With pious care, as Orpheus gives command,
They place Apollo's tripod on the ftrand;
That thofe aufpicious Powers the coaft who guard, 1835
Pleas'd with th' oblation, may their toils reward.
Clad like a youth, before them ftood confefs'd
The mighty Triton: in his hands he prefs'd
The gather'd foil; this amicable fign
He to the heroes held, and fpoke benign: 1840

' The

' The hofpitable pledge my hand extends,
' The beft I now can give, accept, my friends.
' Would you o'er ocean's paths your courfe difcern,
' And learn the tracks, which ftrangers wifh to learn,
' Hear: from my fire, the monarch of the main, 1845
' I boaft my fcience; o'er thefe feas I reign.
' Perchance ev'n you, though diftant far you came,
' May recognife Eurypylus's name,
' In Libya born.' He faid: Euphemus took
The proffer'd foil, and thus refponfive fpoke, 1850
" If fuch thy knowledge, friendly chief, explain
" Where Atthis lies, where rolls the Cretan main.
" Reluctant fail'd we towards the Libyan coaft,
" By angry heaven and adverfe tempefts toft:
" By land, with Argo o'er our fhoulders caft, 1855
" We toil'd, and launch'd her in this lake at laft.
" Nor can we yet our certain courfe devife,
" Where full in profpect Pelops' realms will rife."
He faid: his hand out-ftretching, Triton fhew
The lake's wide mouth, and fea expos'd to view. 1860
' Where the lake blackens, and its waters fleep,
' Expect,' he cries, ' a paffage to the deep.
' Obferve the cliffs high towering on each fide,
' And through the ftreight they form your veffel
  guide.

          ' There,

' There, above Crete, where, mingling with the skies,
' Yon ocean spreads, the land of Pelops lies.   1866
' When to the right th' expanded lake ye leave,
' And the safe seas your mighty freight receive,
' Still cautious coast along the winding strand,
' Till you the cape's projecting sides command : 1870
' Your course, that cape once doubled, safe pursue,
' Your ship uninjur'd, and undaunted you.
' Thus gladden'd go; nor let your vigorous arms
' Droop with fatigue, and shake with vain alarms.'
   Heartening he spoke: the decks they re-ascend, 1875
And, rowing brisk, to cross the lake contend.
The proffer'd tripod friendly Triton takes,
And hides his head beneath the dimpling lakes.
Thus with the costly prize the God withdrew,
Instant invisible to mortal view.   1880
Inspir'd with joy, that some superior guest
Had comfort given them, and with counsel bless'd,
The choicest sheep they bade their leader slay,
And to the Power benign due honours pay.
He to the galley's poop with speed convey'd   1885
The choicest sheep, and, as he offer'd, pray'd:
   ' Dread Deity, who late conspicuous stood
' On the clear margin of this rolling flood,
               U   ' Whether

' Whether great Triton's name delight thine ear,
' Triton, whom all the watery Gods revere; 1890
' Or ocean's daughters, as they found thy fame,
' Thee mighty Nereus, or thee Phorcuns name,
' Be bounteous ſtill: bid all our labours ceaſe,
' And reinſtate us in our native Greece.'
 Thus pray'd the chief, as on the poop he ſtood, 1895
And ſunk the ſlaughter'd victim in the flood.
His head above the billows Triton rear'd,
And in his proper ſhape the God appear'd.
 As when, intent his fiery ſteed to train,
The horſeman leads him to the duſty plain, 1900
His floating mane firm twiſted in his hand,
He runs, yet holds him ſubject to command:
Superb he paces, by his maſter led,
Curvetting ſtill, and toſſing high his head.
His bits, all white with gather'd foam around, 1905
Craunch'd by his reſtleſs jaw, aloud reſound:
Thus Triton's hands the veſſel's head ſuſtain,
And ſafely guide her to the ſeas again.
His every limb, down to his ſwelling loin,
Proclaims his likeneſs to the Powers divine. 1910
Below his loin his tapering tail extends;
Arch'd like a whale's on either ſide it bends.

5   Two

Two pointed fins, projecting from his side,
Cleave, as he scuds along th' opposing tide.
Acute and tapering, these indented thorns   1915
A semblance bear to Phœbe's budding horns.
His arm conducts her, till, from danger free,
She rides imbosom'd in the open sea.
This prodigy the shouting warriours saw,
Imprefs'd at once with gratitude and awe.   1920
Here shatter'd ships Argous' port receives,
Here tokens of her voyage Argo leaves:
To Triton here, high-towering o'er the strand,
And here to Neptune stately altars stand.
For here they linger'd out one useless day;   1925
But with fresh breezes sail'd, at morn, away.
Far to the right they leave the desert land,
And the stretch'd canvass to the winds expand.
Gaining mid ocean with returning light,
The doubled cape diminish'd from their sight.   1930
The zephyrs ceasing, rose the southern gale,
And cheer'd the shouting heroes as they sail.
  * The evening-star now lifts, as day-light fades,
  * His golden circlet in the deepening shades;

☞ The Lines thus marked * are Broome's, who has translated the story of Talus; not without several omissions, which are here supplied.

* Stretch'd

* Stretch'd at his eafe the weary labourer fhares 1935
* A fweet forgetfulnefs of human cares:
* At once in filence fleep the finking gales,
* The maft they drop, and furl the flagging fails;
* All night, all day, they ply their bending oars
* Towards Carpathus, and reach the rocky fhores; 1940
* Thence Crete they view, emerging from the main,
* The queen of ifles; but Crete they view in vain.
* There Tagus mountains hurls with all their woods;
* Whole feas roll back, and tofling fwell in floods.
* Amaz'd the towering monfter they furvey, 1945
* And trembling view the interdicted bay.
* His birth he drew from giants fprung from oak,
* Or the hard entrails of the ftubborn rock:
* Fierce guard of Crete! who thrice each year explores
* The trembling ifle, and ftrides from fhores to fhores,
* A form of living brafs! one part beneath 1951
* Alone he bears, a part to let in death,
* Where o'er the ankle fwells the turgid vein,
* Soft to the ftroke, and fenfible of pain.*
Pining with want, and funk in deep difmay, 1955
From Crete far diftant had they fail'd away,
But the fair forcerefs their fpeed reprefs'd,
And thus the crew difconfolate addrefs'd:

* Attend.

Book IV. APOLLONIUS RHODIUS. 293

' Attend. This monster, ribb'd with brass around,
' My art, I ween, will level to the ground. 1960
' Whate'er his name, his strength however great,
' Still, not immortal, must he yield to fate.
' But from the far-thrown fragments safe retreat,
' Till prostrate fall the giant at my feet.'
   She said : retiring at her sage command, 1965
They wait the movement of her magic hand.
Wide o'er her face her purple veil she spread,
And climb'd the lofty decks, by Jason led.
* And now her magic arts Medea tries;
* Bids the red Furies, dogs of Orcus, rise, 1970
* That starting dreadful from th' infernal shade,
* Ride heaven in storms, and all that breathes invade.
* Thrice she applies the power of magic pray'r,
* Thrice, hellward bending, mutters charms in air;
* Then, turning towards the foe, bids mischief fly,
* And looks destruction, as she points her eye. 1976
* Then spectres, rising from Tartarean bow'rs,
* Howl round in air, or grin along the shores.*
Father supreme ! what fears my breast annoy,
Since not disease alone can life destroy, 1980
Or wounds inflicted fate's decrees fulfil,
But magic's secret arts have power to kill !

U 3   For,

For, by Medea's incantations plied,
Enfeebled foon the brazen monfter died.
* While rending up the earth in wrath he throws 1985
* Rock after rock againft th' aerial foes,
* Lo! frantic as he ftrides, a fudden wound
* Burfts the life-vein, and blood o'erfpreads the ground.
* As from a furnace, in a burning flood
* Pours melting lead, fo pours in ftreams his blood:
* And now he ftaggers, as the fpirit flies, 1991
* He faints, he finks, he tumbles, and he dies.
* As fome huge cedar on a mountain's brow,
* Pierc'd by the fteel, expects a final blow,
* Awhile it totters with alternate fway, 1995
* Till frefhening breezes through the branches play;
* Then tumbling downward with a thundering found,
* Headlong it falls, and fpreads a length of ground:
* So, as the giant falls, the ocean roars,
* Outftretch'd he lies, and covers half the fhores.*

Crete thus deliver'd from this baneful peft, 2001
The Mynians unmolefted funk to reft.
Soon as Aurora's orient beams appear,
A temple they to Cretan Pallas rear.

With

With water stor'd, once more the busy train 2005
Embark, and lash the foamy brine again.
Assiduous all with equal ardour glow
Distant to leave Salmonis' lofty brow.
As o'er the Cretan deep the galley flew,
Around them night her sable mantle threw; 2010
Pernicious night, whose all-investing shade
Nor stars, nor Phœbe's brighter rays pervade.
Thick darkness, or from heaven, or hell profound,
Spread, as it rose, its rueful shades around.
Uncertain whether, on huge billows tost, 2015
Sublime they sail, or sink to Pluto's coast,
Uncertain where the bursting wave may throw,
They to the sea commit their weal or woe.
Jason aloud, with lifted hands, addres'd
The God of day to succour the distress'd. 2020
The tears fast trickling down his sorrowing face,
He vow'd with gifts the Delphic shrine to grace,
He vow'd with choicest gifts, an ample store,
To load Amyclæ, and Ortygia's shore.
Attentive to his tears and meek request, 2025
Phœbus from heaven descends, and stands confes'd,
Where, frowning hideous o'er the deeps below,
The rocks of Melans lift their shaggy brow.

U 4   Awhile

Awhile on one of thefe he takes his ftand,
His golden bow high lifting in his hand; 2030
Affifted by whofe far-reflected light,
An ifle of fmall extent attracts their fight,
Amid the Sporades; againft it ftood
Hippuris, circled by the rolling flood.
Their anchors here they drop. Aurora's ray 2035
Glimmer'd, and funk before the light of day.
A temple here o'er-arch'd with woods they raife,
And bid an altar to Apollo blaze,
On whom the name Æglete they beftow;
For here the God difplay'd his beamy bow. 2040
Here, fince on Argo's crew all bright he fhone,
By the name Anaphe the ifle is known.
The fcanty produce of this barren ifle
To Phœbus they on humble altars pile.
Each fair Phæacian in Medea's train, 2045
Who oft had feen the fatted oxen flain
In king Alcinoüs' court, in laughter joins
At fight of water pour'd on burning pines.
With well-diffembled wrath the chiefs reprove
The laughing damfels, and the mirth they love. 2050
A wordy altercation foon began,
And pleafant raillery through the circle ran.

           Hence,

Book IV. APOLLONIUS RHODIUS.

Hence, to Æglete, on this feftive day,
All who in Anaphe due honours pay,
Maidens and men, a mix'd affembly, join   2055
In friendly contefts and debates benign.

 The halfers now were loofen'd from their hold;
And unreftrain'd in ocean Argo roll'd,
When thus the dream of night, yet uneffac'd,
Revering Maia's fon, Euphemus trac'd.   2060
How, with clofe grafp the facred clod comprefs'd,
Stream'd with a milky current at his breaft.
And from this clod, though fmall, his wondering eyes
Beheld a lovely, female form arife.
Charm'd with the beauteous fair, he foon refign'd   2065
To nuptial joys his love-devoted mind,
Lamenting ftill that he the maid fhould wed,
Whom at his foftering breaft with milk he fed.

 " Thy children's nurfe am I," (the fair began,
Accofting mild the difconcerted man;)   2070
" But not thy daughter : I from Triton came ;
" (Triton and Libya my parents' name)
" He fix'd near Anaphe my watery cell,
" And bade me here with Nereus' daughters dwell.]
" But now I haften towards the fun's bright ray, 2075
" And to thy race the choiceft boon convey."

             This

This dream recurring to his mind again,
He told the leader of the gallant train,
Who, long revolving, thus at length reveal'd
Those myſtic truths the Pythic ſhrine conceal'd: 2080
' Ye Gods! what glory waits thy valorous deeds,
' What fame, Euphemus, to thy toil ſucceeds!
' For, when in ocean's bed this earth you fling,
' Thence (ſo the Gods ordain) an iſle ſhall ſpring;
' Here ſhall thy children's children late repoſe. 2085
' Triton this hoſpitable gift beſtows:
' He tore from Afric's coaſt the treaſur'd ſoil;
' To him, of all the Gods, aſcribe the iſle.'
Thus ſpoke he preſcient, nor in vain divin'd:
Euphemus heard him with attentive mind; 2090
Tranſported with the preſage, forth he ſprung,
And the myſterious clod in ocean flung.
Inſtant emerging from the refluent tides,
Calliſte's iſle diſplay'd its wave-waſh'd ſides,
Nurſe of Euphemus' race: in days of yore, 2095
They dwelt on Sintian Lemnos' ſooty ſhore.
Exil'd from Lemnos by Etrurian force,
To Sparta's friendly walls they bent their courſe:
Ejected thence, Theras, Auteſion's heir,
Bade him to fam'd Calliſte's iſle repair; 2100

His name it took: th' events we now display
Were unaccomplish'd in Euphemus' day.
 Vast tracts of ocean pass'd, the joyous host
Steer'd towards, and anchor'd on Ægina's coast.
They here propose a trial of their skill;   2105
What chief can first the weighty bucket fill,
And, ere his fellows intercept his way,
First to the ship the watery store convey.
For parching thirst, and winds that briskly blew,
To the fleet course inclin'd the gallant crew.   2110
His bucket now, replenish'd at the springs,
Each stout Thessalian on his shoulder brings;
Intent the palm of conquest to obtain,
He scours with speedy foot across the plain.
 Hail, happy race of heroes, and repay   2115
With tributary praise my tuneful lay!
With pleasure still may distant times rehearse
And added years on years exalt my verse!
For here I fix the period of your woes,
And with your glorious toils my numbers close. 2120
Your galley loosen'd from Ægina's shore,
Waves discompos'd, and winds detain'd no more.
Serene ye sail'd beside th' Achaian strand,
Where Cecrops' towers the subject main command,
               Where

Where oppofite Euboea Aulis lies, 2125
And where the Locrian cities lofty rife,
Till Pagafæ her friendly port difplay'd,
Where rode triumphant Argo fafe embay'd.

END OF THE ARGONAUTICS.

THE RAPE OF HELEN;

OR,

The Origin of the *Trojan* War:

A GREEK POEM,

By *COLUTHUS*.

THE
RAPE OF HELEN;
OR,
The Origin of the Trojan War:

A GRK*K POEM,

BY COLUTHUS.

THE
RAPE OF HELEN, &c.

YE nymphs of Troy, for beauty fam'd, who trace
From Xanthus' fertile ſtreams your ancient race,
Oft on whoſe ſandy banks your tires are laid,
And many a trinket which your hands have made,
What time to Ida's hallow'd mount ye throng,   5
To join the feſtive choir in dance and ſong;
No longer on your favourite banks repoſe,
But come, the judgment of the ſwain diſcloſe.
Say from what hills, to trackleſs deeps unknown,
Ruſh'd with impetuous zeal the daring clown;   10
Say to what end, with future ills replete,
O'er diſtant oceans ſail'd a mighty fleet;
What ſeas could this adventurous youth embroil,
Sow diſcord's ſeeds o'er what diſaſtrous ſoil?

Say

Say from what source arose the dire debate, 15
Which swains could end and Goddesses create.
What his decision? Of the Grecian dame
Who to the shepherd's ear convey'd the name?
Speak, for ye saw, on Ida's still retreat,
Judicial Paris fill his shepherd's seat; 20
Venus ye saw, the Graces' darling queen,
As on her judge approv'd she smil'd serene.

What time Hæmonia's lofty mountains rung
With hymeneal songs for Peleus sung,
Officious Ganymede, at Jove's request, 25
Supplied with sparkling wine each welcome guest;
And all the Gods to Thetis' nuptials came,
Sister of Amphitrite, honour'd dame.
Earth-shaking Neptune left his azure main,
And Jove supreme forsook his starry plain: 30
From Helicon, with odorous shrubs o'erspread,
The Muses' tuneful choir Apollo led.
Him Juno follow'd, wife of sovereign Jove:
With Harmony the smiling queen of Love
Hasten'd to join the Gods in Chiron's festive grove.
Cupid's full quiver o'er her shoulder thrown, 36
Persuasion follow'd with a bridal crown.
Minerva, though to nuptial rites a foe,
Came; but no helmet nodded o'er her brow.

Diana

Diana to the Centaur's grove reforts, 40
And for one day forgets her rural sports.
His loose locks shaking as the zephyrs play'd,
Not long behind convivial Bacchus stay'd.
War's God, as when to Vulcan's dome he sped,
No spear his hand sustain'd, no casque his head, 45
Such now, without his helmet or his lance,
Smiling he look'd, and led the bridal dance.
But from these blissful scenes was Discord warn'd;
Peleus rejected her, and Chiron scorn'd.

As by the gadfly stung, the heifer strays 50
Far from its fields, through every devious maze;
Thus, stung with envy, Discord roam'd, nor ceas'd
Her baneful arts to interrupt the feast.
Oft from her flinty bed she rush'd amain,
Then stood, then sunk into her seat again: 55
With desperate hand she tore her snaky head,
And with a serpent-scourge she lash'd her flinty bed.
To dart the forky lightning, and command
From hell's abyss the Titans' impious band,
Jove from his throne with rebel-arm to wrest, 60
Were projects form'd within the fury's breast.
But, though incens'd, she dreaded Vulcan's ire,
Who forms Jove's bolt, and checks the raging fire.

Her purpose changing, she with rattling arms
Dissension meditates and dire alarms; 65
If haply clattering shields can strike dismay,
And from the nuptials drive the Gods away.
But Mars she dreaded, oft in arms array'd,
And this new project with complacence weigh'd.
The burnish'd apples, rich with golden rind, 70
Growth of Hesperian gardens, struck her mind.
Resolv'd contention's baneful seeds to sow,
She tore the blushing apple from its bough,
Grasp'd the dire source whence future battles sprung,
And midst the Gods the golden mischief flung. 75
The stately wife of Jove with wondering eyes
Beheld, and wish'd to grasp the golden prize.
Beauty's fair queen to catch the apple strove;
For 'tis the prize of beauty and of love.
Jove mark'd the contest, and, to crush debate, 80
Thus counsel'd Hermes, who beside him sat:

' Paris, perchance, from Priam sprung, you know;
' His herds he grazes on mount Ida's brow,
' And oft conducts them to the dewy meads,
' Through which his streams the Phrygian Xanthus
    leads: 85
' Shew him yon prize, and urge him to declare
' Which of these Goddesses he deems most fair;

' In

' In whom, of all, his matchlefs fkill can trace
' The clofe-arch'd eyebrow and the roundeft face,
' On fuch a face, where bends the circling bow,   90
' The golden apple, beauty's prize, beftow.'
   Thus fpoke the fire: the willing fon obey'd,
And to their judge the Deities convey'd.
Each anxious fair her charms to heighten tries,
And dart new luftre from her fparkling eyes.   95
Her veil afide infidious Venus flung;
Loofe from the clafp her fragrant ringlets hung;
She then in golden cauls each curl comprefs'd,
Summon'd her little Loves, and thus addrefs'd:
' Behold, my fons, the hour of trial near!   100
' Embrace, my Loves, and bid me banifh fear.
' This day's decifion will enhance my fame,
' Crown beauty's queen, or fink in endlefs fhame.
' Doubting I ftand, to whom the fwain may fay,
' Bear thou, moft fair, the golden prize away.   105
' Nurs'd was each Grace by Juno's foftering hand;
' And crowns and fceptres fhift at her command.
' Minerva dictates in th' embattled field;
' And heroes tremble when fhe fhakes her fhield.
' Of all the Goddeffes that rule above,   110
' Far moft defencelefs is the queen of Love.

X 2   ' Without

' Without or spear or shield must Venus live;
' And crowns and sceptres she has none to give.
' Yet why despair? though with no falchion grac'd,
' Love's silken chain surrounds my slender waist. 115
' My bow this Cestus, this the dart I fling,
' And with this Cestus I infix my sting.
' My sting infix'd renews the lover's pain,
' And virgins languish, but revive again.'
Thus to her Loves the rosy-finger'd queen 120
Told all her fears, and vented all her spleen:
To every word they lent a willing ear,
Round their fond mother clung, and strove to cheer.

And now they reach mount Ida's grassy steep,
Where youthful Paris feeds his father's sheep: 125
What time he tends them in the plains below,
Through which the waters of Anaurus flow,
Apart he counts his cattle's numerous stock,
Apart he numbers all his fleecy flock.
A wild goat's skin, around his shoulders cast, 130
Loose fell and flow'd below his girded waist.
A pastoral staff, which swains delight to hold,
His roving herds protected and controll'd.
Accoutred thus, and warbling o'er his song,
He to his pipe melodious pac'd along. 135
Unnoted

Unnoted oft, while he renews his lay,
His flocks defert him, and his oxen ftray.
Swift to his bower retires the tuneful man,
To pipe the praife of Hermes and of Pan.
Sunk is each animal in dead repofe ;   140
No dog around him barks, no heifer lows :
Echo alone rebounds through Ida's hills,
And all the air with founds imperfect fills.
The cattle, flunk upon their verdant bed,
Clofe by their piping lord repofe their head.   145
Beneath the fhades which fheltering thickets blend,
When Paris' eye approaching Hermes ken'd,
Back he retires, with fudden fear imprefs'd,
And fhuns the prefence of the heavenly gueft;
To the thick fhrubs his tuneful reed conveys,   150
And all unfinifh'd leaves his warbled lays.
Thus winged Hermes to the fhepherd faid,
Who mark'd the God's approach with filent dread:
' Difmifs thy fears, nor with thy flocks abide;
' A mighty conteft Paris muft decide.   155
' Hafte, judge announc'd ; for whofe decifion wait
' Three lovely females, of celeftial ftate,
' Hafte, and the triumph of that face declare,
' Which fweeteft looks, and faireft midft the fair:

' Let

'Let her, whofe form thy critic eye prefers,   160
' Claim beauty's prize, and be this apple hers.'
    Thus Hermes fpoke; the ready fwain obey'd,
And to decide the mighty caufe effay'd.
With keeneft look he mark'd the heavenly dames;
Their eyes, quick flafhing as the lightning's flames, 165
Their fnowy necks, their garments fring'd with gold,
And rich embroidery wrought in every fold;
Their gait he mark'd, as gracefully they mov'd,
And round their feet his eye fagacious rov'd.
But, ere the fmiling fwain his thoughts exprefs'd, 170
Grafping his hand him Pallas thus addrefs'd:
    ' Regard not, Phrygian youth, the wife of Jove,
' Nor Venus heed, the queen of wedded love;
' But martial prowefs if thy wifdom prize,
' Know, I poffefs it; praife me to the fkies, 175
' Thee, fame reports, puiffant ftates obey,
' And Troy's proud city owns thy fovereign fway.
' Her fuffering fons thy conquering arm fhall fhield,
' And ftern Bellona fhall to Paris yield.
' Comply; her fuccour will Minerva lend,   180
' Teach thee war's fcience, and in fight defend.'
    Thus Pallas ftrove to influence the fwain,
Whofe favour Juno thus attempts to gain:
                                ' Should'ft

' Should'ſt thou with beauty's prize my charms
 reward,
' All Aſia's realms ſhall own thee for their lord. 185
' Say, what from battles but contention ſprings?
' Such conteſts ſhun; for what are wars to kings?
' But him, whoſe hands the rod of empire ſway,
' Cowards revere, and conquerors obey.
' Minerva's friends are oft Bellona's ſlaves,   190
' And the fiend ſlaughters whom the Goddeſs ſaves.'
 Proffers of boundleſs ſway thus Juno made;
And Venus thus, contemptuous ſmiling, ſaid:
But firſt her floating veil aloft ſhe threw,
And all her graces to the ſhepherd ſhew;   195
Looſen'd her little Loves' attractive chain,
And tried each art to captivate the ſwain.
 ' Accept my boon,' (thus ſpoke the ſmiling dame)
' Battles forget, and dread Bellona's name.
' Beauty's rich meed at Venus' hand receive,   200
' And Aſia's wide domain to tyrants leave.
' The deathful fight, the din of arms I fear;
' Can Venus' hand direct the martial ſpear?
' Women with beauty ſtouteſt hearts aſſail,
' Beauty, their beſt defence, their ſtrongeſt mail. 205
' Prefer domeſtic eaſe to martial ſtrife,
' And to exploits of war a pleaſing wife.

' To realms extenfive Helen's bed prefer,
' And fcoff at kingdoms, when oppos'd to her.'
' Thy prize with envy Sparta fhall furvey, 210
' And Troy to Paris tune the bridal lay.'

The fhepherd, who aftonifh'd ftood and mute,
Confign'd to Venus the Hefperian fruit,
The claim of beauty, and the fource of woes;
For dire debates from this decifion rofe. 215
Uplifting in her hand the glowing prize,
She rallied thus the vanquifh'd Deities:

' To me, ye martial dames, the prize refign;
' Beauty I court, and beauty's prize is mine.
' Mother of mighty Mars and Vulcan too, 220
' Fame fays, the choir of Graces fprung from you:
' Yet diftant far, this day, your daughters ftray'd,
' And no one Grace appear'd to lend you aid.
' Mars too declin'd t' affert his mother's right,
' Though oft·his brandifh'd fword decides the fight.
' His boafted flames why could not Vulcan caft, 226
' And at one blaze his mother's rivals blaft?
' Vain are thy triumphs, Pallas, vain thy fcorn;
' Thou, not in wedlock, nor of woman born.
' Jove's teeming head the monftrous birth contains,
' And the barb'd iron ripp'd thee from his brains. 231

' Brac'd

' Brac'd with th' unyielding plaits of ruthlefs mail,
' She curfes Cupid and the filken veil.
' Connubial blifs and concord fhe abhors,
' In difcord glories and delights in wars. 235
' Yet know, virago, not in feats of arms
' Triumph weak women, but in beauty's charms.
' Nor men nor women are thofe mungrels bafe,
' Like you, equivocal in form and face.'
In terms like thefe the laughter-loving queen 240
Rallied her rivals, and increas'd their fpleen,
As, lifting high, fhe view'd with fecret joy
Her beauty's triumphs and the bane of Troy.
Infpir'd with love for her, the fair unknown,
By beauty's conquering queen pronounc'd his own,
Ill-fated Paris to the foreft's maze 246
Men vers'd in Pallas' various arts conveys.
At Pericles' command they give the blow,
And lay the glories of the foreft low.
He, artift fam'd, his frantic prince obey'd, 250
And burden'd ocean with the fhips he made.
From Ida's fummits rufh'd the daring fwain,
And to its bowery fhades prefer'd the boifterous main.
Th' extended beach with choice oblations ftor'd,
And his protectrefs Venus oft implor'd; 255

The

The billowy deep his furrowing keel divides,
And in the Hellespont his vessel rides.
But prodigies announce approaching ill,
And with presages sad each bosom fill.
Up-heaving waves heaven's starry concave shroud, 260
And round each Bear is cast a circling cloud.
Clouds and big waves discharge their watery stores;
Full on the deck the bursting torrent pours.
Their sturdy oars with unabating sweep
Far whitening agitate the angry deep. 265
Dardanus pass'd, and Ilion's fertile plains,
The mouth of Ismarus' lake the adventurer gains.
Now, far remote, they view Pangræa's height;
Now Phillis' rising tomb attracts their sight,
And the dull round she nine times trode in vain, 270
To view the faithless wanderer again.
Hæmonia's meads remote, the Trojan spies
Th' Achaian cities unexpected rise:
Phthia, with heroes far-renown'd replete;
Mycenæ, fam'd for many a spacious street, 275
Beside the meads, where Erymanthus glides,
Sparta aspires, that boasts her beauteous brides;
Sparta with joy th' expecting swain survey'd,
Lav'd by Eurotas, by Atrides sway'd.

Nor diſtant far, o'erſhaded by a wood, 280
Beneath a mountain's brow Therapnæ ſtood.
Short was their voyage now : the bending oar
Was heard to laſh the foamy ſurge no more.
The ſailors, ſafe imboſom'd in the bay,
Firm to the beach confine the corded ſtay. 285
In purifying waters plung'd the ſwain,
And, riſing thence, pac'd ſlowly o'er the plain.
For much he fear'd, left his incautious tread
O'er his waſh'd feet the ſpatter'd mire ſhould ſpread;
Or left his hair, beneath his caſque confin'd, 290
Should, if he ran, be ruffled with the wind.
The city's ſplendor Paris' eye detains,
The citizens' abodes, and gliſtering fanes:
Here Pallas' form, in mimic gold portray'd,
Here Hyacinthus' image he ſurvey'd. 295
Him with delight the Amiclæans view'd,
Purſuing Phœbus and by him purſu'd;
But, ſore diſpleas'd at jealous Zephyr's ſpite,
They urg'd the ſtripling to unequal fight;
For Phœbus' efforts ineffectual prov'd, 300
To ſave from Zephyr's rage the youth he lov'd.
Earth with compaſſion heard Apollo's cries,
And from her boſom bade a flower ariſe,

His

His favourite's name, imprefs'd upon whofe leaf,
Still, as the God contemplates, fooths his grief. 305
Now Priam's fon before Atrides' dome
Exulting ftood in beauty's purple bloom.
Not Semele, by Jove's careffes won,
On Jove beftow'd fo beautiful a fon:
(Forgive me, Bacchus, feed of Jove fupreme) 310
Such peerlefs graces round his perfon beam.
Touch'd by fair Helen's hand the bolts recede;
She to the fpacious hall repair'd with fpeed:
Her form diftinct th' unfolded portals fhew;
She look'd, fhe ponder'd, and again withdrew. 315
Then on a radiant feat fhe bade him reft,
And, ftill infatiate, gaz'd upon her gueft.
Awhile fhe likens him in graceful mien
To Love, attendant on the Cyprian queen.
But 'tis not Love, fhe recollects again; 320
Nor bow nor quiver deck this gallant fwain.
'Tis Bacchus fure, the God of wine, fhe faid;
For o'er his cheeks a rofy bloom is fpread.
Daring at length her faltering voice to raife,
She thus exprefs'd her wonder and her praife: 325

 ' Whence art thou, ftranger? whence thy comely
  ' race?
 ' Thy country tell me, and thy natal place.

            ' In

' In thee I mark the majesty of kings:
' But not from Greece thy lofty lineage springs.
' Not sandy Pyle thine origin can shew ; 330
' I know not thee, though Nestor's son I know.
' Phthia, the nurse of heroes, train'd not thee ;
' For known are all th' Æacidæ to me.
' Peleus, and Telamon renown'd in fight,
' Patroclus' courtesy, Achilles' might.' 335
Inspir'd by love, thus spoke the gentle dame ;
And he, thus answering, fann'd the rising flame:
" If e'er recording fame, illustrious maid,
" Hath to thine ear great Ilion's name convey'd,
" Ilion, whose walls on Phrygian frontiers stand, 340
" Rear'd by Apollo's and by Neptune's hand ;
" Him if thou know'st, most opulent of kings,
" Who reigns o'er Ilion, and from Saturn springs ;
" I to hereditary worth aspire ;
" The wealthy Priam is my honour'd sire. 345
" My high descent from Dardanus I prove ;
" And ancient Dardanus descends from Jove.
" Th' Immortals thus forsake the realms of light,
" And mix with mortals in the social rite.
" Neptune and Phœbus thus forsook the sphere,
" Firm on its base my native Troy to rear. 351
" But

" But know, on three fair Goddeſſes, of late,
" Sentence I paſs'd, and clos'd the long debate.
" On Venus, who with charms ſuperior ſhone,
" I laviſh'd praiſes and conferr'd my boon. 355
" The Cyprian Goddeſs, pleas'd with my decree,
" Reſerv'd this recompence, O queen, for me;
" Some faithful fair, poſſeſs'd of heavenly charms,
" Should, ſhe proteſted, bleſs my longing arms;
" Helen her name, to beauty's queen ally'd; 360
" Helen, for thee I ſtemm'd the troubled tide.
" Unite we now in Hymen's myſtic bands;
" Thus love inſpires, and Venus thus commands.
" Scorn not my ſuit, nor beauty's queen deſpiſe:
" More need I add to influence the wife? 365
" For well thou know'ſt, how daſtardly and baſe
" Is Menelaus's degenerate race.
" And well I know, that Græcia's ample coaſt
" No fair like thee, for beauty fam'd, can boaſt."
He ſaid; on earth her ſparkling eyes ſhe caſt, 370
Embarraſs'd paus'd awhile, and ſpoke at laſt:
'To viſit Ilion, and her towers ſurvey,
' Rear'd by the God of ocean and of day,
' (Stupendous labours by Celeſtials wrought)
' Hath oft, illuſtrious gueſt, employ'd my thought.

" Oft

' Oft have I wish'd to saunter o'er the vales, 376
' Whose flowery pasture Phœbus' flocks regales;
' Where, beneath Ilion's walls, along the meads,
' The shepherd-God his lowing oxen feeds.
' To Ilion I'll attend thee: haste, away; 380
' For beauty's queen forbids our long delay.
' No husband's threats, no husband's search I dread,
' Though he to Troy suspect his Helen fled.
The Spartan dame, of matchless charms possess'd,
Proffer'd these terms to her consenting guest. 385
Night, which relieves our toils, when the bright sun,
In ocean sunk, his daily course has run,
Now gives her softest slumbers, ere the ray
Of rising morn proclaims th' approach of day.
Two gates of airy dreams she opens wide; 390
Of polish'd horn is this, where truths abide:
Voices divine through this mysterious gate
Proclaim th' unalterable will of fate.
But through the ivory-gate incessant troop
Of vain, delusive dreams a faithless group. 395
Helen, seduc'd from Menelaus' bed,
Th' adventurous shepherd to his navy led;
To Troy with speed he bears the fatal freight;
For Venus' proffers confidence create.

At morning's dawn Hermione appears, 400
With treſſes diſcompos'd and bath'd in tears.
She rous'd her menial train; and thus expreſs'd
The boding ſorrows of her troubled breaſt:
' Where, fair attendants, is my mother fled,
' Who left me ſleeping in her lonely bed? 405
' For yeſternight ſhe took her truſty key,
' Turn'd the ſtrong bolt, and ſlept ſecure with me.'
Her hapleſs fate the penſive train deplore,
And in thick circles gather round the door;
Here all contend to moderate her grief, 410
And by their kind condolence give relief:
' Unhappy princeſs, check the riſing tear;
' Thy mother, abſent now, will ſoon appear.
' Soon as thy ſorrow's bitter ſource ſhe knows,
' Her ſpeedy preſence will diſpel thy woes. 415
' The virgin-cheek, with ſorrow's weight o'ercome,
' Sinks languid down and loſes half its bloom.
' Deep in the head the tearful eye retires,
' There ſullen ſits, nor darts its wonted fires.
' Eager, perchance, the band of nymphs to meet, 420
' She ſaunters devious from her favourite-ſeat,
' And, of ſome flowery mead at length poſſeſs'd,
' Sinks on the dew-beſpangled lawn to reſt.

' Or

' Or to some kindred stream perchance she strays,
' Bathes in Eurotas' streams, and round its margin
    plays.'   425
' Why talk ye thus?' (the pensive maid replies,
The tears of anguish trickling from her eyes)
' She knows each roseate bower, each vale and hill,
' She knows the course of every winding rill.
' The stars are set; on rugged rocks she lies: 430
' The stars are up; nor does my mother rise.
' What hills, what dales thy devious steps detain?
' Hath some relentless beast my mother slain?
' But beasts, which lawless round the forest rove,
' Revere the sacred progeny of Jove.   435
' Or art thou fallen from some steep mountain's brow,
' Thy corse conceal'd in dreary dells below?
' But through the groves, with thickest foliage
    crown'd,
' Beneath each shrivel'd leaf that strews the ground,
' Assiduous have I sought thy corse in vain: 440
' Why should we then the guiltless grove arraign?
' But have Eurotas' streams, which rapid flow,
' O'erwhelm'd thee bathing in its deeps below?
' Yet in the deeps below the Naiads live,
' And they to womankind protection give.'   445
                    Y   Thus

Thus spoke she sorrowing, and reclin'd her head;
And sleeping seem'd to mingle with the dead:
For sleep his elder brother's aspect wears;
Lies mute like him, and undisturb'd by cares.
Hence the swoln eyes of females, deep distress'd, 450
Oft, when the tear is trickling, sink to rest.
In this delusive dream the sleeping maid
Her mother saw, or thought she saw, portray'd:
Aloud she shriek'd, distracted and amaz'd,
And utter'd thus her anguish as she gaz'd: 455
' Last night, far distant from your daughter fled,
' You left me slumbering in my father's bed.
' What dangerous steeps have not I strove to gain?
' And stroll'd o'er hills and dales for thee in vain?'
" Condemn me not; (replied the wandering dame)
" Pity my sufferings, nor augment my shame. 461
" Me yesterday a lawless guest beguil'd,
" And distant tore me from my darling child.
" At Cytherea's high command I rove;
" And once more revel in the walks of love." 465
    She said: her voice the sleeping maid alarms;
She springs to clasp her mother in her arms.
In vain: no mother meets her wistful eyes;
And now her tears redouble and her cries:

'Ye feathery race, inhabitants of light, 470
'To Crete's fam'd ifle direct your rapid flight.
'There to my fire th' unwelcome truth proclaim,
'How yefterday a defperate vagrant came,
'Tore all he dotes on from his bridal bed,
'And with his beauteous queen abruptly fled.' 475
The reftlefs fair, her mother to regain,
Thus to the winds bewail'd and wept in vain.
The Thracian town diminifh'd from their view,
And fleet o'er Helle's ftrait the veffel flew.
The bridegroom now his natal coaft defcry'd, 480
And to the Trojan port conducts his bride.
Caffandra from her tower beheld them fail,
And tore her locks, and rent her golden veil.
But hofpitable Troy unbars her gate,
Receives her citizen and feals her fate. 485

THE END.

Vulcan in vain inhabitants enlight;
&c. ...... about rapid flight.
T... to ..... transient truth proclaim,
How ..... a desperate vagrant came,
Tore ... Vulcan on from his bridal bed;
And with his beauteous queen abruptly fled.
The restless fair, her march to Cyprus,
Thus to the wind, bewail'd and wept in vain,
The Thracian town diminish'd from their view,
And thro' o'er Hellas skies, the vessel flew.
Thy ......nous nowhere natal coast destroy'd,
And to the ..... pair conducts the bride.
C...... ...... to the caves behold them all,
A .... ; and rent in a golden veil
Her ...... ; Thy Thebais her gate,
.... citizen and club her fate.
....
.... our gods are such as ......

THE END.

NOTES

NOTES
TO THE
ARGONAUTICS.

BOOK I.

V. 1. *INſpir'd by thee,* ---] Thus begins Homer's Batrachomyachia, the 17th Id. of Theocritus, and Aratus's poem.
See alſo on theſe words the Gr. Schol. and Hoelzlinus's note.

V. 3. *Whom Pelias* ---] For Pelias, Æſon, &c. See the preface.

Colchos, now called Mengrelia, is bounded on the north by part of Sarmatia, on the weſt by ſo much of the Euxine ſea, as extends from the river Corax to the mouth of the river Phaſis, on the ſouth by part of Cappadocia, and on the eaſt by Iberia.

V. 5. *Thro' the Cyanean rocks.*]

—————————————when Argo paſs'd
'Through Boſphorus betwixt the juſtling rocks.
Milton's Par. Loſt, B. ii. 1017.

Two rocks at the entrance of the Euxine ſea, called *ſymplegades* by the Grecians, by Juvenal *concurrentia ſaxa*; becauſe they were ſo near, that, as a ſhip varied its courſe, they ſeemed to open and ſhut; or, as Milton

ton expreffes it, to *juftle* one another. They were alfo called *cyanean*, from their dark colour.

V. 13. *Anaurus paft*, ---] A river in Theffaly, according to Apollonius, Callimachus, and others. But fome are of opinion, that Anaurus, as its etymology implies, is the general name of any torrent. Valerius Flaccus, relating the fame ftory, mentions the river Enipeus.

V. 33. *Whom fair Calliope, on Thracia's fhore*] The Pæonians of Thrace lived upon the Hebrus; and all the people of that region were at one time great in fcience. The Grecians acknowledged they were greatly indebted to them; and the Mufes were faid to have come from thofe parts. The Pierians were as famed for poetry and mufic, as the Pæonians were for phyfic. Thamyras, Eumolpus, Linus, Thymœtes and Mufæus, were fuppofed to have been of this country. Orpheus alfo is afcribed to Thrace; who is faid to have foothed the favage rage, and to have animated the very rocks to harmony. *Bryant's Myth.*

V. 35. *Hard rocks, &c.* ---] Mulcentem tigres & agentem carmine quercus.---*Virg. Geor.* iv. 510.

V. 42. *By Chiron's art to Jafon's intereft gain'd.*] Orpheus, in the Argonautic poem afcribed to him, gives the fame account of himfelf.

Καὶ μ' ἴκιχεν κιθάρης πολυδαίδαλον ἐνίνοντα,
Ὄφρα κί τοι μίλπων προχέω μελιγήρυν ἀοιδὴν,
Κηλήσω δί τι θήρας ἰδ' ἑρπετὰ καὶ πιτηνά. Orph. Arg. 71.

V. 71. *Cæneus* ---] It is fabled that this perfon was a Theffalian virgin, the daughter of Elatus, one of the Lapithæ; who, having been violated by Neptune, obtained of him, as the reward of her proftitution, that fhe might be transformed into a man, and rendered invulnerable. Thus changing her fex, fhe changed her name into Cœneus, being before called Cœnis. See Ovid's Met. and Virg. Æn. vi. 448.

V. 79.

V. 79. *From Titaresus ---*] Mopsus was surnamed the Titaresian, from Titaresus, the name of a place and river in Thessaly. Thus Hesiod in Scut. Herc. L. 181.

Μόψοιτ 'Αμπυκίδην Τιταρήσιον——

V. 125. *Theseus ---*] Theseus, by the help of his friend Pirithoüs, had stolen Helen from the temple of Diana, and carried her off: in return for this service, he assisted Pirithoüs in the rape of Proserpine. In order to accomplish this design, they went down to the infernal regions together: but Pluto, having discovered their intentions, exposed Pirithoüs to the dog Cerberus, who devoured him, and chained Theseus to the mountain Tænarus. *Plutarch's life of Theseus.*

V. 138. *Tho' Argus wrought ---*] Apollonius calls him Ἄργος ἀρεςορίδης, the son of Arestor. But Banier remarks that we ought to read (as Meziriac has recommended) ἀλεκιορίδης, the son of Alector. For Argus, the son of Arestor, preceded the time of the Argonauts eight or nine generations: but most of the ancients agree, that the ship Argo was built by Argus, the son of Alector, who lived in the time of the Argonauts. *Banier's Myth. vol. iv.*

V. 147. *--- Pero ---*] Iphiclus had seized upon the oxen of Tyro, the mother of Neleus. These Neleus demands, but is denied by Iphiclus. Pero, the daughter of Neleus, was promised in marriage to him who recovered these oxen from Iphiclus. Melampus undertakes the recovery; but being vanquished is thrown into prison.---See Homer's Od. B. xi. 290.

V. 174. *Prophetic Idmon ---*]. He is mentioned in the same manner by Orpheus and Valerius Flaccus:

————————'Αβαίλος παῖς νόθος ἦλυθε κάρτερος Ἴδμων,
Τόν ῥ᾽ ὑποκυσαμένη τέκεν Ἀπόλλωνι ἄνακτι
Ἀμβρόσιον παρὰ χεῦμα Φερητιὰς Ἀντιάνειρα,
Τῷ καὶ μαντοσύνην ὤπορε καὶ θέσφατον ὀμφὴν
Φοῖβος.   Orph. Arg. 185.
——————— Phebeius

———————— Phebeius Idmon,
Cui genitor tribuit monita prænoscere Divûm
Omina, seu flammas, seu lubrica cominus exta,
Seu plenum certis interroget aera pennis.
Val. Flac. B. i. 228.

V. 180. *Omens from birds, and prodigies from fire.*] There were two grand divisions of the religious ceremonies of the ancients, *viz.* into ἔμπυρα and ἄπυρα, *i. e.* those where fire was heaped upon the altar, and those which were not accompanied with fire. The σήματα ἔμπυρα were observations made from the victims at the time they were burning; which was the province of the Haruspices : the σήματα ἄπυρα referred to the flight of birds, and such observations as the augurs collected from them. Thus Euripides in Bacchæ, v. 257.

Σκοπῶν πλερωτὸς, κᾳμπύρων μισθὸς φέρειν·

V. 197. *And gave the power* ---] Thus Ovid :
———————— cui posse figuras
Sumere quas vellet, rursusque reponere sumptas,
Neptunus dederat, Nelei sanguinis auctor. *Met.* xii. 555.

And Seneca :
Sumere innumeras solitum figuras. *Med.* 635.

V. 222. *Euphemus* ---] The text has Polyphemus ; which is undoubtedly a false reading, as Valerius Flaccus and Pausanias seem to confirm. The annotator to Mr. Pope's Odyssey, not suspecting this, was led into a pleasant mistake. " If Polyphemus (says he, Od. ix. 569.) had really this quality of running upon the waves, he might have destroyed Ulysses without throwing this mountain : but Apollonius is undoubtedly guilty of an absurdity, and one might rather believe that he would sink the earth at every step, than run upon the waters with such lightness as not to wet his feet." As this description of the swiftness of Euphemus is originally taken from Homer's account of the mares

mares of Erichthonius, so Virgil's description of Camilla's swiftness seems copied from these beautiful lines of Apollonius. See Pope's Il. B. xx. 270.

> These lightly skimming, when they swept the plain,
> Nor ply'd the grass, nor bent the tender grain:
> And when along the level seas they flew,
> Scarce on the surface curl'd the briny dew.

> Illa vel intactæ segetis per summa volaret
> Gramina, nec teneres cursu læsisset aristas:
> Vel mare per medium, fluctu suspensa tumenti,
> Ferret iter, celeres nec tingeret æquore plantas.

V. 251. --- *Palæmonius* ---] Our poet in his account of this hero follows Orpheus very closely: Valerius Flaccus makes no mention of him.

V. 273. *They, when on tip-toe* ---] Milton's description of Raphael is similar to this:

> ——————— like Maia's son he stood,
> And shook his plumes, that heavenly fragrance fill'd
> The circuit wide; &c. *Par. L.* B. v. 285.

Apollonius in this beautiful description has far exceeded his venerable master; who says only,

——————— Ταρσοῖσιν ὑπηατίοις πιπόιηπο
Ζήτης καὶ Κάλαϊς, δέμας ἴκελοι ἀθανάτοισιν. Orph. Arg. 219.

V. 287. --- *Minyas' daughter* ---] The Argonauts were distinguished by the appellation of Minyæ: a title which they took as being descended from the daughters of Minyas, a Bœotian prince, the son of Orchomenus, who built a city of that name in Bœotia.

V. 291. --- *Iolchos* ---] A city of Thessaly, and the birth-place of Jason. It was also called Larissa (as Pomponius Mela asserts); hence Larissæus Achilles. *Virg.*

V. 292. --- *the Pagasæan bay.*] Pagasæ is a town and promontory of Thessaly. Here Argo was built; and

and from that circumftance, ἀπὸ τῆς ναυπηγίας, the bay is fuppofed to have derived its name.

V. 319. --- *Phrixus* ---] For an account of Phrixus fee the preface.

V. 327. *Alcimeda embrac'd her fon with tears*,] This affecting fcene is extremely natural, and drawn by our poet in a manner the moft mafterly. He is no where happier than in the execution of thefe pathetic pieces. This parting interview, the epifode of Hypfipyla, and the loves of Medea and Jafon have been admired and imitated by the poets of ancient and modern times.

V. 379. *Hafte, royal mother*, ---] Thus Telemachus addreffes his mother in Homer, and Turnus in Virgil.

Tears and apprehenfions of danger were deemed bad prefages, when the people were going to war.

Ne, quæfo, ne me lacrymis, neve omine tanto
Profequere, in duri certamina martis euntem.
Virg. Æn. xii. 72.

——————— O royal mother, ceafe your fears,
Nor fend me to the fight with boding tears. *Pitt.*

V. 384. --- *So moves the God of day*] Virgil has manifeftly borrowed this comparifon, and applied it to Æneas. B. iv. 143.

As when from Lycia, bound in wintry froft,
Where Xanthus' ftreams enrich the fmiling coaft,
The beauteous Phœbus in high pomp retires,
And hears in Delos, &c. *Pitt.*

V. 447. *With beeves return, the beft* ---] It was requifite to referve the beft of the flocks and herds for the altar: they muft be found and perfect in all their limbs, or they would be deemed a very unfit offering for the Gods. Thus Achilles in Homer offers up to Apollo --- ἀρνῶν κνίσσην αἰγῶντε τελείων. τοῖς θείοις ὡς τελείοις προσάγειν χρὴ τέλεια, fays Euftathius on this paffage.

passage. It is the precept of Virgil, that the cattle which are designed for the plough, for breeding and *sacrifices*, should be distinguished by particular marks, and separated from the rest.

— Continuoque notas, & nomina gentis inurunt.
Georg. iii. 158.

V. 456. *Example fir'd* ---] The poet through this whole description is agreeably circumstantial. He paints the busy scene before us in the liveliest colours. We are present to all the labours of his heroes. We see them constructing, launching and manning their ship, choosing their seats, erecting their altar, and offering sacrifice. We feel ourselves already interested, and cannot help joining with Jason in his prayer, that success may crown their enterprize.

V. 503. *Embasian Phœbus*, ---] Embasian and Ecbasian are epithets which they applied to their tutelar God at the instant of their embarkation, and when they were about to land.

V. 551. *Tho' various toils* ---] This speech of Idmon is calculated to excite our admiration and pity. We cannot but admire the courage and calmness of the hero, when he discloses to his comrades the purpose of Apollo. He tells them, in a prophetic strain, that they would be exposed to dangers, but successful at last; that, as to himself, he knew his doom, which was, that he must die in a distant country long before their return. Homer represents his hero *weeping* at his fate, "Ὡς ἄρ ἔφη δακρυχέων: our poet reserves the tears of sorrow for them, from whom they fall with a better grace;

——— the hoſt the fate of Idmon mourn.

V. 581. *Now by this lance* ---] This circumstance seems to be borrowed from that noble one of Achilles swearing by his sceptre in Homer; which passage
both

both Virgil and Valerius Flaccus have closely imi-
tated.

V. 599. --- *the Aloïdæ* ---] Iphimedia, the daughter of Triopas and wife of Alöeus, fell in love with Neptune, by whom she had two sons, Ephialtes and Otus. Presuming on their gigantic strength, they attempted to dethrone Jupiter; but were slain (as Homer and Pindar relate, and after them Apollonius) by Apollo at Naxus, and thrown into Tartarus by Pluto.

V. 617. *'Twas then*, ---] The following lines, to v. 720. are taken from Mr. West's translation of the song of Orpheus, and the setting out of the Argonauts; but many passages are much altered.

V. 621. *How at the first*, ---]

> Namque canebat, uti magnum per inane coacta
> Semina terrarumque animæque marisque fuissent, &c.
>
> *Virg. Ec.*

For a full illustration of the propriety and beauty of this song, which Scaliger condemns, I beg leave to subjoin Mr. Wharton's judicious criticism, in his *Observations on Spenser's Fairy Queen*. " Scaliger finds great fault with the subject of this song, and prefers to it the subject of Orpheus's song in Valerius Flaccus. By this piece of criticism he has betrayed his ignorance of the nature of ancient poesy, and of the character of Orpheus. But the propriety of the subject of this song is easily to be defended without considering the character of Orpheus. The occasion of it was a quarrel among the Argonauts, whom Orpheus endeavours to pacify with the united powers of music and verse. To this it may be added, that a song whose subject is religious, and which asserts the right of Jupiter to the possession of Olympus, was even expedient, as one of the chiefs had but just be-

fore

fore-spoken blasphemy against him. Nor were the auditors of so mean a rank as Scaliger would represent them : he terms them *Viri Militares*; but it should be considered, that they were *Princes* and *Demi-Gods*. There is one circumstance belonging to the song of Orpheus in Apollonius, which gives it a manifest superiority to that of Orpheus in Valerius Flaccus, I mean the design of it, which was, to express the vehemence of the passions, at once so agreeable to the well-known character of Orpheus, and so expressive of the irresistible influence of music. In the Latin poet, Orpheus sings upon no occasion, and to no end, unless to make the night pass away more pleasantly."

V. 636. *Ophion*, ---] Milton has undoubtedly copied this passage, Par. L. B. x. 580.

——————— how the serpent whom they call'd
Ophion with Eurynome, the wide
Encroaching Eve perhaps, had first the rule
Of high Olympus, &c.

Apollonius, as well as Milton, has hinted that Ophion was of the serpent-race. ——— the vast species of the serpent-breed.

The upper part of Eurynome was a perfect figure of a woman; the lower part, from the thighs downward, terminated in the tail of a fish. *Lucian*.

V. 649. *Here the sweet bard* ---] The effect, which the harp and voice of Orpheus had upon the Argonauts, is here elegantly described. When the poet had ended his song, they, intent and bending towards him, still listened, and imagined him still singing. Milton follows Apollonius very close:

The angel ended, and in Adam's ear
So charming left his voice, that he awhile
Thought him still speaking, still stood fix'd to hear.
Par. L. B. viii. 1.

V. 57. *Then on the flaming tongues* ---] It was the custom

custom of the ancients at their solemn festivals, before they went to rest, to sacrifice the tongues of the victims to Mercury, the God of eloquence, pouring on them a libation of wine. This was done, either with a design to make an expiation for any indecent language that had been spoken (as was the case about fifty lines above) or to signify, that what had been there spoken, ought not to be divulged or remembered afterward.

V. 669. *Endu'd with voice.* ---] The ancient writers, as well historians as poets, are full of these wonders. The speech of Achilles's horse to his master is well known. Among the many prodigies, which are said to have appeared at the death of Julius Cæsar, this, Virgil informs us, was one, --- *pecudesque locutæ.* Appian expressly says that an ox spoke with an human voice. Livy has given us the speech of one of these animals on a certain occasion.

Quod maximè terrebat, Confulem Ch. Domitium, bovem locutum, "Romà tibi cave." *Lib. xxxv.*

V. —— This ship was indeed built out of some sacred timber from the grove of Dodona, which was sacred to Jupiter Tomarias; and on this account it was said to have been oracular, and to have given verbal responses.

V. 670. *Itonian* ---] Minerva was so called from Itonis, a city of Thessaly, where she was worshipped.

V. 698. *The parted ocean whitening* ---] The poets are fond of expressing the activity of the rowers, and the velocity of the ship, by the effect which the stroke of their oars, and the track of the keel produce on the waters.

—— λευκαινον ὑδωρ ξεςτῃς ἐλάτῃσιν. Od. μ'. 172.

Totaque remigio spumis incanuit unda. *Catull.*
Et freta caneſcunt, ſulcam ducente carinâ. *Manil.*

V. 701.

V. 701. *Th' immortal Powers ---*] Apollonius, anxious to imprefs on his readers a juft idea of the importance of his fubject, has, in the true fpirit of Homer, reprefented all the Gods looking down upon Argo, as if interefted in the fuccefs of her voyage.

V. 717. *With Chiron came ---*] Achilles was educated under Chiron. The circumftance of Chariclo's raifing up young Achilles in her arms, to fhew him his father Peleus, is exceedingly beautiful and ftriking. From this action we may alfo fairly conjecture, that this famous expedition preceded the fiege of Troy, probably, about thirty years; *viz.* from the infancy of Achilles to his arrival at perfect manhood.

V. 752. *Corn-crown'd Theffalia ---*] On the epithet ϱιπίη, which the poet here applies to Theffaly, and which feems to have perplexed the commentators, Mr. Bryant makes the following ingenious remark: " The Pelafgi fettled very early in Theffaly, to which they gave the name *Aëria*. This was the ancient name of Egypt, from whence this people came. They likewife called the fame country Ai Monah, Regio Lunaris; which the poets changed to Hæmonia."

V. 759. *And Dolops' tomb; ---*] The fcholiaft tells us, this Dolops was the fon of Hermes, and flain at Magnefia; where they erected a monument, near the fhore, to his memory.

V. 766. *--- Aphetæ ---*] The place from which they fet fail was named from that event *Aphetæ*. It is a town and port of Magnefia in Theffaly.

V. 778. *Tall Athos ---*] Plutarch and Pliny affert, that this mountain is fo high, as to project its fhade, when the fun is in the fummer-folftice, on the market-place of the city Myrina. *Univ. Hift.*

————— ingenti tellurem proximus umbrâ
Veftit Athos, nemorumque obfcurat imagine pontum.
Stat. Theb.

V. 793.

V. 793. *For angry Venus* ---] "The defcription of Venus, enraged againft the men of Lemnos for neglecting her temple, reprefents her (fays Mr. Spence in his Polymetis) rather as the Goddefs of Jealoufy, than of Love. There is no figure of her under this character, nor any defcription in any of the Roman poets *before the third age.*" Had the learned author confulted Apollonius, he would have feen to whom Valerius was indebted for this defcription of Venus, as the Goddefs of Jealoufy. The paffage is indifputably borrowed from our poet. So true is it, what Mr. Gray has obferved of this writer, that had he confulted the Greek authors, they would have afforded him more inftruction on the very heads he profeffes to treat, than all the other writers put together. See Gray's 5th letter to Mr. Walpole.

V. 826. --- *like the Bacchanalian band,*] The Lemnian women are here reprefented as favage as the Thyades, who delighted in bloody banquets. Upon this the fcholiaft obferves, that the Mænades and Bacchæ ufed to devour the raw limbs of animals which they had cut or torn afunder. In the ifland of Chios it was a religious cuftom to tear a man limb from limb by way of facrifice to Dionufus: the fame in Tenedos. Hence we may learn one fad truth, that there is fcarce any thing fo impious and unnatural, as not at times to have prevailed. *Bryant's Myth. vol.* ii. *p.* 13.

V. 852. *For Boreas* ---] There is a judicious note on this paffage, inferted in an elegant edition of our poet, lately publifhed at Oxford; which I fhall venture to give the reader: "Licet ventus Boreas Argonautis ad curfum continuandum *fecundus* effet, non tamen folverunt." Mihi perfpectum eft nihil veri his ineffe. Non enim ventus Aquilo fecundus eft tendentibus in Pontum, fed *adverfum tenet*. Hoc ergo
Apollonius

Apollonius indicat. Minyas non folviffe illo mane, ex infulâ Lemno, quod Aquilo, qui ipfis in Pontum porrecturis adverfus erat, flaret. *Weffeling. Obferv. p.* 130. This obfervation appears to be juft. Yet is it no unufual thing with the poets to put one wind for another. The moft judicious and accurate of the Roman poets is not exempt from errors of this kind. " The defcription of the departure of Æneas from Carthage is not only inconfiftent with truth and probability, in this refpect, but contradictory to itfelf. He fails in the morning with a *weft* wind, which is very improperly called favourable; but before he is out of fight of Carthage, we find him purfuing his courfe with a *north* wind, which is ftill more contrary to his intended courfe." See *an Effay on the original Genius and Writings of Homer.*

V. 913. --- *Hypfipyla arofe,*] Dido is the Hypfipyla of Virgil. The latter, as Hoelzlinus fpeaks, is the archetype of the former.

V. 949. *A mantle* ---] This mantle, which Pallas gave to Jafon, and the fimile of the ftar, to which he is compared, are beautiful fpecimens of our poet's talent for defcription. We fhall find him, in the more defcriptive parts of his poem, rifing greatly above that equal mediocrity which fome critics have afcribed to him.

V. 971. *Behind, Amphion* ---] The fable of Thebes being built by the power of mufic is not in Homer, and therefore may be fuppofed to be of later invention. See *Pope's Od.* B. xi. 320.

V. 982. *The Taphians,* ---] The Teleboans, or Taphians (fo called from the ifland Taphos which they inhabited) coming to Argos, ftole the oxen of Electryon, the father of Alcmena: a battle enfued, in which himfelf and fons were flain.

V. 988. *This Pelops drove,* ---] Hippodamia was

the daughter of Œnomaüs, king of Elis and Pifa. She was a princefs of great beauty, and had many admirers. Œnomaüs having been informed by the oracle, that he fhould be flain by his fon-in-law, endeavoured to deter the fuitors from paying their addreffes to his daughter, by propofing a chariot-race. The terms were; that he who conquered him in the race fhould obtain his daughter, but that he who proved unfuccefsful fhould be put to death. Pelops, whom Hippodamia was moft attached to, accepted the dangerous conditions, and contended with Œnomäus. The plan which his daughter had concerted with Myrtilus, the charioteer, of loofening the pin of the wheel, fucceeded to her wifh. The pin flew out, the chariot was overthrown, and victorious Pelops claimed the lady as his prize.

V. 997. *At mighty Tityus aim'd,* ---] Elara being pregnant by Jupiter, he, to avoid the jealoufy of Juno, concealed her in a cavern of the earth, where Tityus was born: who, from his being immerfed in worldly cares, and from his centering all his affections on the earth, as if he had fprung from it, is fabled to be the fon of the earth.

V. 1132. *And let him revel* ---] This is an oblique, but very fevere farcafm on Jafon.

V. 1161. *And if with offspring* ---] That there was offspring appears from Homer's Il. B. vii.

> And now the fleet, arriv'd from Lemnos' fands,
> With Bacchus' bleffings cheer'd the generous bands.
> Of fragrant wines the rich Eunæus fent
> A thoufand meafures to the royal tent;
> Eunæus, whom Hypfipyle of yore
> To Jafon, fhepherd of his people, bore.

Thefe verfes, fays Mr. Pope, afford us the knowledge of fome points of hiftory and antiquity: as that Jafon had a fon by Hypfipyle; who fucceeded his mother

ther in the kingdom of Lemnos: that Samos was anciently famous for its wines; and that coined money was not in use at the time of the Trojan war; but the trade of the countries carried on by exchange in brafs, oxen, flaves, &c. as appears by two lines farther:

> Each, in exchange, proportion'd treafures gave,
> Some brafs, or iron, fome an ox, or flave.

V. 1187. *That there initiated* ---] All that were initiated into the Cabiritic myfteries were thought effectually fecured from ftorms at fea, and all other dangers: and the influence of the Cabirian priefts was particularly implored by mariners for fuccefs in their voyages. *Potter. Bryant.*

V. 1193. *Thence the black main* ---] So named from a bay, which lies weft of the Thracian Cherfonefus; called Melas from a river of that name.

V. 1207. *An ancient ifland* ---] Cyzicus, or Cyzicum according to Strabo, is an ifland in the Propontis, joined by two bridges to the continent. The ftrait, over which thefe bridges were thrown, being in a courfe of years filled up, an ifthmus was formed, and the ifland became a peninfula: to this ifthmus the poet alludes. *Strabo. Hoelz.*

V. 1235. *Here the rope-faften'd ftone* ---] It is obfervable that the name of an anchor does no where occur in Homer. The fhips of which he fpeaks had only a rudder and ballaft. Neither was there any metal employed in the conftruction of them; the timbers were faftened together with pegs.

We muft not therefore wonder at the rude expedient, to which the Argonauts had recourfe, in thefe ftill earlier times.

V. 1299. *As near* ---]
Ac veluti magnâ juvenum cum denfa fecuri
Silva labat ; cuneifque gemit grave robur adactis;
Jamque abies, piceæque fuunt : fic dura fub ictu
Offa virûm malæque fonant, fparfufque cerebro
Albet ager. *Val. Flac.* L. iii. 163.

V. 1380. *There ftands the tomb*, ---] The moft ancient tombs were very fimple : they were nothing more than hillocks of earth heaped up over the grave. This the Romans called *Tumulus*. Sometimes we find an oar, or pillar erected over it in honour of the deceafed. Thus we read in Homer ;

Τύμβον χιύαλις, καὶ ἐπὶ ϛηλην ἐρύσαλις,
Πήξαμεν ἀκροτάτω τύμβω ἐυῆρις ἐριτμὸν.
See *Bp. Lowth's note on Ifaiah* liii. 9.

V. 1384. --- *round her neck fhe tied*] Some nicer critics may be offended that Clita fhould die in fo vulgar a manner : but this objection is owing to a want of confidering the notions and manners of different ages and countries. Amata, the mother of Turnus, in the 12th book of the Æneid, hangs herfelf. In the 11th book of the Odyffey Jocafta dies in like manner, and likewife in the Œdipus of Sophocles.

V. 1399. *Sift coarfeft meal, and at the public mill.*]
It was cuftomary for families to grind their own corn. For this purpofe they made ufe of hand-mills. Wind and water-mills were a later invention. They employed their flaves at this work : and fometimes it was inflicted on them as the heavieft punifhment.

Molendum in piftrind, vapulandum, habendæ compedes.
Ter. Phorm.
See *Bp. Lowth's Ifaiah*, page 217.

Here we find, not a fingle family, but a whole people, annually, in token of mortification and forrow,
labouring

NOTES to the ARGONAUTICS. 341

labouring together at one common mill, and partaking of the bread of affliction, which is of the coarser kind, and unbaked.

V. 1406. *A beauteous Halcyon,* ---] Ceyx, king of Thrace, married Alcyone, the daughter of Æolus. On a voyage to confult the Delphic oracle, he was fhipwrecked. His corpfe was thrown afhore in fight of his wife, who, in the agonies of love and defpair, threw herfelf into the fea. The Gods, in pity to her fidelity, changed her and her hufband into the birds which bear her name. The halcyons very feldom appear, but in the fineft weather: whence they are fabled to build their nefts on the waves. The female is no lefs remarkable than the turtle for her conjugal affection. When the halcyons are furprized by a tempeft, they fly about as in the utmoft terrors, and with the moft lamentable cries.

V. 1418. *There Cybele* ---] The worfhip of Cybele was famous in Phrygia. Her priefts, founding their tabrets and ftriking their bucklers with fpears, danced and diftorted their whole bodies. To thefe dances and diftortions they add fhrieks and howlings; whence they were called Corybantes. Thus it was that they deplored the lofs of their Goddefs's favourite Atys; thus they drowned the cries of Jupiter, concealed among the Curetes in Crete; and thus they ftifled the grief of thefe Dolians for their flaughter'd monarch. See *Banier's Myth.*

V. 1422. --- *by Cybele the vaft profound,*] Orpheus, in his hymn to this Goddefs, has afcribed to her the fame unlimited dominion:

Μήτηρ μίντι θιῶν ἠδὶ θνητῶν ἀνθρώπων,
Ἐκ σοῦ γὰρ καὶ γαῖα καὶ οὐρανὸς ἰυρὺς ὑπερθεν,
Καὶ πόνιος, ποιαίτι.   Orph. Hymn. 13.

V. 1448. *This trunk they hew'd,* ---] It fometimes happens,

happens, that the roots and branches of aged trees bear a faint likeness to the human fabric. The ancients seem to have taken advantage of this fancied similitude, which they improved by a little art; and their first efforts towards imagery were from these rude and rotten materials. *Bryant's Myth.* vol. i.

V. 1461. *Idean Dactyli* ---] The Dactyli were the priests of Cybele: they first inhabited mount Ida in Phrygia; hence they were stiled *Idæi.* They were originally five in number, as their name, derived from the fingers of the hand, imports.

V. 1463. --- *Oaxis rolls his wave.*] There is a river of this name, not only in Mesopotamia, but in Crete.

Thus Virg. Ecl. i.

Et rapidum Cretæ veniemus Oaxem.

V. 1469. --- *martial dance* ;] Called also the Pyrrhic dance, from fire, with which it was accompanied. It was esteemed a martial exercise, and was performed by persons in armour, who gave it the name of Berarmus, from the temple of the Deity, where it was probably first practised; or from the regularity of their movements in dancing. *Schol. Bryant.*

V. 1478. *Boughs bend with fruit,* ---] It was the general opinion of the ancients, that when they had appeased their Deities by sacrifice and prayer, the tokens of reconciliation would appear by an uncommon fertility of the soil.

The poets have not failed to avail themselves of this popular opinion. It is customary with them to represent fruits and flowers of every kind, as springing up and coming to perfection in a manner, that seemed to indicate the immediate agency of some propitious Deity.

Besides; Cybele was taken for the Earth; on which account she was called the mother of the Gods; for the earth gives birth to all things. Hence her worſhip was blended with ſeveral circumſtances which bore a relation to the earth. Its fertility therefore, at the inſtant of the celebration of her feſtival, is ſomething more than a poetical embelliſhment.

V. 1509. *--- Ryndacus ---*] A river of Myſia, which empties itſelf into the Propontis. Near its banks, as ſome aſſert, ſtood the tomb of Ægæus or Briareus.

V. 1525. *--- Arganthon ---*] A mountain near Cios. Cios is the name of a river, and of a city in Myſia.

V. 1530. *Some bring dry wood, ---*] Thus Theocritus, ſpeaking of the employments of the Argonauts, when they landed in the country of the Bebrycians, ſays,

Ευναις τ' ιςόρνυῖο, κ. τ. λ. Id. 22.

On the dry beach they rais'd the leafy bed,
The fires they kindled, and the tables ſpread.

V. 1556. *Meanwhile, preparing ---*] This ſtory is told with great ſimplicity and elegance by our poet's rival and contemporary Theocritus; Id. 13. Nor has his faithful imitator, Valerius Flaccus, neglected to embelliſh his poem with the ſame ſtory. The learned editor of Theocritus, publiſhed in 2 vol. at Oxford, portions out to each poet his ſhare of merit in the following words: Egregiè quidèm Valerius Flaccus Herculis vehementem & repentinam perturbationem depingit: qui, veſperi reverſus, Hylam ad ſociorum menſas, in littore conſtructas, non deprehendit. Nihil niſi dictionem Virgilianam, caſtam, teretem, ſimplicem, pro turgidulâ illâ, & duriuſculâ, deſidero. Conferatur & Hercules Apollonii Rhodii: quem credibile eſt omnes intendiſſe nervos, ut in ſimili materiâ poetam coævum ſuperaret. Pulchrum profectò illud Herculis, a manu abietem abjicientis. At fortaſſis, fortaffis, ad fummum, fimpliciora Theocriti & luculentiora fatebere, & minus frequentata circumftantiis & elaborata. *Not. ad V.* lv. Id. 13.

V. 1568. *But know, Alcides* ---] Hercules, arriving at the country of the Dryopians, a people of Epirus, applied to their prince Theodamas for refreshment. Upon his refusal, he unyoked one of the oxen with which he was plowing, and facrificed it. Theodamas, attempting to redrefs this grievance by force of arms, was killed, and his fon Hylas was carried off by the conqueror. Some attribute this exploit to the rapacity of Hercules, others to his defire of civilizing an inhofpitable people. Callimachus, fpeaking of the rapacity of Hercules, fays,

Οἱ γὰρ ὅγε Φρυγίῃ περ ὑπὸ δρυῒ γυῖα θεωθεὶς
Παύσατ' ἀδηφαγίης· ἐπὶ οἱ παρα νηδὺς ἰκείη
Τῇ ποτ' ἀροτριόωντι συνήντετο Θειοδάμαντι. In Dian. 159.

V. 1576. *In Dian's praife* ---] Thus Callimachus, in his hymn to Diana, celebrates her as encircled with a choir of nymphs :

—— αἱ νύμφαι σε χορῷ ἔνι κυκλώσονται
'Αγχόθι πηγάων. In Dian. 170.

V. 1598. *As when a lion* ---] Virgil has clofely imitated this fimile in the following lines, where, fpeaking of the impetuofity of Turnus, he thus compares him ;

Ac veluti pleno lupus infidiatus ovili,
Cum fremit ad caulas, ventos perpeffus & imbres,
Nocte fuper mediâ ; tuti fub matribus agni
Balatum exercent : ille afper & improbus irâ,
Sævit in abfentes : collecta fatigat edendi
Ex longo rabies, & ficcæ fanguine fauces.

Æn. B. ix. 59.

V. 1626. *As when a bull, whom galling gadflies wound,*]
Apollonius,

Apollonius, within the compafs of a very few lines, makes ufe of two different words to exprefs the fame animal, μύωψ and οἶςρος. The former, he tells us, is the more general appellation: ἐν [οἶςρον] μύωπα βοῶν κλείουσι νομῆες. B. iii. 276.

The correfpondent names in Latin are *afilus* and *tabanus*: *afilus vulgò tabanus vocátur*, fays Servius.

——————— cui nomen afilo
Romanum eft, æftron Græci vertere vocantes.
Arcebis gravido pecori.   *Virg. Georg.* iii.

Homer alfo fpeaks of this fly as being very pernicious to cattle:

Οἱ δ' ἰφίζονίο κατὰ μέγαρον, βόες ὡς ἀγελαῖοι,
Τὰς μέντ' αἰόλος οἶςρος ἐφορμηθεὶς ἐδόνησεν.   Od. xxii. 299.

Confus'd, diftracted thro' the rooms they fling,
Like oxen madden'd by the breeze's fting.

This fimile is common to the poets: Virgil, Coluthus, and Tryphiodorus have made ufe of it.

V. 1676. *And one ftill moves*, ---] It was ufual with the ancients to place one vaft ftone upon another for a religious memorial. The ftones thus placed they poized fo equally, that they were affected with the leaft external force: a breath of wind would fometimes make them vibrate. Thefe were called rocking ftones. Of fuch an one Apollonius is here fpeaking, as being moved by the wind, and the admiration of fpectators. *Bryant.*

V. 1746. *A land projecting* ---] The coaft of Bebrycia; the ancient name of Bithynia, a country of Afia Minor, near Troas, bounded on the north by the Euxine fea.

Orpheus has given us, at the beginning of his poem, a catalogue of the heroes that accompanied Jafon son to Colchis. Apollonius has followed his example: And he has shewn himself a judicious imitator of Homer, by diversifying and enlivening his narration with an account of the family, character, and birth-place of his Argonauts. He constantly inserts some little history or anecdote, which may serve to imprefs their names on our memory, and to interest us in their future fortunes. He has contrived to throw the utmost variety into the voyage, by describing particularly the situation of the coasts, and the customs and manners of the inhabitants. The launching of Argo, the episode of Hypsipyla, the night-adventure of the Dolians, the story of Hylas, the sacrifices and similes, are severally possessed of such distinguished merit, as cannot fail to give the reader a favourable idea of our poet's taste and genius.

NOTES TO BOOK II.

V. 16. *TILL match'd with me ---*] This encounter between Amycus and Pollux is described likewise by Theocritus, who, in the opinion of Casaubon, far surpasses Apollonius; but Scaliger gives the preference to our author, who has certainly furnished Virgil with many circumstances in his description of the contest between Dares and Entellus. See Æn. B. v.

Neither Apollonius nor Theocritus have lost sight of Homer's description of the combat of the cæstus, Il. xxiii. 683.

Mr.

Mr. Warton, in his valuable edition of Theocritus, delivers his opinion of the defcription of this combat, by the three poets, Apollonius, Theocritus, and Valerius, in the following words: " Apollonio fane, auctore fuo, Flaccum inferiorem cenfeo; quippe quod Flaccus minus fimplex fit, & omnia, fublimitatis affectato ftudio, magnificentius efferat & inflatius. Utroque præftantior Theocritus, quod utroque fimplicior. Tantum illi cedit Apollonius, quantum Flaccus Apollonio."

V. 112. *Like bulls* ---] This fimile is borrowed by Virgil, Æn. xii. 715.

> With frowning front two mighty bulls engage,
> A dreadful war the bellowing rivals wage, &c. *Pitt.*

V. 163. *As fwains with fmoke,* ---] Virgil has alfo taken this fimile from Apollonius; a poet, as Catrou obferves, very rich in beautiful comparifons. See Pitt's Virg. Æn. xii. 832.

> So when the fwain invades with ftifling fmoke
> The bees, clofe-clufter'd in a cavern'd rock,
> They rife; &c.

It was the cuftom of the ancients to force bees out of their hives by fumigation. To this practice the poets frequently allude. Thus Ovid de rem. amor. L. i. 185.

> Quid, cum fuppofitos fugiunt examina fumos,
> Ut relevent dempti vimina curva fagi?

——— τύφι πολλῷ τῷ καπνῷ.   Ariftoph. in vefp.

V. 178. --- *an iron-land.*] The land of the Chalybes, which bordered upon that of the Mariandyni.

V. 199. --- *their brows with laurel crown'd.*] Crowns and garlands were thought fo neceffary to recommend men to the Gods, and were fo anciently ufed, that

fome

some have derived the custom of putting them on at feasts, from the primitive entertainments, at which the Gods were thought to be present. *Potter*.

V. 221. *Fronting Bithynia's coast,*] The storm drove them to Salmydessus, a city on the coast of Thrace opposite to Bithynia.

The Scholiast speaks of more than one Bithynia. There is a country of that name, he tells us, both on the coast of Europe and of Asia. The storm drove the Argonauts to Salmydessus, which is opposite to the Asiatic Bithynia.

V. 224. --- *sad Phineus* ---] Phineus was a king of Thrace, or, as some say, of Arcadia. He ordered the eyes of his two sons to be torn out, to satisfy their mother-in-law. The Gods punished his cruelty: they struck him with blindness, and sent the Harpies to him, who took the meat from his mouth; so that he would have perished with hunger, if Zetes and Calaïs had not delivered him from them, and pursued them to the Strophades, where they gave over the chace. These Harpies were called out of hell, and seem to be of the number of the furies. A permission was given them to dwell upon earth to punish the wicked: by which the poets would represent to us the remorse of a bad conscience. *Catrou*.

V. 237. *For, lo! descending* ---] Apollonius has furnished Virgil with many hints on this subject of the Harpies. See Æn. B. iii. 225.

At subitæ horrifo lapsu de montibus adsunt
Harpyiæ; &c.

When from the mountains, terrible to view,
On sounding wings the monster-harpies flew. *Pitt*.

The Harpies were a kind of birds which had the faces of women, and foul, long claws. When the table was furnished for Phineus, they flew in, and
either

either devoured or carried away the greater part of his repaſt, or polluted what they left. *Raleigh.*

V. 256. *Like ſome pale, lifeleſs, viſionary ſhade.*] The perſon and diſtreſſes of this old man are repreſented to us in a manner the moſt ſtriking and pathetic. Virgil had this deſcription in view, when, ſpeaking of Achemenides, he ſays,

> Cum ſubitò e ſilvis, macie confecta ſupremâ,
> Ignoti nova forma viri, miſerandaque cultu
> Procedit, ſupplexque manus ad litora tendit,
> Reſpicimus: dira illuvies, immiſſque barba,
> Conſertum tegmen ſpinis ——   Æn. iii. 590.

V. 346, 347. *By every woe--- And by theſe eyes ---*] Thus Telemachus ſwears, not only by Jupiter, but by the ſorrows of his father.

> By great Ulyſſes, and his woes I ſwear.
>   See *Pope's Odyſſ.* xx. 406.

Adjurations of this ſort are frequently to be met with in the Greek Tragedians.

V. 377. *As when ſwift hounds, ---*] Virgil has cloſely copied the concluſion of this compariſon: the eager hound, ſays he,

> Hæret hians, jam jamque tenet, ſimiliſque tenenti
> Increpuit malis, morſuque eluſus inani eſt. *Æn.* xii. 754.
> They ſnap, and grind their gnaſhing teeth in vain.

V. 393. *--- the dogs of Jove: ---*] The ancient name of a prieſt was Cahen, rendered miſtakenly χυν, and *canis.* Hence the Harpies, who were prieſts of Ur, are ſtiled by Apollonius *the dogs of* Jove. Iris, accoſting Calaïs and Zetes, tells them, it would be a profanation to offer any injury to thoſe perſonages. The Sirens and Harpies were of the ſame vocation. *Bryant's Myth.* vol. ii.

V. 404.

V. 404. *The Strophades* ---] The word *Strophades* is derived from a Greek verb that fignifies to *turn*. Thefe iflands therefore were named Strophades, becaufe near them the fons of Boreas left off purfuing the Harpies, and *turned* back to the houfe of Phineus.

V. 437. *Two rocks* ---] This is very fimilar to a paffage in the Odyffey, B. xii. v. 71.

> High o'er the main two rocks exalt their brow,
> The boiling billows thundering roll below;
> Thro' the vaft waves the dreadful wonders move,
> Hence nam'd *erratic* by the Gods above.——
> Scarce the fam'd *Argo* pafs'd thefe rapid floods,
> The facred *Argo*, fill'd with demigods!
> Ev'n fhe had funk, but Jove's imperial bride
> Wing'd her fleet fail, and pufh'd her o'er the tide. *Pope.*

It is obferved in the note on this paffage, "that Homer, to render his poetry more *marvellous*, joins what has been related of the Symplegades to the defcription of Scylla and Charybdis.---The ftory of the dove being reported of the Symplegades might give him the hint of applying the crufhing of the doves to Scylla and Charybdis." But we muft remember that Argo paffed, in her *return*, through *Scylla* and *Charybdis*, and that Apollonius, as well as Homer, has mentioned thefe rocks by the name πλαγκταὶ, *erratic*, which is fuppofed to be more ftrictly applicable to the Symplegades. If the Cyanean rocks were called Symplegades from their juftling together, and that appearance was occafioned by the different views in which they were feen, fometimes in a direct line, and fometimes obliquely, why might not Scylla and Charybdis, for the fame reafon, be faid to juftle together, and confequently without impropriety be called πλαγκαὶ or erratic? *Minerva*, according to Apollonius, guided Argo through the Symplegades; but her courfe through *Scylla* and *Charybdis* was directed by
Thetis

Thetis, at the interceffion of *Juno*, agreeable to what Homer here mentions.

V. 448. --- *a nimble dove let fly*,] The dove which returned to Noah with a leaf of olive, and brought the firft tidings that the waters of the deep were affuaged, was held in many nations as particularly facred: it was looked upon as a peculiar meffenger of the Deity, an emblem of peace and good fortune. Among mariners it was thought to be particularly aufpicious; who as they failed ufed to let a dove fly from their fhips, to judge of the fuccefs of their voyage. The moft favourable feafon for fetting fail was at the Heliacal rifing of the feven ftars, near the head of Taurus; and they are, in confequence of it, called Pleiades. It was at their appearance that the Argonauts fat out upon their expedition. Ἄμος δ'ἀντέλλονli πελειάδες.—Theoc. Id. xiii. 25. When firft the pleafing Pleiades appear. And this was thought a fortunate time for navigation in general. The Argonauts, in a time of difficulty and danger, made the experiment of letting a dove fly, and formed from it a fortunate prefage. *Bryant's Myth.* vol. ii. 285.

It is indeed the opinion of many learned men, that the fcience of augury, or of predicting future events by the flight of birds, arofe from the difmiffion of the raven and the dove from Noah's ark at the time of the deluge. This fpecies of divination is undoubtedly very ancient: it is mentiond in many places of the Old Teftament, and made a confiderable part of the religion of the heathen world.

V. 479. --- *Acherufia* ---] Is a cave, through which, according to the fable, is a paffage to the regions below. Hercules is faid to have defcended through it to bring up Cerberus. Tokens of which exploit they fhew, fays Xenophon, even to this day.

Near

Near this spot stands the principal city of the Mariandyni, named from Hercules, Heraclea. Here, as our poet informs us, runs the river Acheron, so called from the abovementioned lake.

V. 493. --- *Halys* ---] This river, which rises in Cappadocia, and empties itself into the Euxine, took its name from the beds of salt through which it runs. *Strabo*. Tornefort says, this country is so full of fossil-salt, that it is to be found in the high roads and plowed lands.

V. 498. --- *Thermodon* ---] This river, says Strabo, after having received many others, runs through Themiscyra, formerly inhabited by the Amazons, and then falls into the Euxine sea.

V. 502. --- *the Chalybes* ---] It is commonly believed, that the ancient Chalybes were the descendents of Tubal; for they are celebrated by the ancients for their extraordinaty skill in working of iron, and making of steel-armour; whence they are said to have had their name. *Univ. Hist.*

Strabo is of opinion, that they are the same whom Homer mentions by the name of ἀλύβες. For he joins them with the Paphlegonians, and characterizes them thus, ὅθεν ἀργύρε ἐςὶ γενέθλη.

Chalybes nudi ferrum —— *Virg. Georg.*

V. 505. --- *the Genetæan hill.*] A promontory, so named from Genetes, a neighbouring river, which ran through the country of the Chalybes. A temple was erected here to Jupiter the hospitable.

V. 530. --- *Phasis* ---] Pliny informs us, that the bird called the *Pheasant*, derives its name from this river, whose banks they frequented in great abundance; and that they were first brought over into Greece by the Argonauts.

Argivâ

Argivâ primum funt tranfportata carinâ;
Ante mihi notum nil nifi nomen erat. *Mart.*

V. 535. *A hideous dragon ---*] *Tarchon*, which, according to the learned and ingenious Mr. Bryant, signifies a hill with a tower, or temple on it, was in later times rendered *Trachon*; from whence the region Trachonitis received its name. This word, it seems, was ſtill further ſophiſticated by the Greeks, and expreſſed Δρακων, *Dragon*: from whence in a great meaſure aroſe the notion of treaſures being guarded by *Dragons*. The Gardens of the Heſperides, and the Golden Fleece at Colchis were entruſted to a ſleepleſs ſet. The dragons are repreſented as ſleepleſs; becauſe in towers there were commonly lamps burning, and a watch maintained. The eyes of the dragon were windows in the uppermoſt part of the building, through which the fire appeared. *Bryant's Myth.*

V. 553. *Lies Colchos, ---*] All the countries which lie on the north and north-eaſt parts of the Euxine, the region of Colchos, and the country at the foot of Caucaſus, were of old eſteemed Scythia, and theſe the Greeks looked upon to be the boundaries, northward, of the habitable world.

V. 556. *--- Æa ---*] The region termed Aια, above Colchis, was a name peculiarly given by the Amonians to the places where they reſided. Among the Greeks the word grew general; and Aια was made to ſignify any land. But among the Egyptians, as well as among thoſe of Colchis Pontica, it was uſed for a proper name of their country.

It was owing to this, that the name given to the chief perſon of the country was *Aiates*. *Bryant's Myth.*

V. 626. *--- coeval tree, ---*] It was the common opinion

opinion of the ancients, that the *Hamadryads* lived and died together with their trees, and therefore were extremely grateful to thofe, who at any time preferved them. The Scholiaft tells a remarkable ftory to this purpofe: A perfon called Rhœcus, obferving a beautiful oak ready to fall, ordered it to be fet upright and fupported. The nymph of the tree appeared to him, and bade him, in return, afk whatever he pleafed. She being exceedingly handfome, Rhœcus defired he might be entertained as her lover: which fhe promifed, and accordingly fent a bee to fummon him. But the young man, happening to be playing at dice when the bee came, was fo offended with its buzzing, that he drove it from him. The nymph, provoked at this uncivil treatment of her embaffador, in revenge deprived Rhœcus of the ufe of his limbs. He alfo fpeaks of another nymph, who was grateful to the man that preferved her oak.

———— τότι δρύες ἠνίκα νύμφαι.
Call. Hymn. in Del. v. 83.

V. 662. *The names of Agreus and of Nomius*] Thus Callimachus:

Φοῖβον κ᾿ Νόμιον κικλήσκομεν, ἐξ ἔτι κείνε
Ἐξότ᾿ ἐπ᾿ Ἀμφυρσῷ ζευγήτιδας ἔτρεφεν ἵππους,
Ἠϊθέου ὑπ᾿ ἔρωτι κεκαυμένος Ἀδμήτοιο.
Hymn. ad Ap. 47.

Ἀγρεὺς and Νόμιος were undoubtedly the names of Apollo; but they were alfo beftowed on his fon Ariftæus, on account of his fondnefs for a country-life, and his many ufeful difcoveries.

Ἀνδράσι χάρμα φίλοις,
Ἄγχιστον ὀπάονα μήλων,
Ἄγρεα καὶ Νόμιον
Τοῖς δ᾿ Ἀρισταῖον καλεῖν. Pynd. Pyth. ix. 115.

V. 671. *To him they gave their numerous flocks to feed,*] Almoft all the principal perfons, whofe names occur in the mythology of Greece and Italy, are represented as shepherds. It is reported of the Muses, that they were of shepherd-extraction, and tended flocks, which they entrusted to their favourite Aristæus; the same whom Virgil stiles *Pastor* Aristæus. *Bryant.*

V. 685. --- *showery Jove,*] Jupiter is frequently represented under the character of *pluvius*, or the dispenser of rain, both by poets, painters, and statuaries. For it was his province, as chief ruler of the air, to direct not only the thunders and lightnings, but the rain. Virgil has given us a noble description of the *Jupiter pluvius* in the following description:

——— cum Jupiter, horridus austris,
Torquet aquosam hiamem, & cælo cava nubila rumpit.
Æn. ix. 670.———*Spence's Polym.*

V. 693. --- *and by these winds detain'd,*] For these Etesian winds, the history of which the poet has just given us, blew north-east, and consequently in a direction the most unfavourable for them who were sailing up the Euxine.

V. 735. *Old ocean thunder'd*;] This storm seems to have been copied by Virgil, Æn. i. by Lucan, Ovid, and Valerius Flaccus.

V. 813. *With cold indifference ---*] The great outlines of Jason's character are piety, humanity, and valour. The sentiment before us is replete with philanthropy, and prejudices us highly in favour of the hero of the poem.

V. 861. *His golden locks, ---*] Milton thus describes Adam's hair:

——————————— hyacinthine locks
Round from his parted forelock manly hung
Clust'ring.   B. iv. 303.

The circumstance of the hair hanging like bunches of grapes has been justly admired. But it is literally translated from the description of Apollo's hair in the Greek poet.

χρύσιοι δὲ παρειάων ἑκάτερθι
Πλοχμοὶ ΒΟΤΡΥΟΈΝΤΕΣ ἐπιρρώοντο κιόντι.

The word βοτρυόεντες could hardly be rendered into English by any other word than by *clustering*. *Warton's Observ.*

V. 867. *Nor dar'd the heroes,* ---] Thus Hesiod in Scuto, speaking of Hercules,

———————————— ὀδί τις ἀυτοῦ
Ἔτλη ἐς ἄντα ἰδὼν σχεδὸν ἐλθεῖν.

There was probably, in the old pictures of Apollo, a certain brightness beaming from his eyes, and perhaps diffused all over his face; in the same manner, as the body of the principal figure is all luminous and resplendent in the famous nativity of Correggio, of the Transfiguration by Raphael. What made me then suspect this, was the ancient poets speaking so often of the brightness of Apollo's face, and the beaming splendours of his eyes. Virgil does not only compare his Æneas (under whom is generally supposed to be meant Augustus) to Apollo for beauty; but, in another place, he seems to call Augustus himself (who was really very beautiful) by the name of this God. *Spence's Polym.*

V. 771. *Then like an arrow* ---] Virgil has adopted this comparison, where he represents Cloanthus's ship as moved forward by Portunus:

———— Et pater ipse manu Portunus euntem
Impulit: illa noto citius volucrique sagittâ
Ad terram fugit, & portu se condidit alto. *Æn.* v. 241.

V. 900.

NOTES to the ARGONAUTICS. 357

V. 900. --- *with curls unclipp'd,*] Nothing was deemed by the ancients more effential to the beauty of a young perfon (and Apollo was always reprefented a youth) than fine, long hair. Hence the epithets *crinitus* and *intonfus* are fo often given to Apollo.

——————— crinitus Apollo,
Nube fedens. *Virg. Æn.* ix. 638.

——————— fic tibi fint intonfi, Phœbe, capilli. *Tibull.*

V. 946. *The Megarenfians Soönautes nam'd*] They are called by our poet in this place, and by Theocritus, Id. xii. 27. Νισαῖοι Μεγαρῆες ; from Nifa, which, as the Scholiaft informs us, was the name of their dock. It was fo named from Nifus, fon of Pandion, and king of this people.

The Megarenfians, going out to plant a colony in Heraclea, were driven by diftrefs of weather into the river Acheron, which, from the protection it afforded them, they called *Soönautes.*

V. 1028. *But fail'd, unhappy!* ---]
Sed non augurio potuit depellare peftem. *Æn.* ix. 328.
The fate of others he had oft forefhewn,
But fail'd, unhappy! to prevent his own, *Pitt.*

V. 1029. *Here, in a covert* ---] This defcription of a boar hid among the rufhes, and the terror of the neighbourhood, reminds us of the following beautiful lines of Ovid, who is defcribing the Caledonian boar:

Concava vallis erat, quo fe dimittere rivi
Affuerant pluvialis aquæ: tenet ima lacunæ
Lenta falix, ulvæque leves, juncique paluftres,
Viminaque, & longæ parvâ fub arundine cannæ :
Hinc aper excitus, medios violentus in hoftes
Fertur, ut excuffis elifus nubibus ignis.
Ov. Met. L. viii.

V. 1167.

V. 1167. --- *Parthenius* ---] This river rifes in Paphlagonia, and derives its name from the cheerful meadows through which it flows. *Strabo.*

V. 1176. *Thy groves, Cytorus,* ---]
Thy groves of box, Cytorus, ever green. *Pope's Il.* B. ii.

Hence things made of box were called *Cytoriaca.*
Sæpe *Cytoriaco* deducit pectine crines.

V. 1204. *The Amazonian cape* ---] The Greeks, who would fain deduce every thing from their own language, imagined, that by the term Amazon was fignified a perfon without a breaft. From this wrong etymology proceed all the abfurdities with which the hiftory of this extraordinary people abounds. They were in general Cuthite colonies from Egypt and Syria; and as they worfhipped the Sun, they were called Azones, Amazones, Alazones; which are names of the fame import. The moft noted were thofe, who fettled near the river Thermodon, in the region of Pontus.

Quales Theïciæ, cum flumina Thermodontis
Pulfant, & pictis bellantur Amazones armis. *Æn.* xi. 658.

V. 1229. *From Mars and Harmony* ---] The Amazons worfhipped the Deity from whom they received their name; viz. Azon and Amazon, the fame as Ares, the Sun. They worfhipped alfo Harmon, the Moon; which the Grecians changed to a feminine, *Harmonia.* So that by γενεὴ Ἄρεος καὶ Ἁρμονίης is meant the children of the Sun and Moon. *Bryant's Myth.*

V. 1251. --- *Tibarenians* ---] It is remarked of this people, that they are uncommonly addicted to laughter and buffoonery. Some have accounted for the

the abfurd cuftom, here alluded to, from this caufe. But it is difficult to affign a reafon for the many abfurd cuftoms which different nations have adopted. It has been recorded by grave hiftorians, that the ancient Spaniards and the Americans follow the practice of the Tibareneans.

V. 1260. *Moffynes call'd*, ---] Xenophon gives us the moft authentic account of this people in the fifth book of his Anabafis. He tells us, that they do thofe things in private, which others do in public; that they talk to themfelves, laugh by themfelves, and dance alone, as if they were fhewing their fkill in public. Savage and indecent as the cuftom, alluded to by our poet, may feem, Strabo afcribes the fame barbarities to the Irifh, and Cæfar makes the fame obfervations on the ancient Britons.

V. 1269. *But if his judgment err*, ---] Thus Pomponius Mela, L. i, c. 19. Reges fuffragio deligunt, vinculifque & arctiffimâ cuftodiâ tenent; atque ubi culpam pravè quid imperando meruere, inediâ totius diei afficiunt.

V. 1301. *But when he rung a cymbal* ---] This cymbal, or crotalum, was made, the Scholiaft tells us, by Vulcan; Hercules received it from Pallas. The defcription of this inftrument is differently given by different authors. Our poet tells us it was made of brafs; others reprefent it as formed of a rod or reed cut in two; both parts of which, when ftruck together, emitted a found after the manner of caftanets. This latter defcription agrees with the opinion of Suidas, and the Scholiaft of Ariftophanes.

V. 1386. *The laws of hofpitable Jove revere.*] Thus Virgil, Æn. i. 784.

Jupiter (hofpitibus nam te dare jura loquuntur)

Almighty Jove! who pleads the ſtranger's cauſe;
Great guardian God of hoſpitable laws. *Pitt.*

And Homer, in the words of Mr. Pope; Od. B. ix.

The poor and ſtranger are Jove's conſtant care;
To Jove their cauſe and their revenge belongs,
He wanders with them, and he feels their wrongs.

V. 1430. --- *round the altar ſtood*;] The tombs, of which frequent mention is made by the ancient writers, were in reality high altars or pillars, and not, as has been ſuppoſed, monuments erected in honour of the dead. Such an one the Argonauts are ſaid to have found in the temple of Mars, when they landed upon the coaſt of Pontus. This was the expreſs object to which the Amazonians paid their adoration; as they lived in an age when ſtatues were not known. *Bryant's Myth.*

V. 1472. --- *Typhaonia's cave,*] Apollonius mentions an ancient Typhonian Petra in the hollows of the mountain. It was an Ophite temple, where the Deity was probably worſhipped under the figure of a ſerpent. Hence the poet ſuppoſes the ſerpent, with which Jaſon engages, to have been produced in thoſe parts. *Bryant's Myth.*

V. 1497. *Where Saturn firſt fair Philyra* ---] Saturn, to avoid being diſcovered by his wife Ops, while he was engaged with Philyra his miſtreſs, turned himſelf into a beautiful horſe.

Chiron, the famous Centaur, was the ſon of this nymph Philyra.

V. 1547. *Where on an oak* ---] The Greek here, and at v. 1399, is δρυὸς; but at v. 534 the word is φηγοῖο, *a beech:* both which trees bearing maſt, they may perhaps be indiſcriminately uſed.

NOTES TO BOOK III.

V. 2. *AND teach thy poet, Erato,* ---] Apollonius with great propriety invokes Erato, the Mufe who prefided over love-affairs. For this book contains the loves of Medea and Jafon, and abounds with the moft beautiful fentiments defcriptive of the tender paffion. Virgil's invocation of Erato, *Nunc age, qui reges, Erato,* &c. is a tranfcript of Apollonius, Εἰ δ' ἄγε νῦν, 'Ερατώ, &c. Virgil feems to have copied our poet in this inftance, at the expence of his judgment: for it is difficult to affign a reafon for his invocation of this Mufe, when he was about to fing, as he informs us, *reges & tempora rerum.*

The fourth book of Virgil, Servius tells us, is borrowed from this of Apollonius Rhodius. Virgil's Æneid, fays Hoelzlinus, would not have been enriched with the epifode of Dido, had not the amours of Hypfipyla and Medea been worked up ready to his hand by Apollonius.

V. 10. *Juno and Pallas* ---] Having conducted his heroes to the banks of the Phafis, our poet fhifts the fcene, and takes occafion to introduce the two Goddeffes, Juno and Pallas, confulting for the fafety of Jafon. There is a neceffity for fuch machinery, in order to preferve the dignity of Epic poetry. And the propriety of its introduction in this place will be acknowledged, if we recollect, that on the fuccefsful application of thefe Goddeffes to Venus the future fortunes of Jafon depend. There needs no greater proof of the beauty of this paffage, than that it has been imitated by Virgil in that part of his firft book, where Cupid is commiffioned by his mother to kindle in Dido's breaft a paffion for Æneas.

V. 46.

V. 46. *A floating isle* ---] The Greek is Νήσοιο πλαγκτῆς. Homer has a similar expression, Πλωτῇ ἐνὶ νήσῳ. Odyss. x. 3.

> A floating isle! high-rais'd by toil divine. *Pope.*

V. 50. *Sat Cytherea on a polish'd throne.*] This whole passage is imitated by Claudian, who, speaking of Venus, says,

> Cæsariem tunc forte Venus subnixa corusco
> Fingebat solio: dextrâ lævâque sorores
> Stabant Idaliæ: largos hæc nectaris imbres
> Irrigat; hæc morsu numerosi dentis eburno
> Multifidum discrimen arat; sed tertia retro
> Dat varios nexus, & justo dividit orbes
> Ordine, neglectam partem studiosa relinquens.

V. 74. *To free Ixion,* ---] He, for making love to Juno, and boasting afterwards that he had dishonoured Jupiter, was hurled headlong by him into Tartarus, and bound to a wheel, which he was doomed to turn without intermission.

V. 79. --- *as o'er the world I stray'd,*] It was the opinion of the ancients, that the Gods frequently assumed the human shape. Thus Homer, Odyss. xvii. v. 485.

> They (curious oft of mortal actions) deign
> In forms like these to round the earth and main,
> Just and unjust recording in their mind,
> And with sure eyes inspecting all mankind. *Pope.*

> ——————— summo delabor Olympo,
> Et Deus humanâ lustro sub imagine terras.
> *Ov. Met.* L. 1.

V. 131. *With golden dice,* ---] The Greek is ἀστραγάλοισι. Homer has the same expression, Il. xxiii. 88. but it is omitted in Pope's translation.

V. 141. --- *Adrastea gave,*] She was nurse to Jove when an infant. Thus Callimachus;

——— εἰ

NOTES *to the* ARGONAUTICS. 363

———————— οἱ δὲ κούμισεν Ἀδρήστεα
Αἴπηῳ ἐνὶ χρυσέῳ. Hymn. ad Jov. v. 47.

V. 149. *A sweet round ball*; ---] It is partly from the wanton and playful character of these little Cupids, that they are almost always given us under the figures of children.
Thus Ovid;

> Et puer es, nec te quicquam nisi ludere oportet:
> Lude, decent annos mollia regna tuos. *Ov. Rem Am.*

In conformity to this puerile character, Venus promises to reward her favourite boy with playthings.

V. 210. *To blameless Phrixus.* ---] See the Preface.

227. *At Colchos still this barbarous rite prevails :*] These extraordinary rites of the Colchians are mentioned by Ælian, in his fourth book. The earth and air are said to be the principal objects of their worship. *Hoelz. and Schol.*

V. 235. --- *but friendly Juno shrouds*] Thus Pallas spreads a veil of air around Ulysses, and renders him invisible:

> Propitious Pallas, to secure her care,
> Around him threw a veil of thicken'd air.
> *Homer's Odyss.* B. vii.

Thus Venus conceals Æneas and his companions:

> At Venus obscuro gradientes aere sepsit.
> *Virg. Æn.* L. I.

V. 251. --- *the Pleiads set or rose,*] The Pleiades are said to be the daughters of Atlas by the nymph Pleione. They were seven in number. Their name is derived, either from their mother, or their number, or, more probably, from the Greek word, which
signifies

signifies *to sail.* They are called in Latin Vergiliæ, from the vernal season when they rise. They rise about the vernal equinox, and set in autumn. See a further account of them in the Note on v. 448, B. ii.

V. 260. --- *Phlegræan war.*] The battle between the gods and giants is supposed to have been fought at Phlegra, near Pallene, in Thessaly.

V. 299. --- *Athamas's fancied wealth to gain,*] These sons of Phrixus and Chalciope had sailed from Colchis to Orchomenos, a city of Bœotia, to receive the inheritance of their grandfather Athamas.

V. 327. *As some good housewife,*---] Virgil seems to have copied this simile from Apollonius. *Æn.* viii. v. 408.

> What time the poor, laborious, frugal dame,
> Who plies her distaff, stirs the dying flame;
> Employs her handmaids by the winking light,
> And lengthens out their tasks with half the night;
> Thus to her children she divides the bread,
> And guards the honours of her homely bed. *Pitt.*

V. 356. *On Mars's isle,*---] One of those islands called the Strophades, in the Ionian sea.

V. 387. --- *the fierce Sarmatians*---] The Sarmatians, or Sauromatæ, were Scythians, who dwelt in the country that lies between the river Tanais and the Borysthenes.

V. 413. *Had ye not first my feast partook* ---] The table was looked upon by the ancients as a sacred thing; and a violation of the laws of hospitality was esteemed the highest profanation imaginable.

V. 562. --- *a maiden dwells,*---] Virgil's description of the Massylian priestess is taken from this passage:

Hæc

Hæc fe carminibus promittit ——
Siftere aquam fluviis, & vertere fidera retro;
Nocturnofque ciet manes: mugire videbis
Sub pedibus terram, & defcendere montibus ornos.
Æn. L. iv. 487.

V. 705. —— *whom her friends had join'd*
In marriage ---] The chief power of difpofing of their daughters in marriage, even among the heathens, was in their parents, without whofe confent it was not held lawful. Thus Hermione in Euripides:

Νυμφευμάτων δὲ τῶν ἐμῶν πατὴρ ἐμὸς
Μέριμναν ἕξει, κ' ἐκ ἐμὸν κρινεῖν τάδε.

V. 797. *Now rifing shades* ---] Here Dr. Broome's tranflation begins, and continues to v. 1087; but not without confiderable omiffions which are fupplied. Virgil has copied this exquifite defcription from our author. Both the poets defcribe minutely the profound calm and ftillnefs of the night, in order to render the agonies of the reftlefs heroines more affecting by fuch a contraft. It is impoffible to give us a more lively idea of their reftlefs fituation, than by reprefenting it in oppofition to that general tranquillity which prevails through the whole creation. The filence of the night, which difpofes others to reft, ferves but to encreafe their anguifh, and to fwell the tumult of their paffion.

> 'Twas night; and weary with the toils of day,
> In foft repofe the whole creation lay.
> The murmurs of the groves and furges die,
> The ftars roll folemn thro' the glowing fky;
> Wide o'er the fields a brooding filence reigns,
> The flocks lie ftretch'd along the flowery plains;
> The furious favages that haunt the woods,
> The painted birds, the fifhes of the floods;
> All, all, beneath the general darknefs fhare
> In fleep a fweet forgetfulnefs of care;
> All but the haplefs queen.   *Pitt.*

That

That sudden and beautiful tranfition at the clofe of the defcription, *At non infelix animi Phæniffa*, is copied with the utmoft exactnefs from the correfpondent line in our poet,

'Αλλὰ μάλ' ἃ Μήδειαν ἐπὶ γλυκερὸς λάβεν ὕπνος.

V. 813. *As from the ſtream-ſtor'd vaſe* ---] Virgil has imitated this fimile, Æn. viii. 22.

> Sicut aquæ tremulum, &c.
>
> So from a brazen vafe the trembling ſtream
> Reflects the lunar, or the folar beam :
> Swift and elufive of the dazzled eyes,
> From wall to wall the dancing glory flies :
> Thence to the cieling ſhoot the dancing rays,
> And o'er the roof the quivering fplendor plays.   *Pitt.*

V. 911. *This plant, which rough Caucaſean mountains bore.*] Caucafus is called by Propertius, B. i. El. 12. the Promethean mountain; becaufe the magic herbs, for which it was famous, were faid to have fprung out of the blood of Prometheus.

> ——— An quæ
> Lecta Prometheis dividet herba jugis.   *Potter.*

V. 935. *As when her limbs divine* ---] We meet with this fimile in the fixth book of Homer's Odyſſey, who applies it to Nauſicaa fporting with her fair attendants in the meads. Virgil applies the fame fimile to Dido, walking in the midſt of the city, with the Tyrian princes. See *Pope*'s note on v. 117. Od. vi. Some of the critics have thought that no paffage has been more unhappily copied by Virgil from Homer, than this comparifon. But, it ſhould feem from fome circumſtances in his fimile, that the Roman poet rather imitated this paffage of Apollonius, than that of Homer.

V. 936.

V. 936. — *the Amnesian waves*,] or, rather, Amnisian, according to Callimachus:

———— 'Αμνισίδας ᾱ́κοσι νύμφας.

They were so named from Amnisus, a city and river of Crete.

V. 988. *And croaking, thus Saturnia's mind express'd.*] Some birds were of use in divination by the manner and direction of their flight; others by the sounds they uttered; these were called *oscines*, of which kind were crows.

Oscinem corvum prece fuscitabo
Solis ab ortu. *Hor.* Od. xxvii. l. 3.

V. 1005. *Meanwhile the maid* ---] No poet has succeeded better in any description than Apollonius has in the following. The anxiety with which Medea expects the arrival of Jason, expressed by her inattention and aversion to every other object, by her directing her eyes every way in search of him, and by her trembling at every breeze, are admirable strokes of nature. The appearance of Jason, flushed with all the bloom of youth, advancing hastily towards her, like the star, to which he is compared, rising from the ocean; the embarrassment which his presence occasions, the silent admiration in which they stand gazing at each other, like two tall trees in a calm, are particulars which none but the imagination of a real poet could have put together, and can never be sufficiently admired.

V. 1099. *The following night in equal shares divide*;] We have here a curious account of the ceremonies made use of in their sacrifices to the infernal Deities. Hecate, the same with the Moon or Diana, was so called, either from her being appeased by hecatombs, or from the power she possessed of obliging those who were

were unburied to wander an hundred years. Virgil applies to her the epithet of *ter geminam*, and Horace that of *triformis*. She was called in heaven Luna, or the Moon, on earth Diana, and in hell Proserpina, Hecate, and Brimo from her terrifying appearance.

It seems extraordinary that Diana, who is the goddess of chastity, should be represented as dispensing her favourable influence in illicit amours. But the mythologists inform us, that Diana and Venus are but one and the same divinity. The Scholiast on Theocritus, Id. ii. says, that it was customary, among the ancients, for the men to implore the sun, and women the moon in their amours. Cicero, speaking of three Dianas, observes, that the first was thought to be the mother of winged Cupid. *De Nat. Deor.* L. 3.

V. 1095. *With honey, sweetest labour of the bees.*] Honey was a favourite ingredient with the ancients in their oblations to the gods, whether of heaven or hell. Homer, in his hymn to Mercury, calls it

——— Θεῶν ἡδεῖαν ἰδωδήν.

Bees and honey are subjects which the Greek poets are particularly fond of introducing; and their country was plentifully supplied with these commodities.

V. 1155. *Where from Prometheus good Deucalion came,*] Apollonius Rhodius, according to the common opinion, supposes Deucalion to have been a native of Greece, the son of Prometheus, the son of Japetus; but in these ancient mythological accounts all genealogy must be entirely disregarded. He represents him as the first of men, through whom religious rites were renewed, cities built, and civil polity established in the world; none of which circum-
stances

stances are applicable to any king of Greece. We are assured by Philo, that Deucalion was Noah. *Bryant.*

V. 1245. *This baneful monster was by Cadmus slain,*] Upon the report of the rape of Europa, her father, Agenor, sent every where in search of her, and ordered his son Cadmus not to return home till he had found her. Cadmus having traversed a part of Greece without gaining any information of her, settled in Bœotia, where he built the city Thebes. Having sent his associates into a grove, consecrated to Mars, to fetch water, a serpent, which guarded the place, devoured them. Cadmus, to revenge their death, slew the monster; from whose teeth, which he had sown, a body of armed men sprung up. This is the fabulous account to which Apollonius alludes.

No colony, says Mr. Bryant, could settle any where, and build an Orphite or serpent temple, but there was supposed to have been a contention betwixt a hero and a dragon. Cadmus was described in conflict with such an one at Thebes.

V. 1247. *An heifer to his feat* ---] πομπαῖες relates properly to divine influence, and πομπή is an oracle. An ox or cow was by the Amonians esteemed very sacred and oracular. Cadmus was accordingly said to be directed πομπῇ βοὸς. *Bryant.*

V. 1285. --- *Amaranthine Phasis* ---] This river is supposed to have derived its source from a nation of that name. The poet, in describing the effects of this infernal evocation, has heaped together with great judgment, and in the true spirit of poetry, every circumstance that is capable of exciting terror and astonishment.

V. 1288. *And now on Caucasus,* ---] Apollonius introduces his heroes on the plains of Mars with the utmost pomp and magnificence, thus artfully preparing us for the solemnities of the ensuing combat, on which the fate of Jason depends.

NOTES TO BOOK IV.

V. 1. *O Goddess,* ---] The first and second books contain, as we have seen, the voyage of the Argonauts to Colchis. In the book we are now entering upon, the poet has given us an account of the route they took on their return. And, in order to throw the utmost variety into his poem, he has conducted them to Greece by a way altogether new and unknown. He makes them sail up the Ister, and by an arm of that river, to the Eridanus, and from thence to the Rhone. Apollonius's geography is, in many instances, very exceptionable. The licence which poets are allowed, *quidlibet audendi*, is his best excuse for inaccuracies of this kind. Scaliger, who seldom spares our author, does not scruple to assert, that, ' quod attinet ad situm ' orbis terrarum, sanè imperitus regionum fuit Apol-' lonius. De Istro, dii boni! quas nugas.' But let it be remembered, that not only poets have trifled in their descriptions of this river, but that historians and geographers, who have attempted to explain its course, have given very different and inconsistent accounts of it. Many curious traditions, and entertaining pieces of ancient Greek history are in-

terspersed

terfperfed throughout this book. The fpeeches of Medea can never be enough admired. Her fentiments are admirably fuited to her condition; they are fimple, unaffected, and calculated to raife our pity. Our poet has difplayed a luxuriant fancy in his defcription of the nuptials of Jafon and Medea; and he has painted the diftreffes of his Argonauts, on the coaft of Africa, in the moft glowing colours. This book appears indeed, in every view of it, equal, if not fuperior to any of the foregoing. We meet with fome obfcurities. The tranflator confeffes his inability to afcertain the true fenfe of every intricate paffage. Let it, however, be fome alleviation of his errors, that his guides have been but few, and they not always the moft intelligent; and that no part of this book, except only the ftory of Talus, has appeared in an Englifh drefs, before the prefent verfion was publifhed.

V. 32. *Clung round each door*, ---] The cuftom of kiffing beds, columns, and doors, before they were obliged to quit them, occurs frequently in the Greek tragedians.

V. 33. *A lock fhe tore* ---] It was cuftomary for young women, before the nuptial ceremony was performed, to prefent their hair to fome deity, to whom they had particular obligations. Medea, therefore, previous to her departure and marriage with Jafon, prefents a lock of hair to her mother, to be depofited by her in the temple of fome deity to whom it was confecrated.

V. 64. *I to the cave at Latmos* ---] Latmos was a mountain in Caria, in whofe cave the moon was faid by the poets to vifit Endymion. Thus, in Valerius Flaccus, who feems to have had this paffage in his eye, we read;

B b 2   Latmius

Latmius æstivâ residet venator in umbrâ,
Dignus amore deæ : velatis cornibus et jam
Luna venit.   Lib. viii. 29.

V. 92. *Whose knees embracing,---*] Several parts of the body were considered by the ancients as the seats of virtues and vices, of good and bad qualities. Modesty was assigned to the eyes, sagacity and derision to the nose, pride and disdain to the eye-brows, and pity to the knees; which, it was customary for suppliants, when they made their requests, to touch and embrace with reverence.

V. 123. *At twilight, ere---*] Xenophon, de Venatione, makes the same observation, ἐξιέναι πρωΐ, exire diluculo. The same remark is made by Oppian and others.

V. 143. *Colchians, far distant:--*] This noble hyperbole has been copied by Virgil, Book vii. v. 515. where, speaking of Alecto, he says,

> With her full force a mighty horn she winds.;
> Th' infernal strain alarms the gathering hinds.
> The dreadful summons the deep forest took ;
> The woods all thunder'd, and the mountains shook,
> The lake of Trivia heard the note profound ;
> The Veline fountains trembled at the sound :
> The thick sulphureous floods of hoary Nar
> Shook at the blast that blew the flames of war:
> Pale at the piercing call, the mothers prest
> With shrieks their starting infants to the breast.   *Pitt.*

This circumstance of the mothers clasping their infants to their breasts, is a very tender and affecting one. The poets seem particularly fond of it. We meet with it in the Troades of Euripides ; and Camoens, in his imitation of these striking passages in Apollonius and Virgil, was too sensible of its beauty to omit it :

Such

Such was the tempeſt of the dread alarms,
The babes that prattled in their nurſes' arms
Shriek'd at the ſound: with ſudden cold impreſt,
The mothers ſtrain'd their infants to the breaſt,
And ſhook with horror. — *The Luſiad*, B. iv. p. 124.

V. 203. *The gallant band beheld with wondering eyes;*] Mr. Warton is of opinion, that Virgil had this beautiful paſſage in his eye in the following lines :

Expleri nequit, atque oculos per ſingula volvit,
Miraturque, interque manus et brachia verſat.
                                    Æn. viii. v. 618.

And thus *Spenſer*, in his *Fairy Queen:*
But Triſtram then deſpoiling that dead knight
Of all thoſe goodly ornaments of praiſe,
Long fed his greedy eyes with the fair light
Of the bright metal, ſhining like ſun-rays;
Handling and turning them a thouſand ways.
                        B. vi. c. 2. ſt. 39.

V. 292. --- *And, ere bright Cynthia* ---] By Selene, and Selenaia, is meant the ark, of which the moon was only an emblem; and from thence the Arcades, or Arkites, had the appellation of Selenitæ. When therefore it is ſaid, that the Arcades were prior to the moon, it means only, that they were conſtituted into a nation before the worſhip of the ark prevailed, and before the firſt war upon earth commenced. *Bryant.* This boaſt of the Arcadians, that they were a nation before the moon gave light to the world, is alſo thus accounted for by ſome ingenious writers: the Greeks generally ordered their affairs according to the appearances of the moon, eſpecially thoſe two of the new and full moon. The Spartans held it criminal to begin any great deſign till after they had conſidered the moon, as ſhe appeared when new and at the full. The Arcadians, contrary to this general cuſtom of the Greeks, tranſacted all their buſineſs of importance

importance before the appearance of the new moon, or that of the full; and were therefore called in derision, προσέληνοι, for their neglect of this religious ceremony. Which term of reproach the Arcadians applied to their commendation, and shrewdly affirmed, that they were entitled to this epithet, because their nation was more ancient than the moon.

V. 301. *Hence rose the matchless chief* ---] Sesostris not only overran the countries which Alexander afterward invaded; but crossed both the Indus and the Ganges; and thence penetrated into the eastern ocean. He then turned to the north, and attacked the nations of Scythia; till he at last arrived at the Tanais, which divides Europe and Asia. Here he founded a colony; leaving behind him some of his people, as he had just before done at Colchis. He subdued Asia Minor, and all the regions of Europe; where he erected pillars with hieroglyphical inscriptions, denoting, that these parts of the world had been subdued by the great Sesostris or Sesoosis. *Diodorus Sic.* L. i. p. 49. Apollonius Rhodius, who is thought to have been a native of Egypt, speaks of the exploits of this prince, but mentions no name; not knowing, perhaps, by which properly to distinguish him, as he was represented under so many. He represents him as conquering all Asia and Europe; and this in times so remote, that many of the cities which he built, were in ruins before the æra of the Argonauts. *Bryant.*

V. 311. --- *recording tablets keep*] The Colchians, says the Scholiast, still retain the laws and customs of their forefathers; and they have pillars of stone, upon which are engraved maps of the continent and of the ocean. The poet calls these pillars κύρβεις: which, we are told, were of a square figure, like obelisks. These delineations had been made of old, and

and transmitted to the Colchians by their forefathers; which forefathers were from Egypt. The Egyptians were very famous for geometrical knowledge. All the flat part of this country being overflowed, it is reasonable to suppose, that they made use of this science to determine their lands, and to make out their several claims, at the retreat of the waters. *Bryant.*

V. 451. *Rise may my Furies,* ---] Thus Dido, in a fit of despondency and rage, threatens Æneas:

> Et cum frigida mors anima seduxerit artus,
> Omnibus umbra locis adero. *Æn.* iv. 385.

V. 526. *Curse of mankind!* ---] Our poet, whenever he introduces moral sentences, which is but seldom, takes care to do it with the utmost propriety; at a time when the occasion warrants the use of them, and gives additional force and lustre to the truths which they convey. Virgil has adopted this sentiment of Apollonius on a similar occasion:

> Improbe amor, quid non mortalia pectora cogis!
> *Æn.* iv. 412.

V. 412. From the Greek word Εϱως, in the original, Mr. Bryant has taken occasion to give us the following curious account of Cupid and his emblems: Iris, the Rainbow, seems to have been expressed Eiras by the Egyptians. Out of Eiras the Greeks formed Eros, a God of Love; whom they annexed to Venus, and made her son. And finding that the bow was his symbol, instead of the Iris, they gave him a material bow, with the addition of a quiver and arrows. Being furnished with these implements of mischief, he was supposed to be the bane of the world.

V. 550. *Turn'd from the murderous scene* ---] The remorse and concern of Medea are very strongly expressed by this simple action, of turning aside and concealing her face from the scene of barbarity. Signs are sometimes more significant than words, however eloquent and pathetic; and silence is often the surest indication of heart-felt sorrow.

V. 613. *Where Cadmus' and Harmonia's tomb* ---] Cadmus settling in Bœotia, married Harmonia, or Hermione, the daughter of Venus by Mars. A conspiracy being formed against him, he was obliged to quit Bœotia, and retire with his wife into Illyricum. They are said by the poets to have been transformed into serpents. Of this transformation, and of the tomb, which the people of Illyricum erected to their memory, Dionysius thus speaks:

>――――――― ἰδαις περικυδέα τύμβον,
> Τύμβοι, ὃν Ἁρμονίης Κάδμοιό τε φῆμις ἐνίσπει.
> Κεῖθι γὰρ εἰς ὀφίων σκολιὸν γένος ἠλλάξαντο,
> Ὁππότ' ἀπ' Ἰσμηνοῦ λιπαρὸν μετὰ γῆρας ἵκοντο.

V. 644. *Of blood yet streaming from his children slain,*] By Megara, the daughter of Creon king of Thebes, Hercules had several sons, whom he slew in a fit of madness. Soon after this slaughter he left Thebes, and received expiation for the murder at Athens, according to some; but according to our poet, at Macris.

V. 689. *Wak'd the brisker gales in Argo's aid.*] In the original,

> Μηδομένη δ' ἄνυσιν τοῖο πλόυ, ὦρσεν ἀέλλας
> Ἀντικρύ·

Juno, anxious for the safety of her crew, and knowing they must visit Circe's isle, raised a storm for that purpose; which drove them back, up the Chronian sea, as far as the island Electris. By thus changing

changing their direction, she shortened their voyage, and hastened their approach to the island of Circe.

V. 727. *To the far Hyperborean race* ---] There are so many inconsistent fables among the ancients, respecting the country and situation of the Hyperboreans, that modern geographers have not been able to reconcile them. See *Gesner de Navigationibus extra columnas Herculis, Præl.* 2.

Callimachus, in his hymn to Delos, speaks of them as a people of high antiquity. Pindar places them near the isles of the Blest, which were supposed to have been opposite to Mauritania, and celebrates their rites. See *Olymp. Od.* iii. and *Pyth.* x.

V. 728. *Griev'd for his favourite Æsculapius* ---] Jupiter, incensed that Æsculapius had restored Hippolitus to life, destroyed him with his thunder. Apollo, willing to revenge the death of his son, directed his darts against the Cyclops, by whose hands the thunder of Jupiter was formed. The god, for this offence, banished him from heaven. See *Virg. Æn.* vii. v. 764.

V. 775. *With chalks* ---] In the original,

— ἵνα ψηφῖσιν ἀπωμόρξαιτο καμόντες
Ἰδρῶ ἅλις· χροιῇ δὲ κατ' αἰγιαλοῖο κέχυνται
Εἴκελοι.

The first line is obscure; for it may either mean, that they made use of the ψῆφοι as ϛλεγγίσματα, or strigiles, for rubbing; or that, in rubbing, the sweat dropped on the stones, ψηφῖσιν, and discoloured them. If this sense be the true one, the following lines may, perhaps, be somewhat less exceptionable than those already given:

To cleanse their sides from copious sweat they toil,
Which, trickling down, distain'd the chalky soil.

This

This paffage will receive fome illuftration from Ariftotle, περὶ θαυμασίων ἀκυσμάτων; who afferts, that among other monuments of the Argonautic expedition this was one, τὸ ἐπὶ τῶν ψήφων λεγόμενον. παρὰ τὸν αἰγιαλὸν ψήφους φασὶν εἶναι ποικίλας. ταύτας δὲ οἱ Ἕλληνες, οἱ τὴν νῆσον οἰκοῦντες, λέγουσι, τὴν χροιὰν λαβεῖν ἀπὸ τῶν ςλεγγισμάτων, ὧν ἐποιοῦντο ἀλειφόμενοι.

V. 783. *Here faw they Circe*, ---] We have the fulleft defcription of Circe and her habitation in the 10th Odyff. of Homer: from which book fucceeding poets have been fupplied with ample materials, to affift them in dreffing out this entertaining fiction.

It is entertaining to obferve, how different poets have written on the fame or fimilar fubjects. And according as they have acquitted themfelves in working them up, we may form a judgment of their tafte and genius.

V. 932. *Till Themis thus* ---] Others afcribe this difcovery to Prometheus, for which Jupiter promifed to releafe him from his chains.

V. 946. *Shall in Elyfium's blifsful plains* ---] The ftory, here alluded to, is mentioned by feveral of the ancient mythologifts. Medea, when in Elyfium, or the Fortunate iflands, gained the affections of Achilles, who then dwelt in thofe regions, and married her. The ancients are by no means confiftent in their accounts of thefe Elyfian fields. Some affirm them to be in the moon, others in the milky way. But it is more generally fuppofed, that they are fituated in fome fertile and pleafant region on earth. See *Homer's Odyff.* B. iv. and the note to v. 765 of Pope's *Tranf.* and *Gefner de Infulis beat. Præl.* 2.

V. 1016. *Her young Achilles o'er the flame* ---] Thus Ceres, when fhe undertook to bring up Triptolemus, in order to render him immortal, fed him all day with
celeftial

celestial food, and covered him all night with burning embers. His father Eleusinus, observing this, expressed his fears for his child. Ceres, displeased with this behaviour, struck him dead, but conferred immortality on his son.

V. 1047. The Syrens were Cuthite and Canaanitish priests, who had founded temples, which were rendered more than ordinary famous on account of the women, who officiated. With their music they enticed strangers into the purlieus of their temples, and then put them to death. The female part of their choirs were maintained for a twofold purpose; both on account of their voices and their beauty. They were said to be the children of the Muse Terpsichore; by which is meant only, that they were the daughters of harmony. *Bryant.*

Orpheus, in the Argonautics ascribed to him, has not only mentioned these Syrens, but given us the song, alluded to by Apollonius, which was so efficacious as to prevent the ill effects of the Syrens' music. We have the most particular description of these enchantresses in the 12th book of Homer's Odyssey.

V. 1054. *Who lur'd, in times remote,* ---] Among others, whom Ceres sent in search of her daughter Proserpine, were the Syrens. She is said to have given them wings, to enable them to explore the country with greater ease and expedition.

V. 1086. *From whose cleft summits flames* ---] These flaming billows must have been very alarming to the sailors, who were ignorant of the cause of them. The poet has therefore, in his description of Scylla and Charibdis, with great judgment selected these remarkable appearances, which could not fail to excite terror and astonishment.

V. 1091. *Here o'er the sailing pine the nymphs preside,*]

fide,] Virgil, in his 1ft Æn. has made ufe of the affiftance of the fea-nymphs on a fimilar occafion.

> Cymothoe fimul & Triton adnixus, acuto
> Detrudunt naves fcopulo.

And Camoens, who feems to have been particularly pleafed with this defcription, has, in imitation of it, fummoned together a vaft number of fea-nymphs to refcue the navy from deftruction. See B. ii. p. 48.

V. 1151. *His father caftrated:* ---] One would not expect to find in fo grave a writer as Hefiod any thing like that low kind of wit, which the double fenfe of words gives rife to. The tafte of the ancients, it has been faid, was too good for thefe fooleries. Yet his learned annotator is of opinion, that Hefiod has availed himfelf of the ambiguity of the word μῆδος. He thus difcuffes this curious fubject in a note on v. 180 in Theog.

Omninò exiftimo Hefiodum, & qui eum hac in re antecefferunt, aut fequuti funt, *lufiffe in ambiguo*. Vox μῆδος duo fignificabat, *pudenda* & *confilium*, cumque audiffent Saturnum patri ἀποτεμεῖν μῆδος, data operâ ita rem acceperunt, quafi narraretur ei pudenda refecuiffe, ut τερατολογίαις, quas hac de re habent, locus daretur; quamvis probè fcirent confilium feu confiliarios intelligi, quorum fuafu Theffaliâ excedere coactus fuerat Saturnus. Hofce confiliarios fugavit, & navibus in Afiam redire coegit.

V. 1281. *Thus Pyƈteus*, ---] (*Note*, it ought to be *Nyƈteus*.) Antiope, the daughter of Nyƈteus, was deflowered by Jupiter in the form of a fatyr. To avoid the anger of her father, fhe fled to Sicyon, a city in Peloponnefus: where fhe was protected by Epops. Nyƈteus at his death requefted his brother Lycus to lay fiege to Sicyon, but to fhew no compassion to Antiope. He, willing to comply with the request of Nycteus, besieged the city, killed Epops, and took Antiope prisoner.

V. 1283. *Thus Danaë,* ---] Danaë was the daughter of Acrisius. Having been informed by the oracle, that his grandson should bereave him of his life and crown, he shut her up in a tower of brass. But Jupiter, according to the fable, made his way through the roof in a shower of gold. The meaning of which fable is; Prætus, who was surnamed Jupiter, bribed the keepers, and having thus gained access to the prisoner, made her the mother of Perseus. Acrisius being apprized of this illicit commerce, and the fruits of it, ordered the mother and her son to be locked up in a chest, and thrown into the sea.

V. 1338. *Snatch'd from the flames,* ---] Jupiter being in love with Semele, Juno concerted the following scheme for the destruction of her rival. She appeared to Semele in the shape of Beroë, a nurse, and insinuated to her, that if her lover were really Jupiter, he would not disguise himself like a mortal: and that the certainty of his divinity could no otherwise be ascertained, than by his appearing before her with the same majesty, which he assumed when he visited Juno. Semele followed her advice; and Jupiter having sworn by Styx to grant her whatever she might ask, approached her in the full blaze of his glory, and Semele was consumed by his lightning. Jupiter being desirous to preserve the infant Bacchus, of whom Semele had been for some time pregnant, commissioned Mercury to deliver him from the flames, by taking him out of her womb, and conveying him to Eubœa. Here he was committed to the care of Macris. But Juno's resentment being not yet subsided, she forbade her favourite island Eubœa to give protection to the nurse of Bacchus; who now fled for refuge to Phæacia.

V. 1505.

V. 1505. *As when* ---] " The principal image (fays Pope, Il. xiv. in a note on v. 457.) is more ſtrongly impreſſed on the mind by a multitude of fimiles, which are the natural product of an imagination labouring to expreſs ſomething very vaſt: but finding no ſingle idea ſufficient to anſwer its conceptions, it endeavours by redoubling the compariſons to ſupply this defect." Since then the heaping together of fimiles, when the occaſion requires, is conſidered as a proof of true poetical enthuſiaſm, it muſt be allowed that our poet, in this inſtance, as well as in many others, has ſhewn himſelf capable of riſing above that uniform mediocrity, which has, perhaps too haſtily, been aſcribed to him. For we have here an accumulation of compariſons the moſt elegant and appoſite. The deſpondent heroes are likened to fpectres and ſtatues diſtilling drops of blood. Medea's fair attendants, lamenting their misfortunes, are compared to ſwallows, bereaved of their neſts and ſcreaming for their mother; and, immediately after, to the plaintive notes of dying ſwans.

This ſimile of the ſwallow is copied by Virgil, Æn. xii. 473.

V. 1649. *In Atlas' realm :* ---] In Africa, where, according to Virgil, Atlas reigns:

Ultimus Æthiopum locus eſt, ubi maximus Atlas——

V. 1651. *The fair Heſperides* ---] They were the daughters of Heſperus, the brother of Atlas, and ſhepherdeſſes. Hercules carried off their ſheep (which, for their exquiſite beauty, were called golden) and ſlew the ſhepherd, whoſe name was Draco. The Greek word μῆλα, which ſignifies apples as well as ſheep, is ſuppoſed to have given riſe to the fiction.

Some are of opinion, that the fable of the ſerpent, who guarded the golden apples, and was ſaid to have
been

been slain by Hercules, derives its origin from the Mosaic account of the fall.

V. 1749. *Thus sees the clown,* ---] Translated by Virgil, Æn. vi. 453.

───── qualem primo qui surgere mense
Aut videt aut vidisse putat per nubila lunam.

V. 1791. *For when brave Perseus*---] It has been already remarked, that Danaë was inclosed in a chest by the command of her father Acrisius, and thrown into the sea. This chest was cast upon the island Seriphus, one of the Cyclades in the Ægæan sea. It was found by a fisherman, who brought it to Polydectes, king of the island. He received the mother and child with great tenderness: but falling in love with Danaë, and fearing the resentment of Perseus, now grown to manhood, he planned the following scheme for his destruction. Having invited the neighbouring princes to an entertainment, he desired each of them to bring with him some rarities for the feast. Perseus was required to bring on this occasion the head of Medusa, one of the Gorgons: an enterprize which the king imagined would prove fatal to him; but by the assistance of Minerva, he cut off the Gorgon's head; which, when he carried it to the island, turned its inhabitants into stone, and among the rest, their king, Polydectes, who had sent him out on the expedition. See *Pindar's Pyth. Od.* xii.

V. 1817. *His corse the bright-arm'd heroes thrice surround,*] Virgil takes occasion to mention the same custom in the following words:

Ter circum accensos cincti fulgentibus armis
Decurrere rogos : ter mæstum funeris ignem
Lustravare in equis, ululatuque ore dederunt. *Æn.* xi.

1870. *Your course, that cape once doubled,*---] It would

would contribute towards clearing this obscure passage, if instead of ἰϑύς, we read ὑπέρ. This conjecture may the more readily be admitted, as we meet with the same expression, ἀγκῶνος ὑπὲρ τρεχοντος, at v. 1626.

V. 1943. *There Talus* ---] The following is Broome's note, prefixed to his translation of the story of Talus.

The following verses from Apollonius will appear very extravagant, unless we have recourse to their allegorical meaning. Plato in his Minos writes thus:

Talus and Rhadamanthus were the assistants of Minos in the execution of his laws. It was the office of Talus to visit all parts of Crete thrice every year, to enforce them with the utmost severity. The poet alludes to this custom in these words:

Fierce guard of Crete! who thrice each year explores
The trembling isle, and strides from shores to shores.

Talus is fabled to be formed of brass, because the laws, which he carried with him in his circuit, were engraven upon brazen tables. It is not improbable, but the fable of the bursting the vein above the ankle of Talus, by which he died, arose from the manner of punishment practised by him; which was, by the opening of a vein above the ankles of criminals, by which they bled to death.

V. 2093. *Instant emerging* ---] See on this subject Pindar's Pyth. Od. iv. towards the beginning.

V. 2096. ---- *Sintian Lemnos* ----] The Sintians were orginally Thracians; but settled afterwards at Lemnos.

V. 2118. *And added years to years exalt my verse.*] It was customary with the Greeks, not only to sing hymns, but to recite heroic poems in honour of the gods and heroes at their festive meetings.

NOTES

TO THE

RAPE OF HELEN.

COLUTHUS LYCOPOLITES, a Theban poet, flourished in the reign of the emperor Anaſtaſius, about five hundred years after Chriſt. He is ſaid to have been the author of ſeveral poems; none of which have come down to us except this, which in many paſſages is corrupt and mutilated. There is an excellent edition of this poem by *Lennep*. There is alſo an old tranſlation of it by *Sir Edward Sherburne*; to whom I acknowledge myſelf indebted for ſome of his uſeful annotations.

Did the inſertion of this little poem ſtand in need of an apology, it might be made by obſerving, that the ſubjects of the two poems are not wholly diſſimilar. In the one is celebrated *the rape of Medea*, in the other *the rape of Helen*; two events of equal celebrity in ancient ſtory.

On the title of this poem Sir Edward Sherburne makes the following not unpleaſant remark: "The word

word *rape* must not be taken in the common acceptation of the expression. For Paris was more courtly than to offer, and Helen more kind-hearted than to suffer such a violence. It must be taken rather for a transporting of her with her consent from her own country to Troy: which Virgil seems to insinuate in the first book of his Æneid, where, speaking of Helen, he says,

<blockquote>Pergama cum *peteret*, ———</blockquote>

The word *peteret* implies that the quitting of her country, and going along with Paris, was an act she desired, as well as consented to; and thus much the ensuing poem makes good."

V. 2. *From Xanthus' fertile streams* ---] The most celebrated river in Troas: it derived its source from mount Ida.

V. 10. --- *clown.*] The ancients esteemed the art of husbandry to be of all others the most honourable. The hands of princes sustained at the same time the crook and the sceptre. Paris, the son of Priam, king of Troy, is represented in this poem under the character of a shepherd. In our times the care of flocks and herds is committed to the lowest orders of the people. Shepherd and clown are terms with us nearly synonymous. But we must endeavour to separate from them the ideas of churlishness and ill-breeding, when applied, as the ancients applied them, to heroes and kings.

V. 24. *With hymeneal songs for Peleus sung,*] It was a fiction of the poets, that Peleus, the son of Æacus, and pupil of Chiron, married Thetis the daughter of Nereus; and that all the Gods attended at their nuptials on mount Pelion, except Eris or Discord, in whose presence agreement and harmony could not

long

long subsist. See on this subject *Catullus de Nupt. Pel. & Thet.* and *Valerius Flaccus*, L. i. v. 129.

V. 42. *His loose locks* ---] The correspondent lines in the original ought to be placed after v. 33. as *Lennep* rightly observes: to that place (immediately after the poet's mention of Diana) the translator has restored them.

V. 56. *With desperate hand* ---] The conjectural reading of *Vossius* is here preferred; as it seems to contain more sense and more poetry than any other. He reads,

———————————— χειρὶ δὲ λαιῇ
Οὐδὲ τι κόλλοπ' ἔρυξε, κ̀ ἣν ἐφυρασσατο μίτρην.

V. 79. *For 'tis the prize of beauty and of love.*] Apples were esteemed the symbol of love, and dedicated to *Venus*. They were also considered as allurements of love, and were distributed as presents among lovers. Hence the expressions μηλοβολεῖν, and *malo petere*, in Theocritus and Virgil.

V. 89. *The close-arch'd eyebrow,* ---] The ancients looked upon such eyebrows, which our poet calls βλεφάρων συνοχὴν, as essential to form a beautiful face. See *Anacreon*'s description of his mistress, and *Theocr.* Id. viii. 72.

V. 99. *Summon'd her little Loves,* ---] They were supposed to be very numerous:

——————— volucrumque exercitus omnis amorum.
Val. Flac. vi. 457.

V. 116. *My bow this Cestus,* ---] The Cestus of Venus, of which Homer makes particular mention, Il. xiv. 216. derives its name ἀπὸ τῦ κεντεῖν. To which

which stimulating quality our poet alludes in the following line,

And with this Cestus I infix my *sting*.

V. 205. *Beauty, their best defence, their strongest mail.*]
———— κάλλος,
'Απ' ἀσπίδων ἀπασῶν
'Απ' ἰγχίων ἀπάντων.   Anacr. Od. xi.

V. 267 and 268. --- *Ismarus* --- *Pangræa* ---] Mountains in Thrace. The former is also the name of a lake.

V. 269. *Now Phillis' rising tomb* ---] Demophoon, son of Theseus, on his return from Troy passed through Thrace, where he was hospitably received by Phillis, its queen, who fell in love with and married him. He having expressed his desire to visit Athens, his native country, Phillis consented to his departure, upon condition that he would return on a certain day which she should appoint. Demophoon promised to be with her on the appointed day. When the day came, Phillis, tortured with the pangs of an impatient lover, ran nine times to the shore, which from this circumstance was called in Greek *Enneados*: but unable any longer to support his absence, she in a fit of despair hanged herself. See *Ovid's Epist.* ii. *Phillis to Demoph.*

V. 274. *Phthia* ---] A province and city of Thessaly; the birth-place of Achilles. But, for a more particular account of Coluthus's geography, the reader may consult *Lennep*'s note on v. 215. where he shews, (to make use of his own words) *quam fuerit in Geographicis hospes Coluthus.*

V. 296. *Him with delight* ---] Hyacinthus was a young prince of the city Amyclæ in Laconia. He had

had made so extraordinary a progress in literature, that he was considered as a favourite of Apollo. As he was playing with his fellows, he was unfortunately struck on the head by a quoit, and died of the blow. The poets have enlarged on this simple story in the following manner.

The wind which blew the quoit aside, and gave it the fatal direction, they have called Zephyrus; whom they have represented as the rival of Apollo. Zephyrus, having received for his kindnesses to Hyacinthus the most ungrateful returns, was resolved to punish him for his insolence: and having challenged him one day to a game of quoits, he struck the unfortunate youth a blow on the temples.

The inhabitants of Amyclæ, says the poet,

——————————— δηϊῶ᾽ ἀήτου
Σκυζόμενος, καὶ τοῦτον ἀπήγαγεν.———

were displeased with the contest proposed by Zephyrus, and withdrew Hyacinthus from the fight; or, perhaps (still better to connect this with the following sentence) they brought him out, and spirited him on to the fight, presuming that his favourite God would enable him to come off victorious; --- αὐταρ Ἀπόλλων, &c.

This is *Lennep*'s conjectural reading; which, whether the true one or not, must be allowed to affix a tolerable meaning to a passage that was before very unintelligible.

V. 302. *Earth with compassion* ---] From the blood that was spilt on the ground Apollo produced a flower, called after the name of his favourite youth. See *Ovid. Metam.* L. x.

V. 331. --- *Nestor's son* ---] Antilochus, mentioned frequently in Hom. Il.

V. 333.

V. 333. --- *Æacidæ* ---] The defcendants of Æacus. He was the fon of Jupiter and Ægina: his offspring were Phocus, Peleus, Teucer, and Telamon.

V. 390. *Two gates of airy dreams fhe opens wide*;] The fiction to which our author in this place, and Virgil in Æneid vi. allude, is borrowed from B. xix. of Hom. Odyff. It is imagined, that this ftory of the gates of fleep may have had a real foundation, and have been built upon the cuftoms of the Ægyptians. See the note on v. 656. B. xix. of Pope's Odyff. Our poet has reprefented thefe fanciful gates as opened by *Night*; and with great propriety.

" The ancients, fays *Sir Edward Sherburne*, painted Sleep like a man heavy with flumber, his under garment white, his upper black, thereby expreffing day and night; holding in his hand a horn, fometimes really fuch, fometimes of ivory in the likenefs of one; through which they feigned that he conveyed dreams: true when the fame was of horn, falfe when of ivory." Some have affigned as a reafon, why true dreams pafs through the gate of horn, and falfe ones through the gate of ivory; that horn is a fit emblem of truth, as being tranfparent, and ivory of falfehood, as being impenetrable.

V. 448. *For fleep his elder brother's afpect wears,*] Virgil, Æn. vi. 278. calls Sleep *confanguineus lethi*.

V. 450. *Hence the fwoln eyes of females*, ---] Hence, i. e. by reafon of the likenefs there is betwixt thefe two affections.

V. 464. *At Cytherea's* ---] The line in the original is obfcure, and ufually mifplaced. It is given to Hermione, but without the leaft reafon. It is here reftored to its proper place; and is an obfervation which comes naturally enough from the mouth of Helen. See *Lennep's* note on the paffage.

V. 482.

V. 482. *Caſſandra from her tower ---*] Caſſandra was the daughter of Priam, and prieſteſs of Apollo. Apollo gave her the gift of prophecy; but, on her refuſing to comply with the conditions on which it was given her, he rendered it ineffectual, by ordaining that her predictions ſhould-never be believed. Hence it was, that, when Paris ſet ſail for Greece in purſuit of Helen, her prophecy, that he ſhould bring home a flame, which ſhould conſume his country, was not regarded. Her appearance therefore on the preſent occaſion is quite in character; and our poet has ſhewn his judgment by the repreſentation he has given of her.

END OF THE NOTES.

www.ingramcontent.com/pod-product-compliance
Lightning Source LLC
Chambersburg PA
CBHW020100020526
44112CB00032B/687